Voices from Death Row

Voices from Death Row

Second Edition

Bruce Jackson *and* Diane Christian

Cover drawing by Billy Hughes, 1980. Billy had been a farrier before his conviction. He spent much of his time on the Row painting watercolors of and drawing cartoons about horses. He appears frequently in this book and in our documentary film, *Death Row* (1979). The last time we spoke with him was when he called us from a county jail. His second trial had just ended with another conviction and another death sentence. Billy was executed January 24, 2000.

Published by State University of New York Press, Albany

Printed in the United States of America

For information, contact State University of New York Press, Albany, NY
www.sunypress.edu

Library of Congress Cataloging-in-Publication Data

Names: Jackson, Bruce, 1936– author. | Christian, Diane, 1939– author.
Title: Voices from death row / Bruce Jackson, Diane Christian.
Other titles: Death row
Description: Second edition. | Albany : State University of New York Press, [2022] | Earlier edition published in 1980 as: Death row.
Identifiers: LCCN 2021055426 | ISBN 9781438489292 (hardcover : alk. paper) | ISBN 9781438489315 (ebook)
Subjects: LCSH: Death row—Texas. | Capital punishment—Texas. | Death row inmates—Texas—Case studies.
Classification: LCC HV8699.U5 J3 2022 | DDC 364.6609764—dc23/eng/20220127
LC record available at https://lccn.loc.gov/2021055426

10 9 8 7 6 5 4 3 2 1

For all the victims

Contents

Where would Christianity be if Jesus got eight to fifteen years, with time off for good behavior?

—New York State Senator James H. Donovan,
New York Times, April 2, 1978

If Senator Donovan can get resurrection into the death penalty, I might be willing to give it a second look.

—New York Governor Hugh L. Carey,
New York Times, April 2, 1978

People who are well represented at a trial do not get the death penalty. I have yet to see a death case among the dozens of eve-of-execution stay applications in which the defendant was well represented at trial.

—Justice Ruth Bader Ginsberg, Associated Press, April 10, 2001

No man, brought to Sing Sing to be legally slain, expected to be executed. The old Latin parody, written by Terence, "We know we must die, but we don't believe it," applies to the men in the death-cells and describes their condition up to the very moment, sometimes, and always to within a few hours of the time when they are led out to the chair. When finally the conviction is borne in upon them that there is no possible hope of escape, that justice is relentless and has them in her clutch, they accept the situation with amazing complacency and walk to their death the most composed and reliant of all who assist at the tragedy. Occasionally some ill-regulated soul, unprepared for its flight, or uneducated to meet the inevitable in the school of life, resists, and the man has to be carried; but, as a rule, they die becomingly and with dignity.

—Number 1500, *Life in Sing Sing, 1904*

Note

Earlier versions of some of the material in the introduction to this edition appeared in our article "Time on Death Row," in *Living on Death Row: The Psychology of Waiting to Die,* ed. Hans Toch, James R. Acker, and Vincent Martin Bonventre (Washington DC: American Psychological Association, 2018), and in our book *"In This Timeless Time": Living and Dying on Death Row in America* (Chapel Hill: University of North Carolina Press, 2012).

Comments in the introduction and photograph captions about commutations, execution dates, and deaths from other causes are derived from the Texas Department of Corrections Death Row and Inmate Information web pages (https://www.tdcj.texas.gov/death_row). Quotation marks indicate exact language from those sites.

National capital punishment data is from the Death Penalty Information Center website (https://deathpenaltyinfo.org).

Our 1979 film *Death Row* is available for streaming, free, at the Folkstreams website (https://www.folkstreams.net/films/death-row).

We gave no real names in the 1980 edition, either in the text or with the photographs. Everyone's case was then still pending. The cases are now all resolved, so there are names in the captions to the photos (most of which were not in the 1980 edition) and in the preface to this edition.

Our thanks to Rodney Appleby for his help with the transcription of Brandon's rant, and to Michael Lee Jackson and Rachel Jackson for their careful review of the introduction to this edition.

BJ and DC
Buffalo, New York, August 23, 2021

Preface to the Original Edition

This is not a book meant to argue the legitimacy or illegitimacy or the social utility or disutility of capital punishment. It would take a book of nearly this length to adequately note, explain, and argue the statistical distortions, evidential inadequacies, and syllogistic manipulations in Walter Berns's recent attempt to make the death penalty morally attractive.[1]

Our concern here is simpler: we want to add evidence to the dialogue about what the death penalty really means. Even if adequate counsel were supplied at trial to everyone charged with a capital offense, even with a Supreme Court that does not find execution offensive in itself, there is still a long time between sentencing by a trial judge and ultimate disposition—death, a prison term, or release. Most capital cases consume only a few weeks of court time; the act of killing takes only a few minutes.

Death Row is years and years.

When we began gathering material for this book in early April 1979, 105 men were on Death Row in Texas; another nine were out on bench warrants for hearings or new trials. We taped interviews with twenty-six of these men, and with four Death Row porters, two custodial officers, and one medical assistant. We did not interview the prison doctor, who could not speak English very well, or the Baptist minister, who refused to discuss his work with us.

The selections from the interviews in this book are not attributed. Most names have been changed, and, to further prevent identification, we have altered a few dates and geographical locations. These changes were not made when it seemed they would affect the substantive content of the

1. Walter Berns, *For Capital Punishment: Crime and the Morality of the Death Penalty* (New York: Basic Books, 1979).

statement. When a statement could not be altered without also significantly changing its content, we left it out. There were very few such statements, however. What is presented here is a fair sample of the things said to us on Death Row.

We are aware that the lack of attribution may create some inconveniences for a reader. It would be nice, and perhaps useful, to know that a statement on page 50, say, was made by the same person interviewed on page 141.

There are dangers. Lives are in balance on the Row. Almost everyone is fighting to have a new trial, and in trials anything can be used by either side. It is difficult to know beforehand what might be used against a prisoner, what passing remark might turn out to be deadly in an unsuspected context. Several men on the Row told us of former cell neighbors or porters who came to new trials and testified for the state. We wanted to let these men say something about their lives on the Row, but we were not willing to let our work endanger their lives further. For that reason, we decided not to attribute any of the statements.

The extracts are drawn from transcripts of slightly over sixty hours of interview material, most of them done by Diane. A small portion of the extracts is from recordings made during work on our film documentary, *Death Row* (Buffalo, New York: Documentary Research, 1979). We have received several hundred letters from men on the Row and have incorporated some material from those letters in this book. All statements in quotation marks are from their letters; all statements or questions in italics are by one of us; all other statements are by men from the Row.

Diane did most of her interviews in the prison visiting room, which is not used by regular prisoners during the week. That is why so many of the men talk about "down there." The place they refer to—J-wing of Ellis Unit of the Texas Department of Corrections—is about one-eighth of a mile away but in the same building. It is separate enough in their minds, and in reality, from the rest of the prison for them not to say "here." The Row is a place all its own.

We included little about the specific cases that brought the condemned men to Death Row. The merits of the cases and the legitimacy of the legal procedures involved are beyond the scope of this book. This book is about how they survive and endure life on the Row; how they fill their time, maintain contact, preserve their sanity; what they expect will happen. The segments about lawyers and courts are included primarily to give some sense of the fragile connections they have, the curious ways some arrived, and how they try to get out.

Three kinds of editing were done on the transcripts. The first was the most obvious and the least troublesome: we cut out passing comments or observations by us (such as *Oh? Really? Why? What do you think of that? Can you give a little more detail?*), and we cut from the inmates' statements false starts and repetitions (things one says in conversation but not in a written statement). We took those liberties in part to make the transcript material more readable, but also because of what we think is a real difference in the way people express themselves in conversation and in writing. When one writes a letter or an article or a book, one is far more careful about those false starts and repetitions; one has the luxury of rereading. We have gotten many letters from the men on the Row whose conversations are transcribed here, and, based on those letters, we don't think we have betrayed their speech by making minor modifications. Had we presented literal transcriptions, we would have given you something like the dialect writing of the nineteenth century: some people, perhaps, did talk like those Joel Chandler Harris characters, but the print versions always read like caricatures. We added nothing to the statements.

Second, and more important, were the decisions about which interview segments to include. Some choices were easy: one man would say something another man had said or repeat something he said before. We selected the "better" statement of the two, the one we thought made the point more accurately or efficiently. Sometimes the choice was more difficult. Some statements were, we thought, exaggerated or flatly untrue; some were based on rumors and wishes rather than observations or participation. We included some of those statements, because the book is as much about how men on the Row read their world as it is about the appearance of that world.

The third significant editorial decision had to do with the juxtaposition of statements. Three statements in sequence, like three photographs in a line on the same wall, are seen differently than if the three statements were read or the three photographs were seen in isolation. The juxtapositions create or reveal a narrative, an argument, a logic. One reflects upon, looks forward or backward to, the others. Those are judgment calls; there is no way to explain or justify or codify them. Some adjacent remarks support or complement one another, others contradict one another. The perceptions of the world held by the men on Death Row are no more homogeneous than perceptions of any group anywhere: about some things there is great consistency and agreement, about others there is very little. We selected remarks to give a fair sample of both the agreements and the contradictions.

The problematic aspect of this kind of sociological document is that it is based on the perceptions of researchers that are not in themselves documentable, that are probably only partly conscious. The quality of life on Death Row—what a day is like, what those days do to the men who endure them—will never reduce to statistical descriptions. If you want to know what that place is like and you cannot go there, you can't get much help from numbers, averages, or standard deviations.

That means we ask you to trust us, to believe that we have sensed the measure of that world and are delivering it to you, or that we are at least presenting a fair approximation. Those editorial decisions are all based on our own assumption that we learned enough in our brief visits to offer you a fair sample of the residents' perceptions of their world. We are fully aware of the hubris in this assumption.

Different interviewers, even asking the same questions, elicit different responses from people. Sometimes it is a matter of trust: a person will tell one interviewer things he won't tell another. Sometimes it is a matter of sex or age reaction: a person will talk differently to a man than to a woman, to an older person than to a younger person. Sometimes it is a matter of personal perception: an interviewee who wants to help will go into far more detail for an interviewer he thinks is naive than for one he thinks is very informed. For that reason, extremely sophisticated interviewers often miss completely a lot of basic, important information.

That doesn't mean that studies based on interviews are unreliable or untrue, but it does mean that they can never be totally true or totally reliable. The characteristics of the information gatherer influence the quantity and quality of the information gathered—a 35 mm camera with a wide-angle lens records a different kind of visual information than an 8 × 10 view camera with a six-inch lens. Both produce legitimate information, but knowing something of each instrument permits the viewer to know something of how to read the resultant photographs.

In a book such as this one, based on interview material and observations, there is no way to control for the difference in interviewer, personal idiosyncrasies, or contextual influences. All one can do is describe them.

We have our own opinions of the function of the death penalty in our society and the function of Death Row in Texas at this time. We have tried, as best we could, to keep those opinions in some kind of intellectual escrow during the interview selection process. There is no way, from here, from our point of view, from our place, to know how well we succeeded. Total objectivity is probably impossible in an investigation of this kind, so we have appended to this study a statement about our own positions so you might know how they may have determined or modified our collection and presentation of the data. We tried to be fair.

Funds for work on this book and the film were provided by grants from the American Film Institute, the Playboy Foundation, the Polaroid Foundation, the Edna McConnell Clark Foundation, the Levi Strauss Foundation, the State University of New York at Buffalo, and the Fund for Investigative Journalism. We are grateful for their aid. We are also grateful for their courage: many foundations we approached, as well as a number of corporations, made it clear that they would be happy to support us on almost any other project, but they just didn't want their names connected with Death Row.

For their help, we also would like to thank Ann Christian, Ruth Christian, Esther Lawton, Julia Jackson, W. J. Estelle, Jr., Andrew Holt, Don Reed, A. L. Hart, R. L. Cousins, John Price Hayter, Oscar Savage, and George Beto. We also want to thank Murriel "Donnie" Crawford of J-23 for his three poems.

Most of all, we want to thank the residents of and workers on Death Row in Texas. Some of them took real risks in talking with us. We hope they think it was worth it.

Bruce Jackson
Diane Christian
Buffalo, December 1979

Preface to the Second Edition

1. Voices

Voices from Death Row consists primarily of things said to us by Death Row inmates and Death Row porters (all of whom are trusties) in Texas about living in the limbo between a sentence of death and ultimate resolution of that sentence in execution, death by murder or natural causes, commutation to a term or life sentence, or exoneration. The book also contains commentary and analysis by us having to do with the death penalty in general and Texas Death Row in particular.

We don't know of any other book that has such first-person accounts. The accessibility we had to Texas Death Row in 1979—to sit in the cells and listen and to have uninterrupted private conversations with those condemned men in the prison's visiting room—is unimaginable in today's closed prison environment.

Some things have changed since our visits to the Row. Conditions of confinement are far more punishing and brutal now.

2. Killing

The Supreme Court voided all death penalty statutes in *Furman v. Georgia*, 1972. That decision didn't outlaw the death penalty; it merely said that the states had to clean up the way they went about administering it. Four years later, in *Gregg v. Georgia* (1976), the Court allowed states that created death penalty statutes meeting the objections raised in *Furman* to start killing again. The case of Jerry Jurek, whose photograph appears in this book, was included in the *Gregg* decision.

The first post-*Gregg* execution was Gary Gilmore in Utah (January 17, 1977). Gilmore went to court to block appeals on his behalf. The court gave him what he wanted. The second was John Spenkelink in Florida (May 25, 1979). He fought all the way to the electric chair.

We did our work on Texas Death Row in April 1979, after Gilmore and before Spenkelink.

Texas resumed executions with Charlie Brooks (December 7, 1982). Brooks was the first American executed by lethal injection.

In the four decades since *Gregg*, 1,534 men and women have been put to death by state governments and sixteen by the federal government. Public support for the death penalty is at its lowest level since the 1960s. The number of death sentences has declined, but the number of sentences of life without parole has increased hugely.

Texas, with 572 executions, accounts for 37.6 percent of the total.

There were no federal executions from 1964 to 2001. The federal government executed two men in 2001 (one of them Timothy McVeigh, the Oklahoma City bomber) and one in 2003. There were no more federal executions until the final year of the Trump administration. The first of these was on July 14, 2020. The Trump administration would, over the following six months, execute eleven more men and one woman, the last three of them during Trump's final week in office.

Since 1974, 185 condemned prisoners have been exonerated by the courts. The most common official reasons are perjury, false accusation, official misconduct, mistaken witness identification, and inadequate legal defense. Most exoneration cases had more than one cause for exoneration. The case of Rickey Newman (Arkansas, convicted 2002, charges dismissed 2017), for example, had false or misleading forensic evidence, false confession, perjury or false accusation, official misconduct, and inadequate legal defense.

No one knows how many of the executed were innocent: investigatory resources are scant and are dedicated to the living.

3. Access

Voices from Death Row is not, as we note in the introduction to the first edition, about capital punishment. It is about living in a special prison defined nowhere in law, a prison that is a collateral consequence of a death sentence by a court, a limbo in which people live for decades between the moment that sentence is declared and final resolution in exoneration, commutation, or death.

This book could not be done now. When we were working on *"In This Timeless Time": Living and Dying on Death Row in America* (University of North Carolina Press, 2012) we tried repeatedly to visit Texas's current Death Row. None of our letters or emails was answered. A retired warden, who himself had presided over many Texas executions, urged the prison administration to let us visit. His calls and emails were also ignored.

Our 1979 access was perhaps grounded on a fluke. In 1978, after giving a lecture at the Criminal Justice Institute at Sam Huston State College in Huntsville, Texas, Bruce had been asked to testify in a prisoners' civil rights case, *Ruiz v. Estelle,* about how the Texas prison system had changed since he'd done his earlier ethnographic work there in the mid-1960s. He agreed to do so, but only if he could first revisit all the prisons on which he'd worked a decade earlier. In the course of a conversation about that with then-director James Estelle, Bruce said he'd thought he was through visiting prisons, that he was on to other kinds of work now.

"Any time you want to do any projects here," Estelle said, "you have the same access you had under Dr. Beto ten years ago."

Bruce, and in all likelihood Estelle, thought that was an offer that would never be called. But it was.

Bruce started his prison visits and, for the first time, visited Death Row. He'd avoided it in his earlier work. He realized that Death Row differed from all other parts of Ellis prison farm, and all other Texas prisons, and that all death rows differed from all other prisons in exactly the same way.

That July, in Hailey, Idaho, Bruce told his editor at the *Nation*, Carey McWilliams, what made death row unique. "Someone should do a book about it, a film about it," he said.

"Yes," McWilliams said. "You have to do it."

"Why?" Bruce said.

"Because you have the access," McWilliams said.

The two of us looked at one another, we looked at Carey, and Bruce said, "Yeah, you're right. We'll do it."

Bruce wrote Jim Estelle, saying we wanted to do a film about Death Row. We have no idea what Estelle thought when he got that letter, but there was no way he could walk the offer back. Too many people had been in the room when he'd made it. You just don't make promises in front of people like that and then say, "Well, I didn't really mean it." More important, probably, is that Bruce hadn't yet testified for the state in *Ruiz.*

So, in April 1979, we went to Death Row in Texas. Before we went, we wrote every inmate there, telling them something about who we were and what we hoped to do. When we got there, Diane spent days in the prison's visiting room in conversations that ranged from thirty minutes to six hours. Bruce spent his days filming on the Row, taking still photos during breaks, and sometimes visiting cells in the evening for longer conversations. Each night, in the Holiday Inn, we reloaded our film magazines, set all the equipment batteries to recharging, and talked about what we'd learned. Diane would tell Bruce about something someone had told her that might fit into the film; Bruce would tell Diane about things he'd heard that he thought warranted far more talk.

It ended when we burned out emotionally. Every day, we had conversations with men living under a sentence of death. We were, in our way, doing the same thing as they were: going to work each day as if the situation was normal. But it wasn't. And we had an option they didn't: we could leave.

We had enough film and money for a few more days, but film and money weren't enough. We went home to Buffalo and spent the next nine months working on the book and the film.

Both had the same name: *Death Row.* The first screening of the film was on the Row itself. We ran it through the sixteen TV sets on the walls of J-21 and J-23. We'd promised them that if they thought we'd gotten it wrong, no one else would see the film. They liked it. Afterward, we visited every prisoner on both sides of J-block and talked about it.

That night, we showed the film at Sam Houston State University. Some guards were there with their families. One, who had seen the film earlier, said, "At last my wife can see what I've been trying to tell her about."

The next morning, we had breakfast in the university's hotel. A young man introduced himself. His name was Brent Bullock, Jr. He was a deputy sheriff from Provo, Utah, and he was in Huntsville, he said, to take a course at the Criminal Justice Center. He had been one of the officers who had arrested Gary Gilmore after Gilmore committed two murders in Provo, and he had been a witness when Gilmore had been executed by firing squad. Gilmore's execution, he said, hadn't bothered him at all; he thought Gilmore had it coming. But the film had disturbed him terribly. No one, he said, should have to spend years dangling like that.

We agreed with him.

Time on the Row

The main thing Bruce told Carey McWilliams about Death Row is this: Death Row differs from all other prison situations in one important regard. Nothing done by the prisoners while there influences anything but the conditions under which the prisoners reside while there. A condemned man may get lockdown if he is perceived as troublesome, but that has nothing to do with the death sentence. All decisions about the death sentence are made elsewhere.

Behave badly on the Row and you lose recreation privileges or commissary privileges, or you may be sent down the corridor for a few days in the dark cells of solitary or moved to a part of the Row with fewer amenities—but your bad behavior on the Row doesn't affect the sentence of death. Behave like an angel on the Row and the guards and porters will be nice to you—but it doesn't affect the sentence of death. An ordinary prisoner serving a sentence, even life without parole, may earn modification in his living conditions by behaving in ways of which the prison administrators approve: he is assigned to a cellblock or prison with fewer restrictions and more privileges; if there are prison jobs, the prisoners who behave in approved ways get the best job assignments. For prisoners not serving life without parole, good behavior may result in a reduced sentence. But prisoners on Death Row are not serving sentences and they are not doing time. There is no way to reduce a sentence of death because death is absolute and eternal. Condemned prisoners are, as several of them said to us, "just in limbo."

The single most common slang expression for "serve a prison sentence" is "do time." It conjugates: *I'm doing time, I did do time, I will do time.* It also works as a noun: "Where have you been?" "I've been doing time."

In the penitentiary, if you ask someone, "What are you doing?" you will, even if that person is at that moment reading a magazine, writing a letter, drawing a chicken, get as a temporal answer, *a nickel . . . a dime . . . 25 to life. . . . I'm doing it all.* The answer to "What are you doing?" is for them what the judge said at the end of the trial: the sentence being served.

But there is in the penitentiary one group of inmates who are not doing time at all, who are instead outside of time: the inhabitants of Death Row, the condemned, those who are there not to expiate an act but merely to wait.

Many men and women are in prison for murder, and many of those are in for first-degree murder, which is murder with malice aforethought:

a jury decided they knew what they were going to do, they knew it was a crime, they decided to do it, and they did it. But nearly all those sentenced murderers are doing time. Seventy percent of prisoners serving life sentences are eventually released, and most violent offenders serve only about 50 percent of the court's sentence, so even prisoners doing life sentences are doing time; they just don't know how much time they're doing. But, like all prisoners other than the condemned, they're in the active voice.

Not so the condemned. They are "on the Row" just as mental patients are "in the hospital." Time does not count for the condemned because they are not serving a sentence. If you're on Death Row a year or twenty years, the time you've been there matters not at all when your time there ends. The condemned, unlike all the prisoners in all the other cells in all the other cellblocks, are not there to become better persons or even to be punished. Time spent on Death Row isn't the sentence; it is collateral damage occasioned by the sentence.

If, on the Row, you ask "What are you doing?" you will get as an answer, *reading a magazine, writing a letter, drawing a chicken,* or *use your eyes.*

If you become a nice guy while on the Row, if Jesus fills your heart and you are ready to tend to the lepers without wearing gloves, it matters not at all; if you turn into a brute it matters not at all; if you go mad it matters not at all. The Row is not for improvement and it is not for atonement and no one except outside sentimentalists and your family care if you do either, and their opinions don't matter to anyone who counts. The Row is limbo, a place men and women wait for years between the day a judge pronounces the sentence of death and the final determination in reversal, commutation, pardon, or death.

Jack Harry Smith, 1937–2016, Who Died on the Row

Death comes to those on the Row in four ways: execution, murder, suicide, or the same way it comes to most of the rest of us.

Jack Harry Smith came to the Row on October 9, 1978, when a Harris County jury convicted him of killing Roy A. Deputter, who tried to interfere with Smith's holdup of Corky's Corner convenience store in Pasadena, Texas, on January 7 of the same year. Smith had previously received a seven-year sentence for robbery and assault (1955) and a life sentence for robbery by assault (1960; paroled 1977). He attempted to escape in 1963.

Jack died of cancer in the medical facility of Estelle Unit of the Texas Department of Criminal Justice on April 6, 2016. He had been brought to Estelle from Death Row, which is now located on the Polanski Unit, 50.9 miles southeast of Estelle. He was seventy-eight years old and in his thirty-eighth year on Death Row. He had been sick with cancer for several years by the time of his final move to Estelle.

Jack had been on Death Row in Texas only a few months when we met him there in April 1979. Jack told us that he spent a great deal of time working on his case but it wasn't easy because he didn't have any money so it was hard for him to get copies of official court documents, such as old indictments and transcripts. The state law library, he said, charged him five cents a page for the transcripts, which he thought was fair enough, but most of the time it cost more nickels than he had to buy a transcript. The indictments were far shorter than the transcripts, but the Harris County court charged him a dollar each for copies of his old indictments. "Well, if a man don't have the money," he said, "there's no way I can get these indictments."

There was a further problem: Jack couldn't read very well, so once he got the indictments and other transcripts, he couldn't do much of anything with them unless somebody helped him. Texas prisons had a vigorous literacy program, but Death Row prisoners weren't allowed to take part in it or any other education program. Bruce would often see Jack—who lived in cell 18 on one-row of J-23—with his left hand through the bars of his cell holding a mirror attached with string to two rolled-up newspapers, also held together by string. The mirror on the newspaper tubes let him and Mark Fields in cell 19 look at one another while Fields read to Smith from the transcripts Smith's nickels had purchased from the state law library.

Jerome Lee Hamilton, Smith's partner in the holdup, testified against Smith and, in return, received a life sentence. Hamilton was paroled in February 2004. That is not uncommon in capital cases in Texas when there are two individuals accused of equal responsibility for a felonious killing: one testifies against the other and after a while is set free; the other is given a death sentence and is subsequently executed, commuted to life without parole, dies, is murdered in prison, or, in rare instances, is exonerated.

Three prisoners on Texas Death Row (Clarence Jordan, Harvey Earvin, Raymond Riles) were, by a few months, there longer than Jack Harry Smith, but he was the oldest resident of the Row. Riles (who came to the Row on February 4, 1976) got off the Row in 2021 when an appellate court decided he never should have been sent there in the first place; he did forty-five years in solitary confinement because of that mistake. Earvin (who arrived on the Row on November 26, 1977) and Jordan (who arrived on September 12, 1977) are still there.

Polunsky

When Jack Smith was sent to Death Row, it was located on the Ellis Unit of what was then called the Texas Department of Corrections (the prisons are now part of the Texas Department of Criminal Justice). Ellis is 13.2 miles northeast of Huntsville, Texas, home of the administrative offices of the prison system and the Huntsville Unit, which everyone calls "The Walls." It has that name because it is the only prison in the system bounded by a wall rather than chain-link fences and concertina razor wire. The Walls was and remains the location of the death house—a row of eight cells where inmates were moved before their execution—and the killing room, with the gurney and elaborate system of tubes that delivers to the veins of condemned prisoners the drug cocktail Texas uses for executions.

Having the killing apparatus in one place and Death Row in another means that the prison officials putting someone to death meet that prisoner for the first time the day of the execution. It is more work to haul the condemned from another unit to be killed, but the process is far easier on the staff, since the people knowing the person being put down aren't party to the event, and the people doing it aren't familiar with the person they are killing.

In 1999, Death Row moved to the Allan B. Polunsky Unit, 44.8 miles east of Huntsville. The ostensible reason was that three men had, the year before, escaped Death Row on Ellis, but not one of the three made it off the prison grounds. The real reason was that Polunsky was the Texas prison system's supermax, and the officials in charge wanted its crown jewel to be the max within the max: Death Row.

The Polunsky Unit was originally to have been named the Terrell Unit, after Dallas insurance executive Charles Terrell, but when he learned that the prison would be the location of the new Death Row, he requested his name not be used in connection with it. So the prison system renamed the Ramsey III Unit in honor of Terrell, and the new unit after Allan B. Polunsky, a former chairman of the Texas Department of Criminal Justice.

From the condemned men's point of view, there are two changes resulting from the move of Death Row from Ellis to Polunsky. The first is the length of the drive to the death house at The Walls: with Polunsky being nearly 45 miles from Huntsville, the condemned man's last ride is a good deal longer than the thirteen-mile trip from Ellis (women under death sentences are kept at another prison entirely).

The other is the condition of confinement: Polunsky is far more brutal and vicious.

On Ellis, the condemned were kept in regular cells on the two sides of cellblock J. One side of the block—Row J-23—had been populated when Texas killed with the electric chair, so there were no electric outlets or lights within the cells. The theory was, since Texas killed with electricity the condemned had to be prevented from committing suicide by electricity. All the transparent windows on J-23 (the last row in the prison, so it had a view all the way to the cyclone fence and guard picket and beyond) had been replaced with frosted glass. No one remembered why.

By the time there were enough prisoners to start populating J-21, Texas was killing by lethal injection, so those cells had electric lights and electric outlets for fans and such. And the windows were clear glass. After J-21 began holding condemned prisoners, broken windows on J-23 were replaced by clear glass panes.

Prisoners on J-21 and J-23 were allowed out of their cells one at a time for showers, and in groups of nineteen for three ninety-minute recreation periods a week. If the weather was good and the ground dry, they could go outside to a small exercise yard. If the weather was bad and the ground wet, they were in a dayroom with four steel tables, each of which had four welded steel seats. The dayrooms also had water fountains.

In the day room they could talk and play dominoes; in the yard they could play volleyball or sit on benches and play chess. Opposite the cells were eight television sets bolted to the walls between the windows. During the day they would play soaps; in the evening they would mostly play sports.

In their cells, the prisoners couldn't see people in adjoining cells directly, but they all had mirrors, so they could have conversations with people on either side and with people passing by. They would play chess on handmade chessboards suspended by string between the cells, and dominoes on blankets on the walkways.

Everything changed with the move to Polunsky. There is no more group recreation: individuals are allowed out one at a time in a small walled yard. The yard has two cages, so if someone else is out, that provides a brief opportunity for conversation. It is the prisoners' only such opportunity. There is no more communication with people going by on the walkway or in the next cell: everyone is in a single cell with a solid door, broken only by a small slot through which food trays come and go and hands are thrust to be handcuffed in case of the very rare visit. There is no looking at the outside because the only window is another narrow slit high on the wall: it lets some light in, but there is no way to see anything through it. There is no television. For most prisoners there is no radio, and the few who are allowed radios get only occasional reception because of all the layers of steel and concrete surrounding them. Most prisoners are allowed no more than one book. No family pictures can go up on the walls.

Jack Smith told the Associated Press in 2001, "I feel that the system is waiting for me to pass away of old age. I'm angry at the justice system, at the courts for wasting taxpayers' money for giving me this hospitality." The last legal action of importance in Smith's case was in 2008, when the US Supreme Court rejected an appeal of his 1978 conviction. Since then, he waited to be killed or to die. His body got him before the State of Texas did.

Jack Smith was right. There was no reason to keep a dying old man in silent solitary confinement as his body wound down. There is no reason to keep the other two hundred men on Death Row of Polunsky prison in such hideously cruel conditions. The prison officials cite security; they always cite security. But Death Row murderers differ from non–Death Row prisoners serving time for murder in only one regard: they got the death penalty and the others didn't. Severity of the crime has nothing to do with it; extent of criminal career has nothing to do with it. It is entirely a function of the county where the trial was held and whether or not the defendant had enough money for retained council.

Most other Death Rows aren't much better: 93 percent of all condemned prisoners in the US are in solitary confinement cells twenty-three to twenty-four hours a day. The conditions under which people are kept on Death Row in Texas have been described by the United Nations as torture. The UN is right. Texas does it to prove it is tough; it gets away with it because the Supreme Court has turned a blind eye to what goes on there.

Bruce attempted to visit Polunsky in 2010, but the official who was in control of such visits—Michele Lyons, Texas Department of Criminal Justice Director of Public Information—refused to take or respond to his telephone calls, and neither would she respond to his email requests for assistance. Former Walls warden Jim Willett, who was then running the Texas Prison Museum in Huntsville, was surprised at the official stonewalling: "Ten years ago they let David Isay interview the tie-down team for NPR," he told Bruce.

But Kerry Max Cook, an exonerated prisoner we met there, said he wasn't surprised that Bruce was stonewalled: "What you saw at Ellis was awful. Polunsky is far worse. If you're a prisoner there, you can't talk to anybody. You don't see anybody. People go crazy there all the time. They don't want anybody to see what it's like in there now. If people like you don't get in, then the world doesn't get in—and what's going on there doesn't get out."

Life without Parole

We wrote above that Death Row prisoners are the only American penitentiary prisoners for whom time does not count. Time doesn't count for political prisoners at Guantanamo, and neither does it count for detainees in mental institutions. Neither of those populations is in the criminal justice system or the penitentiary system; they're another discussion. Neither does time count for pretrial detainees who couldn't make or who weren't allowed bail. If they're convicted, the pretrial detention time may be subtracted from the sentence; if they're not convicted, then that pretrial detention is just time stolen from their lives. They're not so much in the criminal system as in limbo at its outer periphery.

But what about people doing life without parole? Their sentence is not to a period of time but to a change in condition: death within prison.

Their condition is nonetheless qualitatively different from Death Row prisoners. They can hope for a change in the law or a reduction in their sentence. Neither is probable—the pattern of LWOP sentences in recent years has been more of them, not fewer, and the minuscule amount of legal assistance for convicted prisoners primarily goes to those facing execution. But either is always possible.

Nonetheless, the difference in the conditions of imprisonment is profound.

From the outside, a prison sentence is the punishment. But once inside, there is a great spectrum of ways of doing time. Prison is a place to which someone is sentenced; once there, it is a place where people live. Most jurisdictions have a wide variety of carceral structures, some easy, some not. Some units within a prison system permit a great deal of movement and interaction; others permit very little of either. A prisoner serving LWOP can, depending on the jurisdiction, do easy time or hard time. For those prisoners, behavior, performance, and relation with the guards and administrators count. In most states, LWOP prisoners serve time under exactly the same conditions as other prisoners.

Kerry Max Cook

One prisoner we met on Death Row, Kerry Max Cook, had three trials. Two resulted in death sentences; another was declared a mistrial. In 1997, before the start of a fourth trial, Kerry agreed to a deal that would let him plead no contest in exchange for release.

"The lawyer told me 'We're sure to win this one,' " Kerry said to us. "I said to him, 'That's what they told me the last three times.' "

In each trial, more of the prosecution's evidence was tossed out: testimony about a jailhouse confession by someone charged with a felony, whose felony charges evaporated immediately after he testified; testimony from a fingerprint "expert" who said that Kerry's fingerprint found outside the crime scene was less than twenty-four hours old (it is impossible to determine the age of a fingerprint), and so on. But, after twenty years at Ellis and then at Polunsky, Kerry wasn't up to taking the risk one more time. Sometime after his release, DNA evidence cleared Kerry of the crime, but because he'd taken that plea, Texas refused to compensate him for the lost years. While still at Ellis, frustrated because no one would listen to him, he attempted to amputate his penis.

Kerry wrote a book about what happened to him—*Chasing Justice: My Story of Freeing Myself After Two Decades on Death Row for a Crime I Didn't Commit* (New York: William Morrow, 2007)—and his story was one of the six that formed the basis of Eric Jensen's and Jessica Blank's award-winning play *The Exonerated* (2002). Richard Dreyfus and Aidan Quinn are among the actors who have portrayed Kerry in the stage version; Quinn also played him in the film version (2005). He is still haunted by his years on the row. Neither writing the book nor being depicted in the play has rid him of that. "Freedom came," he wrote us in 2010, "but the shadow of bars follow me." Because he pled guilty before the DNA exoneration, he remains, technically, a convicted felon, so there are many jobs he cannot take, many social benefits he cannot get. He is still being punished by the State of Texas twenty-four years after his exoneration.

"People often ask me," he said to us in a recent phone conversation, " 'How did you keep from going crazy in there?' I tell them, 'I don't know that I did.' "

Kerry told us of finding a roll of toilet paper on three-row that was full, from the first sheet to the very last, with perfect, tiny writing, words with no spaces between them, like ancient Greek, one word abutting against the next with no punctuation, sheet after sheet, until the writer got to the end of the roll, at which point he had rolled it back up and thrown it away.

Sometimes, Kerry said, he'd find slips of paper on the run in the same minuscule hand. He'd take the sheets back to his cell and would spend hours trying to make sense of them, being a reader doing the writer's process in reverse. He never learned who the writer was. The unknown writer's words and Kerry's failed attempt to make sense of them were equally with or without meaning.

Billy Hughes's Horses

Billy was a young man on the Row that Bruce talked with frequently. Diane met with him several times; she spent more time talking with him than with any of the other prisoners. Billy had been born January 28, 1952, which means he was twenty-seven when we met, and four days short of his forty-eighth birthday when he was put to death on January 24, 2000.

Billy liked to draw horses. He did cartoons that he sold to horse magazines, thereby making enough spending money so he never had to ask his family to send him any, a fact he was proud of and to which he referred on several occasions, even in one of the last letters he sent us.

Billy gave us two beautiful watercolors for our daughters, Jessica and Rachel, and designed a desk pad for Jessica, who was fourteen at the time. He offered to send Bruce a watercolor as well and asked if he had any preferences. Bruce and Billy sat on his bunk and talked about various situations in which horses found themselves. He showed Bruce photographs and his drawings and paintings of Arabians, Morgans, palominos, quarter horses, appaloosas, and other breeds.

Bruce said that he'd rather have a drawing about the Row.

"What part of the Row?" Billy asked.

Bruce told him any part he wished, perhaps a drawing that expressed something of his feelings about being there.

"Okay," Billy said.

Several months later a large manila envelope arrived, addressed to Bruce. It contained a beautiful watercolor of an appaloosa; there was no sky or ground or shadow or any other object or detail, just the spotted horse motionless against the white of the paper. And it contained the drawing on the cover of this book.

Billy's first trial lasted three days and, to go by the transcript, which he lent us for a while, his court-appointed lawyer never went off autopilot. A police officer testified that only six shots were fired at Billy's car; according to forensic testimony, there were seven bullet holes in the car; Billy's lawyer never inquired into the discrepancy. There were guns found in Billy's car, but no evidence was introduced at trial connecting any of those guns to the bullets taken from the slain policeman; Billy's lawyer seems never to have asked for a ballistics report. Would any such inquiry, or any of the others that weren't made, have changed the outcome? We'll never know. Two days after the jury came in with the guilty verdict, Billy was on Death Row at Ellis.

He called us from county jail after his retrial. He told us he'd been convicted again and had just gotten another death sentence. He'd always insisted that he had no memory of the traffic stop in which he was supposed to have killed a policeman. This time, he said, his lawyer put him on the stand and had him hypnotized. While under hypnosis, he admitted to the murder. Afterward, he said, he had no memory of it.

In 2009, we mentioned this conversation to Kerry Max Cook. Kerry was dubious. He wrote: "I can tell you as an expert regarding criminal trials and death penalty law that no attorney in the world would put a client—especially one in a death penalty case where the victim was a Texas Peace Officer (in Billy's case, a State Trooper!)—on the stand—period—much less under any quack science of 'hypnosis.' THAT would be ludicrous. It simply cannot be true, Bruce. That is a case we would still hear about today! I have never heard of it." Every criminal lawyer and prosecutor we've mentioned the conversation to since has agreed with Kerry.

Was Billy telling us a true but hugely anomalous story? Was he rationalizing what just happened in court? Was he giving us a nice version because he wanted us to like him?

John Coetzee visited us a year or two after *Death Row* came out. His third novel, *Waiting for the Barbarians*, had been published about the same time. We talked about writer things, about movie options, and then about the differences in writing fiction and what the two of us were trying to do.

John asked a key question: "Those men you and Diane interviewed and filmed on death row: how can you know when they were being self-serving and how can you know what truth is in what they say?"

Bruce said, "I never know whether they're telling the truth. But I do know that that moment, in that place, that is what they said. There is the truth of utterance."

That applies to just about every statement in this book. And a great deal more.

"Fantastic Dancer of the Mind"

Many men we met on the Row stay with us: Jack Smith, Andy Barefoot, Kerry Max Cook, Excell White, Billy Hughes, Skeet Skillern, and more.

Things happen, words are said, and they come to mind. Over time, one man we met there, Thelette Brandon, has loomed larger and larger in our memory and our sense of the Row. In the text, we refer to him as "Dancer."

He was the only person on the row who seemed sufficiently crazy, so capable of instantaneous gratuitous violence, that Bruce never sat alone with him in his cell. Now, his craziness seems a perfectly lucid response to the world in which, at the age of twenty-six, he found himself.

Brandon's sentence was reduced to life on July 28, 1982. His initial parole eligibility date was August 2, 1984; the prison website currently lists it as December 23, 1990. Those dates are fictions. Texas had no life without parole sentence at the time of his initial conviction, so they couldn't sentence him to that after his death penalty was commuted. They would have been hitting him with a punishment that didn't exist when he was found guilty. Instead, they just set an impossible date for when he flattens out his sentence and can walk free: the year 9999. He has been eligible for parole for decades, but if the parole board doesn't set him free, he's got seven thousand and seventy-eight years before they have to let him out.

Brandon lived in cell thirteen on one-row. Except when he was sitting on his bunk or on his toilet eating, Bruce doesn't remember ever seeing Brandon not in motion. He'd hang on the bars and rock back and forth. He'd stand in the middle of his cell and dance. (In the rest of this book, everything we or prisoners or porters say about "Dancer" is about him.)

The first day Bruce was on the Row one of the porters brought him a note, winked, and said, "From Brandon." He pointed at a tall man who was standing close to the bars of his cell, moving his upper body left and right, dancing to a beat neither Bruce nor anyone else could hear, and grinning at him. The porter rolled his eyes.

The note said: "There are things we should talk about. Thelette J. Brandon. Fantastic Dancer of Mind."

Every night after lights out Brandon had vigorous conversations with two individuals, Emily and George, who he told Bruce lived in the pipe chase (the narrow corridor between J-21 and J-23 through which power cables, water pipes, and sewer pipes ran and into which the cell ventilators fed) behind his cell. Some nights they wouldn't talk to him and he'd get very cross with them; other nights they would talk to him, and the conversations—only one side of which was ever heard by anyone else—would quickly degenerate into fierce arguments that went on for hours. Some nights he sang to them. Everyone else would scream at Brandon to shut the fuck up so they could get some sleep, but the only voices he attended in the dark were the voices of Emily and George. We don't know when or if he slept.

At least six men on the Row told us they'd like to kill Brandon just so they could get some sleep. Others were more sympathetic. Jack Smith, who lived in cell 17 on the same row, said to Diane, "That nut that talks to hisself, three of them jumped him. They beat him up in the day room. Then they carried him out in the hall and put him back in his cell and locked him up. You know why they jumped on him? Because he talks day and night down there. Carries on conversations with hisself. Loud. And sometimes he'll scream out real loud. I don't hold it against him. I blame the officials for not doing something for him. Why don't the doctors do something for him? Why don't the psychiatrists do something for him? I can't destroy that man because I know he's not there or he wouldn't be staying up day and night."

Bruce asked Scott Summerfield, one of the guards, why the medical staff didn't do something for Brandon. He shook his head and said, "The unit psychologist, or whatever he is, doesn't particularly like to come to this tank."

One day, while Bruce was filming, Brandon yelled out, "Hey, Bruce, gimme one of those cigars."

"No," Bruce said.

"Come on," Brandon said.

"I'll give you one if you promise not to argue with Emily and George tonight."

"It's a deal."

"You promise that there won't be any yelling?"

"I promise."

Someone in one of the adjoining cells yelled out, "Don't believe him, Bruce. He's lying. He's always telling people he's not going to do it and then he does it."

"I'll be real quiet," Brandon said. Bruce gave him the cigar.

The next morning Bruce came on the row about 6:00 a.m. Before he was past the shower cell on one-row someone yelled out, "The sonofabitch was arguing with them all goddamned night!"

Somebody else yelled, "I told you!"

As Bruce passed Brandon's cell, Brandon said, "Hey, Bruce, that cigar you gave me didn't work. Gimme another one and let's try it again tonight."

A few days later, Charles Grigsby, one of the porters, said to Diane, "That wasn't right, what Brandon did with Bruce and the cigar."

"You mean promising not to carry on and then carrying on anyway?"

"No. He can't help that. I mean him saying 'gimme one of those cigars.' That's no way to ask for something."

"Bruce says Brandon is kind of crazy."

"Even so," Grigsby said, "that's no way to ask somebody for something."

Bruce was taking a picture of Barefoot, who lived in cell 3 on one-row, when he heard smashing glass. By the time he turned and saw where it was, Summerfield had yelled "Roll 13!" and Summerfield and two porters—Emery Harvey and Charles Rigsby—had rushed toward Brandon, who was standing in front of cell 11, where Donnie Crawford lived, holding a towel and not doing much of anything. Harvey and Rigsby each took Brandon by an arm and then Summerfield pushed him from behind. They propelled and steered him at a trot toward his cell. They got there just as Ronnie Hodges, the guard in the hall picket, got the cell door open. They shoved Brandon in. Summerfield again yelled "Roll 13!" and Brandon's cell door slammed shut.

Harvey told Bruce that on the way back from his shower Brandon had smashed his coffee glass—formerly an instant coffee or peanut butter or mayonnaise jar—against the bars of Donnie's cell. "That's how you blind guys," Harvey said. "The jar hits the bars going fast, it explodes and it sends glass flying into the face of anybody who's looking out." He shook his head. "What's weird is, he and Donnie are friends. I never saw anything bad between then."

"The way you get somebody over here," Andy Barefoot said later, "is you heat you up some water boiling, boiling hot. And when he comes by, scald him. Or either take a mayonnaise jar and throw it through the bars and let it cut people up. 'Cause that glass hitting that bar, and the momentum of it's still going and the sharp edges, will cut you bad."

After everything calmed down and was back to normal, Bruce went over to Brandon's cell and asked him, "Why did you try to blind Donnie?"

"I didn't. I was trying to blind Wolf."

"But you smashed the glass on Donnie's bars. Donnie's in 11, Wolf's in 12. Why did you do that?"

"I just don't know, Bruce. I really don't."

"So why did you want to blind Wolf?"

Brandon shook his head. "I don't know, Bruce. I just don't know."

The next day, Donnie told Diane that the reason Brandon had smashed the glass against the bars of his cell was Donnie had just reached through the bars of his cell and punched Brandon in the head as Brandon was going back to his cell from the shower.

Brandon, Donnie said, had then rushed to his cell, picked up the jar, came back out and smashed it against the bars of Donnie's cell. (Harvey, the porter, and Andy Barefoot had told Bruce that Brandon had the glass with him. When things happen quickly, stories vary.) Diane asked him why he had punched Brandon in the head. "Because he's driving me crazy yelling all night. I can't get any sleep." Donnie told Diane that a few days earlier Wolf had jumped on Brandon in the dayroom and had punched him a few times for the same reason. Someone else told Bruce it hadn't been just Wolf beating up on Brandon in the dayroom: several guys had gotten in on it, and it had happened more than once. That was probably the same beating Jack Smith had described to Diane.

"So that's what that was about," Donnie said. "Him not letting us get any sleep."

"He said he didn't know why he smashed the glass on your cell or why he wanted to blind Wolf."

"By now," Donnie said, "he probably doesn't."

A few months later, Brandon was moved to Rusk, the state mental hospital, for a while. By the time we came to show the film on the Row in December, he was back on the Row.

We visited every cell on J-21 and J-23. That was Diane's first time on the Row. The building major and a guard hovered near her the entire time.

Brandon was now on two-row on J-21. "He was excited about your coming today," the building major said, "so they gave him a whole bunch of tranquilizers to make sure he was all calmed down."

When we got to Brandon's cell he was at the bars and bouncing back and forth the same way he always did. He'd been on cell restriction after he smashed the jar on the bars of Donny Crawford's cell, so he and Diane had never met when we'd worked on the row the previous spring. He looked at her, grinned, and said, "So you're Diane. You're one beautiful mama. I want to shake your hand."

There was dead silence on the run and everybody knew what everybody else was thinking. The building major, who was standing next to Diane, went absolutely rigid. Brandon kept grinning at all of us. Diane said, "Thank you," and put her hand in front of the bars. Brandon took it in his. He drew it to his side of the bars. Brandon was a very large man and Diane's hand disappeared from sight. We all knew that, if he wished, Brandon could pull Diane's arm out of its socket in an instant.

All he did was hold it a moment longer, smile again, and let it go. Everyone relaxed.

Then he said, "And Bruce, my man, now I want to shake *your* hand." He grinned again, knowing exactly what everyone was thinking this time too.

Bruce put his hand out. Brandon took it in his, gently pulled it inside the bars, looked at Bruce, looked at Diane, looked at the building major who was in a condition we thought close to panic, and then he shook Bruce's hand, held it a long time, and finally said, "It's good to see you." And it was.

What Brandon Said

Our documentary film *Death Row* ends with a tracking shot on the third tier of J-23. The shot begins with Brandon, rocking back and forth at the bars in his cell. The soundtrack during that shot is Brandon's voice. Bruce wanted to end the film with what Brandon said because he thought it demonstrated a truth at the heart of the place: Death Row is a crazy place. People do all kinds of things to pretend their world is normal, or to hide from it, but the only thing really going on is waiting to learn whether or not they'll be bundled into an SUV, driven to The Walls at Huntsville, and coolly put to death. Diane wanted to end the film with what Brandon said because she thought he articulated, poetically, what the Row was all about. Now we think we both were right.

There is something astonishing about Brandon's words: they have remained current. In April 1979 he was spot-on about our problems with Iran (the Iran hostage crisis was going on), and with our inability to admit how much of American political and social life is driven by notions of ethnic purity. Every time we show the film, people listen to Brandon and say, "He could have said this yesterday."

As could almost everything these men had to say about their condition and situation forty-three years ago. Some death rows are kinder than the one they describe; most, especially Texas, are crueler. The basic existential fact is exactly the same: a condemned prisoner lives from day to day waiting to learn if decisions made elsewhere by people who may be concerned with nothing the condemned prisoner did or did not do will result in freedom, ordinary prison time, or state-administered death.

This is what Brandon said:

> I'd like to just comment on the present-day situation in the world
>
> As far as what's happening in Asia, Iran to be exact. I believe that it's time that the real issue of religion via politics come into being it has to be one based on separation, separation, and understands what it means to go by the book or the Koran, the holy Koran, for this book is inspired so that man can get some kind of insight into the existence of being religious.

> As far as the condition and the situation, I'm not going to philosophize, because it's not my belief, but I will contend that whatever's happening in Iran we are so concerned about it and in spite that we might never have some impetus into the total outcome. Iran: obviously Iran understood that the people of America, the United States government of America, is one based on the creed of ethnic purity.
>
> We learn through conversations and disagreements but this is our form of politics. When it comes down to spreading love and joy on the world I'd just like to say happy. Be happy that you are to come to understand that for our way of doing things, and you will be something to do with if you're not welcome.
>
> But we would like to send our concern to the whole wide world, people in China, Red China, the people that's in Taiwan, Thailand, Britain, Singapore, Australia, Burma, Finland, Denmark, Britain, Great Britain, France, Russia, Cuba, Africa, South Africa, West Africa, or wherever there's potential of ethnic purities and violations of human rights we are concerned that it is our somewhat our background that some failure so as to the outcome in case of injustice based on one of the attempt to convey and over institutionalize a concept, an idea based on one of separatism.
>
> Understanding the real language that is being, is being spoken.

Palm Trees Painted on the Walls Where the Blood Was

On March 15, 2022, just as this edition was about to go to press, Kerry Max Cook called from Houston. He talked about changes on Ellis Death Row after we were there in 1979, and a bizarre repurposing of the Row in spring 2022. We summarize the conversation in the Postscript. It brings everything you will have read by that point into the present.

Glossary of the Row

The conversation of Death Row inmates includes a fair amount of prison slang or argot. Even though most men on the Row have not done time previously and have almost no contact with other prisoners now, some have done time, and there is the daily contact with the porters and the guards.

There are three locations: *in population* means among convicts not sentenced to death, those who work regular prison jobs and get to move around for meals and recreation; *in the free world* or *on the streets* means any place outside prison or jail; and *on the Row.*

Row has three possible meanings. It may mean Death Row, the administrative unit within Ellis prison where all the condemned men are housed. Death Row is presently the two sides of J-wing. *Row* may refer to either of those sides, J-21 or J-23. It may also mean any one of the three tiers on each of those sides. A speaker might refer to *two-row,* meaning the second tier of J-21 or J-23. He might refer to *this row*, meaning either the tier he is on or the side of the wing. References to the administrative unit will be spelled with a capital *R,* references to the wing sides or the tiers will be spelled with a lowercase *r*. Generally, the meaning will be clear from the context. The walkway in front of the cells may be called a row, but it is often called *the run*. Generally, *row* implies the cells and the run, and *run* means the space outside the cells on this tier level. Sometimes the row is called the *tank*.

The convicts who maintain the wing—serve food, deliver messages and commissary, clean up, carry hot water and toilet paper, do nearly everything but lock and unlock cell doors and deliver prescriptions—are variously called *porters*, *hall boys*, and *wing tenders*. For decades, they were called *building tenders*, but because of a recent court case challenging their abuses, that term has fallen out of use in official statements. Some inmates on the Row, as elsewhere in the prison, still call all inmates with building trusty jobs *building tenders.*

Going for a date means being taken from the prison to the court of original jurisdiction for an execution date. In Texas, the death sentence is pronounced immediately after the punishment phase of the trial (the jury first decides on guilt or innocence; if a guilty verdict is delivered, the jury then determines whether the sentence shall be life imprisonment or death), but the execution date is not fixed until certain preliminary motions are filed and processed and the case is affirmed. Many men spend two or three years on the Row before getting their first date.

Bench warrant is the court order necessary to have a prisoner brought from the Row to court. Prisoners might go out on *bench warrant* because they are getting a date or because they are required in court in connection with an appeal procedure or for a new trial.

The *picket* is the caged-in area at the end of each wing. It can be entered only from the prison's central corridor; there is no access from within the rows. The picket is three tiers high. On each side on each tier is a locking device that controls all the cell doors. The guard in the picket throws a lever for each door he wants moved; he can control any number of cell doors (from one to twenty-one) at once. After he selects the cell doors to be moved, he cranks a large stainless steel wheel. If the locking mechanism in the picket breaks down or jams, there is no way the cell doors can be opened short of cutting the doors open with torches or special blades. No prisoners, not even trusties, are ever allowed in the picket.

Locked down means kept on cell restriction. *Locked up* usually means sent to the solitary confinement cells, which are in another part of Ellis. The solitary cells have limited facilities, reduced light, no television access, and no recreation periods; inmates in solitary are put on a restricted diet. Other names for solitary are the *hole* and, among some older convicts, the *shitter.* The term *shitter* is more commonly used on Death Row to mean the cell toilet.

Stinger is the electric immersion heater used for heating coffee or tea water. Since Texas abandoned electrocution in favor of death by lethal injection, Death Row inmates have been permitted to purchase these devices from the commissary. Commissary purchases are made with *scrip* rather than cash. Inmates are permitted to *draw* a certain amount of scrip every two weeks.

Fall partner is someone arrested on the same charge as the speaker. *People* is one's family. A *home boy* is someone from the same home town. *Laws* are the police. *The Man* is any official in law enforcement or corrections—a police officer, the warden, a guard, or the agency employing such individuals. *He works for the Man* doesn't mean he works for any specific individual but rather that he works for the police or the prison or the FBI or whatever the context indicates. *Boss* is any prison guard or officer. *TDC* is the Texas Department of Corrections.

Pipe chase is the narrow walkway between the two sides of a cellblock. The only entrance is through the hall picket. It is where sink and toilet pipes and drains enter and exit the cells, and where the air vents lead.

A *jacket*, to the officials, is an official record packet. To the inmates, *jacket* means a reputation. *He has a snitch-jacket* means he is known as an informant.

To *have nuts* means to have courage or be brave. To *run it down* means to explain.

Head-strumming is hitting someone. To be a *punk* is to occupy the role of catamite or fellator, generally in exchange for commissary or protection.

My house means my cell. *The County* means the county jail.

Shakedown means search. *Get down* means to do something. *Come down* means come to the prison from the County.

To *go down* means to be executed.

I.

Death by Texas

1. Killing Rooms

The first man to die in the Texas electric chair was Mack Matthews, a black man convicted of murder in Tyler County. He was killed February 8, 1924. Four other black men, all convicted of murder, died in the chair the same day: George Washington (Newton County), Melvin Johnson (Liberty County), Ewell Morris (Liberty County), and Charles Reynolds (Red River County).

Before February 1924, Texas had no electric chair, and its state prison had no Death Row. Men under death sentences were kept in the same county jails they stayed in during their trials, and when the appeals ran out, they were hanged by local officials. After Texas prison inmates built the chair, execution services were centralized at the Huntsville Unit of the Texas prison system. By July 30, 1964, the date of the last execution by electrocution in Texas (Joseph Johnson, black, murder, Harris County), 361 men had died in the Huntsville killing room.

Huntsville Unit is the official name for a prison everyone calls "The Walls." It is the only one of Texas' fifteen prisons with a real wall around it: thick, thirty feet high, guards on top with automatic and semiautomatic weapons. The Walls is the oldest building in the Texas Department of Corrections. It was constructed not long after the Civil War and once held an Indian chief. All the other prison buildings date from the 1930s or later. Most were built in the 1950s and 1960s, and some are under construction. Except for The Walls, all the Texas prisons now have their perimeters secured by single or double cyclone fences and underground pressure-sensing devices. These are easier to maintain, cheaper to build, and easier to watch.

The death house at The Walls has eight cells. They used to be adequate. That was because not very many people were sent down each year, and those who were sent down were processed quickly. The courts now insist that procedures be examined very carefully before the state kills anyone, so after conviction in court and fixing of a death penalty, years pass by before anyone is really at mortal risk.

The old death cells and the execution chamber are between one of The Walls's cellblocks and some of the administrative offices. It is possible to reach the execution chamber without passing through the large brass prison gates and walking through the yard and cellblock. It is just a matter of passing through an office corridor, unlocking a few doors, crossing a small patch of grass, and stepping across the small exercise yard, which is now only a vestige of the days when condemned men actually spent a lot of time there. That route was taken by witnesses to 361 deaths.[1]

The killing room is not large. A gurney is now where the chair used to be. When an execution takes place, the gurney will be taken through the control room into the row of death cells, and the man to be killed will be strapped to it. The gurney will be quickly moved back to the killing room.

An iron rail separates the witness area from the killing area. Three intravenous tubes will be inserted in the condemned man's arm. They lead through a wall to three petcocks and three bottles. One tube and bottle, according to the present plan, will contain water or some other harmless fluid; a second will contain sodium pentothal; the third will contain the killing fluid (it hasn't yet been determined exactly what will be in that third bottle). Presumably, there will be three hands on the three petcocks, preserving the old fiction: none of the three executioners will know for sure who did the killing, so no one will have to feel guilty about it later in the unlikely event that the executioner decides that the death penalty is something the state shouldn't do, and that execution is something he or she shouldn't have helped to do.

There are no chairs for witnesses. A visitor, being shown the room for the first time, said to the guide, "You should have chairs. People may get faint."

"No," the guide said, "that won't be a problem. It will be very quick. And it will look just like the guy is going to sleep. That's the reason for the pentothal. There won't be time for people to get sick. It will be over in seconds."

Of the 361 men who died in that room during the years Texas still used the electric chair, 229 were black, 108 were white, 23 were Mexican American, and 1 was an Indian. Five were executed for armed robbery, ninety-seven for rape, and 259 for murder. Only two women were sent to Death Row during those years, but neither was electrocuted. Emma Oliver (black, murder, Bexar County) had her sentence commuted to life in 1951 and died in prison, and Carolyn Lima (white, murder, Harris County) won a new trial in 1966, got a fifteen-year sentence, served her time, and was released.

When the Supreme Court temporarily outlawed the death penalty in 1972, fifty-two Texans were under sentence of death. Forty-five were on Death Row at Ellis Unit, the others were still in their county jails. All fifty-two death sentences were commuted to life. Between 1924 and 1972, 506 men and women had been placed on Death Row.

The change to execution by lethal injection was made by the Texas legislature in 1977. The electric chair—called "Old Sparky" by some—was crated up. It presently rests along a wall facing the eight old death cells.

In the old days, after a condemned man was strapped into the chair, the executioner would hit him with three jolts. The first was 1,800 volts and lasted one minute; the second was 200 volts and lasted two minutes; the third was 1,400 volts and lasted one and a half minutes. The executioner had to manipulate a rheostat or throw shunting switches to get the different voltages, and he had to watch the clock to make sure the times were right. Sometime in the late 1960s or early 1970s (no one around remembers quite when) the state acquired an automated sequencer. The executioner had only to push one button and the device pumped through the wires clamped to the condemned's body the proper voltages for the proper times. Lights on a chrome panel would inform witnesses of the system's status at any particular moment. When the sequence was finished, the device was programmed to shut itself off. The machine was never used because, by the time the men condemned under Texas' 1974 capital punishment law began getting close to potential execution dates, the state had adopted what it considered the more humane technology of lethal injection. The chair-automator is still in place, ready to be hooked up should the lethal injection technology have problems no one yet anticipates.

The following articles from the Texas Code *of Criminal Procedure* are in force:

> Whenever the sentence of death is pronounced against a convict, the sentence shall be executed at any time before the hour of sunrise on the day set for execution. (article 43.14)
>
> The Director of the Department of Corrections at Huntsville, or in the case of his death, disability or absence, the Warden of the

> Huntsville Unit of the Texas Department of Corrections, shall be the executioner. In the event of the death or disability or absence of both . . . the executioner shall be that person appointed by the Board of Directors of the Texas Department of Corrections for that purpose. (article 43.18, amended by Acts of 1975)
>
> The following persons may be present at the execution: the executioner, and such persons necessary to assist him in conducting the execution, the Board of Directors of the Department of Corrections, two physicians, including the prison physician, the spiritual advisor of the condemned, the county judge and sheriff of the county in which the Department of Corrections is situated, and any of the condemned person's relatives or friends that he may request, not exceeding five in number, shall be admitted. No convict shall be permitted by the prison authorities to witness the execution. (article 43.20)
>
> The body of a convict who has been legally executed shall be embalmed immediately and so directed by the Director of the Department of Corrections. If the body is not demanded or requested by a relative or bona fide friend within forty-eight hours after execution then it shall be delivered to the Anatomical Board of the State of Texas, if requested by the Board. If the body is requested by a relative, bona fide friends, or the Anatomical Board of the State of Texas, such recipient shall pay a fee of [*sic*] not to exceed twenty-five dollars to the mortician for his services in embalming the body for which the mortician shall issue to the recipient a written receipt. When such receipt is delivered to the Director of the Department of Corrections, the body of the deceased shall be delivered to the party named in the receipt or his authorized agent. If the body is not delivered to a relative, bona fide friend, or the Anatomical Board of the State of Texas, the Director of the Department of Corrections shall cause the body to be decently buried, and the fee for embalming shall be paid by the county in which the indictment which resulted in conviction was found. (article 43.25)

The last executioner in Texas was Joe Byrd, assistant warden of the Huntsville Unit. After his death, the cemetery in which unclaimed inmate bodies are buried was renamed the "Joe Byrd Cemetery."

2. The Row

In the later years of the old Texas death penalty, the eight-cell Death Row at The Walls was clearly inadequate. When the Ellis Unit was built in the early 1960s, one side of one wing, J-23, was set aside to be Death Row. The Row was emptied for a time when the Supreme Court created a temporary moratorium on executions in *Furman* v. *Georgia* in 1972.

Ellis is twelve miles from Huntsville. It is Texas' maximum-maximum unit. Ellis takes the inmates other Texas prisons can't or don't want to handle. When the death penalty was suspended, J-23 was Ellis's segregation unit. Segregation is for inmates Ellis can't or doesn't want to handle; it is almost continuous lockup.

After the Texas legislature drafted a law in 1974 that it thought could withstand the confusing and ambiguous constitutional tests littered through the nine separate opinions in *Furman*, the Row was reactivated. At first, the condemned men were put on the lower part of the row, and segregation inmates were locked in the higher cells.

In February 1978, all of J-23 and a small portion of J-21 held condemned men. In April 1979, the condemned had taken over all of the cells on the first run of J-21 and some of the cells on the second run. By July 1979, only five cells in J-21 were not occupied by condemned men.

There were 114 men under sentences of death in April 1979. Sixty were white, forty were black, and fourteen were Mexican American. Only one of the 114 had been condemned for killing a black victim. The median ages were thirty-one for whites, thirty-two for Mexican Americans, and twenty-five for blacks. The oldest man on the Row was fifty-one; the youngest was twenty. One man had been on the Row slightly over five years, another had just arrived. The median age at time of offense was in the early twenties. Several, particularly among the blacks, were there for crimes committed before they were nineteen. Twenty-six percent of the whites, 29 percent of the blacks, and 38 percent of the Mexican Americans had previous Texas Department of Corrections records.

J-23 is the left side of the last wing on the left as you face the prison from the front gate. There are no lights or electrical outlets in its cells: the state didn't want to risk voluntary, premature electrocutions. By the time overcrowding forced expansion into J-21, the method of execution had changed to death by lethal injection, so the J-21 cells were not modified. They have the same light fixtures and electrical outlets over the sinks that all other cells in Ellis prison have. Inmates on J-23 are now permitted to run extension cords from the run into their cells to power their fans, electric razors, and stingers. They are not allowed to run extension lights into their cells.

J-23 cells are always dark. Even on bright days they are dark because one is always looking out at an enormous wall of shimmering translucent glass. Sitting in the cells is not unlike sitting in a small cave. The contrast in light levels makes the cave darker than it may in fact be because the pupils of the eyes narrow in response to the windows' glow. Inmates look out between their bars, squinting into a world that is never more than ten or twelve feet away.

Between the large windows are the television sets bolted to the concrete wall. There are eight of them on J-23. Inmates on the first run can look through their cell door bars and see the television sets clearly, but none of them can look at the sets directly because the lower four sets are positioned so men on the second row can see them also. To watch television, it is necessary to sit close to the bars and tilt up or down. The inmates on the second and third rows look through a wire mesh designed to keep anyone from leaping off the tier or throwing someone else off the tier. Second-tier inmates can see the heads and shoulders of people moving outside the first-tier cells if those people step out from under the run overhang. Men on the third tier see nothing but the television sets, and to do that they must lean forward and look down.

When Ellis was built, J-23 had clear glass in its windows, as did all the other prison rows. Sometime in the past ten years, all the glass on J-23 was replaced. Instead of transparent windows, J-23 now has translucent panes. All the windows—those looking out on the prison grounds from the row, those looking out on the prison grounds and onto the central corridor from the dayroom—are translucent. Until the overcrowding that forced the takeover of J-21, no Death Row inmate could see birds, grass, trees, rain, the sky, or other prison inmates. Inmates on J-21 get to look from their recreation room onto the prison corridor, and from their cells into the parallel cellblock.

The previous paragraph is not quite accurate: someone smashed one pane on J-23, and it was replaced with a clear piece of glass. A few men can see a small piece of the world outside.

They cannot select what comes on television. The radio is piped in through small speakers in each cell; it plays one of three stations they can select. But their choices don't matter much because the speakers are all suspended in the narrow passage between the two sides of the block called the *pipe chase.* The pipe chase reverberates with the sounds of all three stations.

Directly below the speaker, also opening on the pipe chase, is the air vent. If they block off the air vent with towels or sheets, they can hear just one station, but they stifle the flow of air.

Death Row is a world of enormous sensory overload and sensory deprivation.

There is no silence until late at night; the radios come on again at 6:00 a.m. Some men try to sleep all day and get up at night to write and read. Their eyes go bad and they grow old waiting to die.

One man asked us for a Polaroid to send home. We took it and gave it to him. He waited for it to develop, then called us to his cell. "How old do you think that man is?" he asked. We thought he was in his middle or late forties, so we said, "Forty." He nodded. "I just turned twenty-eight. One day you look in the mirror and you know it's you there, but it doesn't look like you."

Using their shaving mirrors, the inmates can see along the run: the world in a five-inch circle of glass. The rest of the time, they see only the rectangle marked by their cell doors and the wall a dozen feet away. At night, the only illumination in the J-23 cells comes from sixty-watt bulbs suspended about two feet outside the cells.

The only times J-21 or J-23 inmates get to focus at any distance is when they come out for showers or recreation, and that does not consume very much time, or when they have visits. For most inmates, visits are rare, and some get none at all. As a result, many of the men who have been on the Row awhile have bad eyes. The muscles atrophy in the murk of the cramped iron space.

The cell sinks are along the back wall, next to the toilet. That is the darkest part of the J-23 cells. The men hang shaving mirrors on the bars and walk back and forth to the sink while shaving. They come to the bars, wait a moment for their eyes to adjust, shave, then move back into the darkness for water.

Razors—safety injector types—are passed out and collected every day. A guard goes down the row with a long tray with each man's razor in a small slot. He carries the tray in one hand, a jar of pink shaving cream in the other. He hands the razor to the inmate, and the inmate reaches out between the bars to take a glob of the pink stuff. A little while later, the guard collects the razors. He makes sure the blade is still in place.

All other Texas inmates are now allowed to keep injector razors in their cells. The guards change blades at regular intervals. Officials say the blades are so small they're not very dangerous, and anyone really wanting to hurt someone can easily find himself a more deadly weapon—a piece of steel from one of the shops, a pitchfork tine, something like that.

There are some five hundred other men at Ellis doing time for murder, but only the Death Row inmates cannot have their razors. The notion is that they would be dangerous with them. Inmates on the Row think that is silly. "You could make somebody bleed with one of them blades," one inmate said, "but it would take all day to kill him." "They claim we're dangerous with the razors," another said, "but you've got everything in here that you could do more damage with than the razor. That mirror there. You could break it and do anything with it. You got glass in here that you could hurt somebody else with a whole lot worse, but they take the razors back. It's just rules, you know, that they go by."

It's more than "just rules." In the late fall and early winter of 1979, a series of incidents on Death Row and in Ellis prison's Isolation Unit (where particularly violent inmates are held) changed the policy about allowable items. An Isolation inmate had his throat cut with one of those little injector blades. The blade was melted into a plastic ballpoint pen. One witness said, "You could stick both hands in that hole." A guard was stabbed by a Death Row inmate who bent into a weapon the hard wire used to hang the shaving mirrors. There were two incidents of glass throwing at porters and guards. In December 1979, all glass was taken out of Death Row and Isolation cells: the mirrors, the coffee and peanut butter jars, nearly everything that could be turned into a weapon.

"It's not fair to punish all of us just because some jerk on the other side stabbed a guard," one inmate said to us. "I didn't stab a guard, but I can't have a mirror anymore. That's not right."

"But how do you know who is going to stab someone before it happens?" Diane asked.

"I don't know, but it's not right to punish us all for what someone else did."

It wasn't clear when, if ever, the restrictive policy would again relax.

During the day, inmate porters work on each of the J-wing rows. They perform a variety of services, ranging from delivery of commissary to loading and collecting food trays to cleaning and mopping. Food comes from the central mess hall in a hot-cart. The porters serve one wing at a time. One week J-21 gets served first, the next week J-23 gets served first. Usually, the two porters from J-23 will come to J-21 to help with food service, then the two J-21 porters will help on J-23. Each tray must be carried to each cell—a lot of running up and down the iron stairs. One porter will load the trays (sometimes the guard on duty will help) and the others carry them. The trays are slid under the cell doors.

At night, only one porter is on duty on each row. He gets the laundry ready for the next day. He lays out fresh clothes and clean towels. He runs errands for inmates on the Row: he gets hot water for those without "stingers" (electric immersion heaters), and he carries notes, newspapers, and magazines. He makes patrols and alerts the guards if anyone is acting strangely.

A guard in the hallway controls access to J-21 and J-23 with a big yellow key. The individual cells are controlled by another guard in the cage—they call it the *picket*—spanning the ends of the two wings. The picket has a stairway so the guard can unlock cells on the second and third runs. He is responsible for letting men in and out of the six separate rows of cells. At certain times of the day, he is constantly running up and down the metal stairs.

The only telephone in the wing is in the picket. If a free person working on the wing has a call, the wing door must be unlocked, then locked again, then the picket door is unlocked and locked again. After the call, the process is repeated in reverse. Prisoners are never near the telephone.

On each row, an iron stairway leads to the second and third tiers. In most of the blocks of Ellis, that stairway is always open, but on Death Row it is frequently locked by a heavy iron door, especially when groups of inmates are moving to and from recreation or when they are showering. By locking the stairway, the guard can have one inmate out on one-row and another out on two-row and not have to worry that they'll meet halfway and get into a fight.

Death Row inmates get showers one at a time. The noun takes a verb form: "I'm going to shower the row now," the guard says. "I'm opening one-row cell 13 to shower Jones." One is "being showered" rather than "taking a shower." The option is the guards', always. The same thing happens with recreation; it becomes a verb: "I'm going to recreate group three now," the guard says, meaning he will let one-quarter of the men on the row out of their cells and into the small dayroom.

Saturday and Sunday are the visiting days for regular convicts. There is a prison rule that Death Row inmates shall never come into contact with other inmates (except for the barber and the porters who service J-21 and J-23), so Death Row inmates have visits Monday through Friday.

Free-world visitors come through the prison's double cyclone fence, enter a doorway, and make an immediate left turn into the visiting area. It is a large room with the visiting tables making two sides of a large U. The closed end of the U is a solid wall. Running the entire length of the tables on both sides is a tight steel-mesh screen that goes all the way from the oak tabletop to the ceiling. There are no contact visits at Ellis for anyone. The screen is fine enough so a cigarette won't pass through; a joint might, but there are always guards close by, watching.

Inmates enter the visiting room from the open top of the U, which passes through a pair of rooms, where they are searched coming and going. Beyond those rooms is the quarter-mile-long central corridor of Ellis.

On weekends the visiting room is crowded. Ellis now has 2,300 inmates, so a fair number of families always makes the trip. But on the Death Row visiting days, when the other convicts are at their jobs in the fields or the factories or in the building, or are in school, the room is usually empty. It is rare for even two Death Row inmates to get a visit at the same time. A guard always sits nearby, presumably to make sure that nothing is passed through the tiny interstices of the screen. Some inmates complain that he sits close enough to overhear the family conversations. "Why would I want to listen to their bullshit?" one guard said. "They got nothing to say I'm interested in."

At first it would seem that Death Row inmates have better visiting options than do other prisoners: five days to two, empty rooms to full ones. But most prison inmates come from poor families, and Texas is a big state. Houston is seventy-five miles away, Dallas is 160, and El Paso and Amarillo are five hundred miles to the west. For some, a trip to Huntsville and a visit consume a whole day; for many, a visit requires far more time. The family of a regular inmate can leave home after work Friday, spend Saturday at the prison, and perhaps get home in time for church on Sunday, or in time for the football game. Who can afford the luxury of taking off two or three days during the week?

Every day, every Death Row inmate takes a shower. The guard in the picket at the front of the wing starts on a row and, one by one, lets the inmates out, watches as they walk to the shower at the near end of the wing, and watches as they pick up clean clothes and go back into their cells. After a man is locked back down, the guard opens the next cell. This continues until he reaches the last man in the last cell. Then he goes up to another row and begins the process over again. Then the last row. During the entire time, he sits at the end of each row, watching. Inmate porters are working around the Row, ready should there be trouble.

The stairway folds back upon itself; there is no point attempting to throw oneself down it. A metal screen rises from floor to ceiling on both two- and three-row, so no one can throw himself to the concrete floor below. The only kind of trouble that can occur during shower time is if one prisoner on the way to or from a shower should attempt to do something to a prisoner locked up in one of the cells he passes.

One day there was an incident. Dancer was going to the shower. He carried with him an empty coffee jar that he said he intended to fill with hot water from the tap. Inmates of the Row have stingers, but if they're going out of the cell they often get water from the tap in the utility room because it is faster. The tap water is extremely hot, hot enough to cause a bad burn if one isn't careful. Shower was Dancer's only time out of the cell: he had been on cell restriction since he had had a fight in the recreation room with another inmate a few months back.

He took his shower, filled his jar, and walked toward his cell, alternately humming and talking to himself. Almost without breaking his stride, he swung his right arm to the left and smashed the jar of scalding water against the bars of cell 13. No one saw the move coming; he had given no signal, no telegraph. He was still humming and talking to himself, again walking toward his cell. Two porters and one of the guards reached him in seconds; they pushed him into his cell, afraid he was about to explode. The guard in the picket spun the big stainless-steel disk, and the cell door slammed shut.

"Sonofabitch tried to burn Donnie," someone yelled.

"Didn't try to burn me," Donnie said. "Tried to blind me. If he'd wanted to burn me, he'd have just thrown the water."

Dancer had smashed the glass against the bars so it would send fragments hurtling toward Donnie's face. None of them did any damage, however.

Donnie swept his cell while Dancer began discussing politics and ethnic purity with the two invisible friends he said lived behind the air vent in the dark shadows of the pipe chase. He talked to his friends in the pipe chase a lot. Sometimes late at night, sometimes all night long, he talked to them, argued with them, screamed at them. Sometimes he sang them songs. It was because of the conversations with the two friends in the pipe chase that he had gotten into that fight in the recreation room. Another inmate told Dancer he had to stop it, no one was getting any sleep. Dancer said he didn't have to stop anything. This went on for days, they argued, and one morning the other inmate punched Dancer in the head. He was still on cell restriction too.

Recreation occurs in three ninety-minute segments each week. J-21 and J-23 are each divided into four recreation groups. Each weekday except Wednesday, which is haircut day, three of the groups are let out.

When the weather is warm and the ground dry, the inmates can go out to a small caged area where there is a concrete bench and a small volleyball court. Playing volleyball is more difficult for J-23 than it is for J-21 because the top of the cage is lower and hitting the ball without hitting the top of the cage is difficult. Hitting the top of the cage counts as a missed point.

On days when the weather is cold or wet, or when the ground is muddy, or when there isn't an extra guard available to sit outside the cage and monitor what is going on, Death Row inmates are allowed into the recreation room but not the yard. The recreation room has a water fountain and three tables. Each table has four backless attached seats. Some men play dominoes. Others sit and talk. Some walk around the room or stand near the window, letting the sunlight hit their bodies. It isn't often that they get to move very far, and, after the tiny cells, even the small recreation room seems like a minor liberty.

Only rarely do all the men in a recreation group come out at once. Some never come out at all, like one man who has snitched several times on the others. Some, like Dancer and the man he fought with, are under cell restriction. Some, like the man on three-row who cut his wrists, are kept on lockup for punishment. And some don't come out for recreation because they don't like other Death Row inmates. "I don't talk to any of them while I'm in my cell," one said. "Why should I come out there and talk to them? I got my coffee here. I got things to do in here."

And some don't come out because one of their soap operas is on. For men on the Row, soaps can become very important. Characters in the soaps are, for some of them, the people they know better than anyone in the world. Family may not visit, free-world friends may drop away, but "All My Children," "The Doctors," and "As the World Turns" continue forever, as reliable as the prison routine. For some men on the Row, the characters in the soaps are the closest thing to a family they will ever again have. All the prisoners have stories about other prisoners who refused or cut short a rare visit because it was time to see what was happening in one of the soaps.

During the first two weeks of April 1979, a Baptist minister visited the Row twice, each time for about five minutes. When we asked to speak with him about the Row and his work there, he said he preferred not to talk about it. One inmate overhearing that conversation said, "That's because all he does down here is play dominoes or get the Bible freaks reading certificates." We saw no other chaplains or priests. There are no church services on Death Row.

A few times each day, the medical assistant came through with his plastic box full of medication for those inmates who had managed to get a prescription from the doctor, and aspirin for those who hadn't. Talking with the doctor, the inmates complained, was not easy because his English wasn't very good, and he handled the problem of difficult communication by not communicating much at all. They would ask for medication for nerves and he would ask what was wrong with them. They would say, "Nerves," and he would nod and say, "Yes, but what is *wrong* with you?" They thought they had already told him and he was awaiting a disease he could hang a pill upon. They had only symptoms, not diagnoses, to offer.

We tried talking with the doctor once. He was very small and, we thought, Asian. One of the inmates said he was Filipino, another said he was Vietnamese. Another said, "Who gives a shit?"

"We'd like to talk with you," we said to the doctor.

His eyes darted and he backed away. "Fine, everything fine," he said, and fled. We didn't see him on the Row again during the visit.

One afternoon, the unit psychologist, a young man very dapperly dressed and combed, came to the wing. He stood against the outside wall for a moment, talked to one inmate, then left.

An assistant warden made a circuit of the wing, presumably listening to requests, complaints, grievances, and needs. He told one inmate, an artist, that he would be allowed to continue receiving his drawing pens. The inmate had been worried because the assistant warden was new and the grapevine had said he thought drawing was unimportant and frivolous.

Other than those visitors, we saw no one on the Row but the porters, the wing officers, and the condemned men. It is possible there were other visits, say, when we were out to lunch, which sometimes took thirty minutes, or at night after we were gone, but no one said anything about other visitors to the wing except to complain: "They bring reporters or citizens' groups through here. They come down and say, 'A woman's gonna be on the wing, get dressed.' Then they come in, they walk through real quick, and they look at us like animals in a zoo. Nobody ever talks to us. They just look in the cage and they go away."

3. Time and Trivia

Many Death Row inmates, like many other Ellis inmates, are convinced that prison officials regularly hold up their mail. They talk of letters that took an inordinately long time to arrive or letters they sent that never arrived at all. One inmate "proved" to us that Ellis officials held up his mail by showing us a letter he had gotten from a friend in New York. The postmark was eight days earlier and he had received the letter the previous evening.

"The only reason that letter could take that long," he said, "is because they were sitting on it up there."

"Why would they sit on a letter from your girlfriend in New York?"

"Don't ask me. Ask them."

We watched the mail room at various times. Officers would be in there most of the day sorting the mail, bundling it for delivery to the wings. There didn't seem to be any special bags for incoming or outgoing mail to be held up for special inmates; we saw no lists of inmates whose mail was segregated or—in the FBI vernacular—given a "cover." Every time we saw the mail sorting, it seemed to be very much like mail sorting in the other institutions we knew: clerks spent their eight hours putting envelopes and folded newspapers and magazines into boxes. The only difference was the slicer, which cut the edges off envelopes for the visual inspection for contraband.

As an experiment, we mailed a letter to ourselves from Huntsville. We put it in the mailbox at the post office near the town square. It took a full week to reach us in Buffalo.

It's not surprising that mail should be such a focal point for the paranoia, for the mail is, even more than visits, the prisoners' primary contact with the free world. The mail is the way one reaches family, obviously, but it is also the way one reaches lawyers, newspapers, judges, and potential friends. There are no telephones for prisoners on Death Row, nor are there for prisoners anywhere else on Ellis prison farm.

Absence of mail or delay of mail means people out there are not bothering to respond or are not responding quickly, or that prison authorities are hiding the mail for some devious reasons of their own. It is easier to think that the prison authorities are hiding the mail than that a judge or a loved one is too busy to send a letter back to Ellis.

Ask why the authorities go to all the trouble of delaying the mail and you get a variety of answers: they want to be mean, they want to keep us off-center, they want to show they're in control, they have it in for me.

A warden says, "I don't want anybody to do hard time. They do hard time and I do hard time. We're all in this place together, everybody knows that." Another says, "I don't have enough men to man the pickets properly. How am I going to spare people to segregate the mail just to harass somebody?"

Many inmates and workers on the Row refer to some inmates' behavior as "paranoid." It is difficult to deal with that term in the context of a community defined only by the knowledge that rational society has carefully decided that nearly everyone in sight is to be put to death. People out there *do* want to kill them, every one of them, so it is hardly surprising that some inmates look upon everyone within sight or sound as dangerous or malevolent.

Several Death Row inmates told us they feared being killed if they were returned to the counties that originally tried them. They were sure that the local sheriffs and police would find some excuse for shooting them down.

Two inmates whose interviews appear here were transferred to the counties of original jurisdiction after their interviews. One was out for a date, the other for a court proceeding. Neither was harmed; both were treated fairly well by the police. One preferred his time in the county jail to his time on Death Row and wanted to stay on there. No Death Row inmate has ever been killed by local police or sheriffs while out on a bench warrant.

One of the saddest things is that no one really cares. Too much time has passed. Police might have killed some of these men had the opportunity and idea arisen before trial, but not now. Local authorities fully expect that, after the court choreographies are done, the state will *do* it, and the hot anger that precipitated the original convictions are long forgotten. It is no longer necessary, because the state will kill them clinically, without anger, without rancor. That is one more unbearable insult.

What was bizarre about the bench warrant experience for the two men was understanding that the communities and organizations that had ordered their deaths were no longer *angry* at them. Something out there was still intending to kill them, but it no longer had a face or a name: it was just a bureaucratic procedure, working its way out.

Prison is an institution of contracts and agreements, most of them unarticulated but nonetheless well understood by all. Most of the contract terms are set forth by the administration, but convicts can modify many of them in certain ways, and they can punish some individual administration workers for failing to carry out their part. The balance of power is with the administration, surely, but it is not total or unilateral. A guard who won't play by the rules, for example, can be sabotaged in various ways. The techniques necessary for keeping the system bilateral reinforce convict culture, and generate brilliant hustling. It probably does nothing for rehabilitation, but it keeps the prison running.

It doesn't work that way on Death Row. On Death Row, none of the usual bargains apply.

Elsewhere in the prison system, the counters are obvious. A convict who behaves badly gets shipped to increasingly restrictive prisons, where he has fewer and fewer personal options and where he earns less and less good time and where the job choices are less and less interesting. A convict who behaves well gets more good time, a better job. If a warden decides a man is trying to make it, he can help the man; if a warden decides a man is trying to be a hard case, he can make the man's life miserable.

On the Row, there is little the wardens can do to or for the men, and equally little the men can do to or for the prison. They don't work, so they can't strike. They don't get good time, so their behavior is meaningless. What they do on the Row—unless they start fights or try to kill themselves—matters to no one.

Most convicts spend their time trying to convince prison officials that they are nice and benign and should be released. The parole board does the releasing, but its decisions are largely based on reports and recommendations generated by the prison officials. A report, which may not be in writing, saying a man is a troublemaker kills a shot at parole. A report, which also may not be in writing, saying a man is really ready may ensure one.

For men on the Row, the opinions of the prison officials count for nothing. The decisions are made elsewhere, by men who never see the Row or the condemned. The decisions are made by judges in Austin or the Texas Court of Criminal Appeals or in New Orleans at the Fifth Circuit or in Washington at the Supreme Court.

Most regular convicts spend most of their energy getting by. Few have any hope of getting a reversal; the time a reversal takes is longer than most will spend in prison anyway. Men with a few years of time to do are not likely to elicit the attention of unpaid lawyers.

Death Row convicts spend their time trying to get out. Getting by means accepting death, getting by too well is itself a form of death. Some of the men keep themselves alive, emotionally and literally, by fighting the case. Some live in the case, think of nothing but the case, talk of nothing but the case.

They talk of two things: their innocence or how procedure was violated in their trials. Most talk is of the procedure, which might strike an outsider as curious—after all, it's the innocence or guilt that matters, right?

Wrong. For the courts considering the appeals, guilt or innocence is irrelevant and immaterial. That decision was made by the jury, long years ago. Appeals courts rarely try to second-guess juries. That would be usurping the rights of the other citizens, their right to say whether one of their peers was guilty or innocent.

Appeals courts review the process by which an individual was convicted. A trial examines evidence for guilt or innocence; an appeal examines a *trial* and the steps leading to it for legitimacy. The decision a Death Row prisoner hopes it will make is that the entire process was somehow contaminated by some official misbehavior, so the trial decision must be reversed, and a new trial is impossible. Second best is the new trial, *absent* the offending information.

So the condemned who elect to fight become passionate devotees of legal trivia, always in the hope that the uncovered item, the discovered decision, the neglected fact will turn out to be reversible error.

This is not such a matter of concern among other convicts because courts generally find minor trial errors "harmless," which means that "the error or misbehavior did occur, but we don't think it affected the outcome enough to warrant starting all over again." Proof of an error isn't enough to get a new trial; one must also prove that the error affected the results. But in a death penalty case, "harmless error" is not so simple. The death penalty is absolute, not relative. It is everything, not just a few years. A minor difference in terms of the trial may not have influenced the decision about guilt or innocence, but it may very well have influenced the decision about prison time versus death.

4. Death

Several Death Row inmates complain about the lack of rehabilitative facilities on the Row. They say conditions make them harder, meaner; that there are no opportunities for self-improvement, but a lot of reasons for developing or worsening antisocial attitudes.

They miss the point.

Death Row is deeded to the notion that these men, of all the criminals in the penitentiary, are special. They are the ones society has said are not capable or deserving of redemption or reform.

To give them schooling, training, or therapy would create an ambiguity the system is not ready to manage and that it has no desire to have become overt: it would acknowledge that residence on the Row is still tentative. In order to deal with the Row and what it means, the prison system adopts the posture of the inmate who says, "We're here for one thing: we're here to die."

Death Row fits none of the rhetorical models of the prison, and in that conceptual hole are bred most of the abominations of the place.

There are four justifications given for the existence of prison in America, or four functions given for the institution: specific and general deterrence (to scare this person or people in general away from doing this act again or doing it at all), incapacitation (keeping the offender from hurting someone for a period of time), rehabilitation (fitting the individual for a law-abiding life), and punishment.

Deterrence and incapacitation have nothing to do with what goes on in a prison, since they are outside concepts, defined merely by the successful existence of the prison. Success in this context is giving the appearance of prison not being a happy place, and being a place no one leaves without authorization. Rehabilitation is known only later. It turns up in statistics compiled after the person leaves; it has nothing to do with day-to-day management. Punishment usually is defined as merely being there; the court sends you to prison *as*, not *for*, punishment.

Most prison workers focus on security and maintenance of order, because those are immediately measurable. Legitimizing those two factors are the other five. They supply the theoretical foundation that permits keeping men locked in tiny cages, forcing them to march in narrow lines, keeping them silent in the mess hall, and subjecting them to all kinds of personal intrusions.

But on Death Row, the foundation is missing. There is no notion of rehabilitation; it is the one place in criminal justice where rehabilitation is denied, ignored, or irrelevant. There is no incapacitation that couldn't be handled as well in one of the wings down the hall. There is no deterrence because deterrence, here as everywhere else, is unmeasurable. There is no punishment (in theory) because the punishment to which these men are condemned is death, not loss of time. Technically, Death Row prisoners more than thirty days away from execution are the legal property of the counties, not the state prisons. The years in the cells are without meaning in the prison logic. No good time accrues, no benefits are conferred for behaving well or working diligently. There is no work to do diligently.

The condemned do not fit the conceptual model that prison workers—wardens, ministers, doctors, guards, convict porters, everyone—have of the prison. So the prison workers abandon them.

The condemned live with the barest services, the minimum contact, the slightest concern. They write letters that go unanswered; they ask for help that does not come; they ask for individual recognition that is not given.

What prisons do best of all is warehouse people; all the rest is rhetoric. Death Row is the most obvious warehouse of all, and prison workers do not like to face that. Death Row inmates have a problem facing where they are, but prison workers have a problem facing what Death Row is, what it says about their industry.

The style of managing people on Death Row is not unlike the style of managing patients in wards for the terminally ill: the condemned/patients are treated as if they were already partially dead, as if they were already partly out of this world.

Death is difficult to deal with in any circumstances, and to deal with people who are more or less certain of meeting it in the near future is, for the kinds of people who handle Death Row inmates and terminal patients, very frightening. The almost-dead are treated as if they were contagious, and the handlers protect themselves by preserving distance.

There are many institutions in most societies for dealing with people in transitional phases of life, what anthropologist Victor Turner calls the "liminal phase," when one is, in his terms, "betwixt and between." Often there is a rite of passage framing this liminal period so that by the end of the period and the rite, one has moved into the new phase and the new role.

Most passages are volitional or serial. That is, one elects to become a priest, to become married, and so one goes into the liminal world in preparation for induction to the priesthood or for ratification of the marriage. For those passages that simply reflect maturation—the coming of age of a hunter or the marriageability of a girl—the community has had the experience of such passages before. All the adults did it: the men with the tipped bows put aside their childish sticks and went through it, the women stopped playing house with the other girls and did it, the boys stopped playing hunter and now go on real hunts and live in their wives' lodges.

But death is a transition like no other, for there is no objective sense of the other side. It is always hypothesis, and the rituals all deal with the remains, with fragments. For many tribes, and for many highly civilized peoples as well, the recently dead are difficult to understand, difficult to accept. It is not just a matter, as Freud suggested, of withdrawing affect. It is also a matter of being incapable of comprehending the transition because there is no objective sense—save for the postulates named in myth—of the other side.

So some funeral ritual has to do with naming the otherness of the recently dead, of saying how that person is now really different from us. In a prescientific world, that otherness is not easy to understand because the change is not at all clear: that motionless thing upon the ground looks like Harvey, but the "Harveyness" has somehow gone away. The thing that has gone has never been seen by anyone, but it is clearly gone. What is the thing that is left, the remains? What relation has it to the Harvey we knew? What relation has it to us?

The Yokuts of central California used to have two funerals. The first took place immediately after death; for it, the body was handled by transvestites. A year later, the "real" funeral was held. The Jewish tradition of the unveiling—when the family comes back a year later to mark the tombstone—is a remnant of the second funeral ceremony. By the time of the second funeral, the change in physical state is unambiguously clear: only bare bones remain, and Harvey has surely gone somewhere else.

As difficult as it is to conceptualize recent death, it is probably even more difficult to conceptualize impending death. That is terribly difficult for those who are dying, and it is also difficult for those who have to deal with those who are dying.

One way of dealing with the dying is to treat them as if they are already dead. Some anthropologists have theorized that the reason people can be killed by voodoo is because people in the community learn of the voodoo curse and then begin withdrawing affect from the cursed person. They begin treating him as if he were already dead, and, even without knowing of the curse, he responds to the treatment by acting appropriately. Terminally ill patients often complain that family members and hospital staffers talk of them in the third person, even within a few feet of their beds. And so do the condemned men on Death Row.

For us, dead bodies are things, not people. That is part of the way we manage them. Immediately, at death, one becomes "it," not "him" or "her." The process is not merely one of neuterizing now that sex is irrelevant but rather one of objectifying now that life is gone. A dead man or woman is a thing, not a person. Making the dead person a thing is one of the ways we deal with the horror of death.

On the Row, the condemned men are treated as things. The authorities don't go out of their way to treat them more cruelly than other convicts (though it sometimes seems that way) because few wardens or guards believe the men on Death Row are any worse than many other convicts in the penitentiary. More controlling is that they are perceived differently in a critical way: none of the usual quantifications apply. There is no question of recidivism, no question of rehabilitation, no relevance of the utility of education.

The limbo period for the condemned—matching the time of transition of motionless thing to fleshless skeleton, or the time of deterioration of the cancer patient, or the time of psychological debilitation of the victim of voodoo—is the period of appeals. For the condemned man, that time is spent trying to get out from under, but for the system, that time is used to pull layers of legal legitimacy over a corpse that hasn't quit moving or complaining yet.

Proponents of capital punishment often lament the long period between sentencing and execution. They fail to understand that only that lengthy period permits the clinical killing to take place without anyone having to feel any guilt or personal responsibility at all. The appeals process doesn't exist just to give the condemned a fair chance at correcting errors; it also exists to let the bureaucracy of death function without the burden of sin.

II

Death Row

1. Arriving

I live in a place
with the tightest security
Where no one cares
about innocence or purity
Where depression hangs
like a giant dark cloud
Where men wait to die
and make the state proud
Where our lives hang
on a court's decision
Where the biggest of men
have tears cloud their vision
Where the dreams are of home
And the world outside
Where we wake up in the morning
knowing we can't hide
Where we have much more
than time to do
A place no one would condone
if only they knew.

—Donnie Crawford, execution number 569, May 18, 1979

Legal Matters

During a plane trip back to New York from Houston last year, the man with the aisle seat interrupted our conversation to ask if we were lawyers. We said we weren't.

"I heard you talking about a case in federal court and I thought you were maybe lawyers," he said. We said we had been involved in a case, but only as expert witnesses. Was it a criminal case? he wondered. We said it was a civil suit about criminal matters. He said he avoided criminal cases whenever possible.

"Or I give them to a junior member of my firm. They're not economical, you know."

"Unless you represent big-time gangsters."

"There aren't many big-time gangsters. Most criminal cases are petty things. Somebody steals something or kills somebody and he's clearly guilty and all you're doing is negotiating with the DA. And later, they get mad at you. They always get mad at you because you didn't write them, because you don't come to see them. Like that's all you've got to do is go up there to Huntsville to see them. You make far more money sticking to your desk. You can't make any money doing those criminal trials. At your desk in a civil case, you tell them, 'I bill so much an hour,' and that's it. There's never any problem, never any question. You do the work and they send you a check and that's the end of it. Criminal cases, they go on and on and on. I hate them. Even after they're convicted, they keep bothering you."

The greatest legal complaint of Death Row inmates doesn't deal with perjured testimony, ambitious DAs, or hostile judges and juries (though those things are mentioned frequently), but with lawyers who don't respond. Few Death Row inmates have retained counsel. Some had retained counsel at the beginning of their trials, but the money ran out quickly. One study done by the Research Department of the Texas Department of Corrections revealed that 73 percent of those charged with capital murder and represented by court-appointed attorneys were sentenced to death, but only 35 percent of those charged with capital murder and represented by retained counsel were sentenced to death.

It is difficult to know how much or how little work actually is done by lawyers on behalf of the men on the Row. They tend to read lawyers' work in terms of the amount of attention they get. They feel if the attorney isn't responding to their letters, he surely isn't pursuing their cases. One lawyer told us, "In many instances that's probably true, but not always. If you're spending your time writing those men progress reports when nothing is really happening—and most of the time nothing is happening in this business because you're just waiting—then you don't have time to be filing motions or whatever. Or taking care of those cases that pay you enough so you can give some time to these indigents."

Few attorneys seem to realize—or care about—how centrally they figure in the lives of the men on Death Row. Their work is the only thing keeping those men out of the death house at The Walls.

Some inmates work very hard on their own cases. They get lawbooks, and they discuss with one another motions, citations, lawsuits. A few worry about the facts of their cases—proving their innocence—but the more sophisticated know that is no longer an important issue. The appellate courts are not concerned with guilt or innocence. No appellate judge addresses the question, "Is this fellow really nasty enough to have to die?" The question is only, "Did he get a fair trial in terms of the present rules of the game?" If the answer is no, the man declared guilty of the most vile crimes imaginable gets a whole new shot, and in some instances may be turned free; if the answer is yes, a man who in other circumstances might have received probation is sent along to die.

Much of the bitterness about the sentences is directed toward the punishment phase of the trials. In Texas, there are two phases to a capital trial. In the first, the jury hears evidence and determines guilt or innocence. If the verdict is guilty, the jury is immediately reconvened to answer two other questions: Did the defendant knowingly act in a way likely to cause the death of someone else? Is the defendant likely to commit further acts of violence in the future? At this point in the trial, the prosecutors usually bring in "experts"—often psychiatrists—who confidently predict future crimes of violence. Sometimes these opinions are based on no conversations at all with the defendant. Few responsible social scientists believe it is possible to predict human behavior in specific terms, especially over a long period of time (what the question really implies is that if the defendant were given a life sentence, would he, after being paroled in fifteen or twenty years, do further violence to the community?), and it is over this issue that the Texas capital punishment law is most likely to be overturned by the Supreme Court.[1] The jury doesn't set the death penalty, it merely answers yes or no to those two questions; if both are answered in the affirmative, then the judge automatically assigns the death penalty. It seems a rather sophistic distinction.

Another point of bitterness is the negotiated plea. Most men on the Row can name individuals doing time in the Texas Department of Corrections (TDC) who committed crimes as bad as or worse than the crimes for which

---

1. See, for example, the harsh criticism of the use of questionable psychiatric testimony in Dallas courts during the punishment phase of Texas capital trials in Smith v. Estelle, 602 *Federal Reporter* 2nd at 694 (1979).

they were convicted, but those others managed to negotiate a guilty plea, for which they got a life sentence. Not infrequently, a prosecutor will use the threat of a capital charge to get a defendant to plead guilty to murder. That does not happen in cases with a lot of anger or local publicity, and it rarely happens with police homicides. It might be that the most criminal murderers are the ones most likely to negotiate a guilty plea: they are court- and prison-wise in a way most Death Row inmates, who have not been in trouble with the police before, are not. Those more seasoned crooks know they have a good chance of being sentenced to death if they go to trial, and they know they can make it through fifteen years in prison, so they take that punishment and avoid the risk. Many inmates on Death Row were offered deals but turned them down. Some have fall partners—men who participated in the same crime—who got a bargained sentence. The first of those partners will be eligible for parole in a few years. It is possible that a man could spend more time on Death Row fighting his case than his partner spends in prison serving out a life sentence.

There is a great feeling of helplessness and impotence in conversations with Death Row inmates about the legal process. Even though they may fight hard, they don't feel very effective. They feel few people listen, few read their letters or complaints or briefs. "They" are all those who have done or wish to do one harm: the police, the courts, the prison administrators. The belief is that "they" can do anything they want to do. One man talks about how only the appeals process keeps "them" from killing everyone right now. He doesn't attempt to reconcile the "them" that operate the appeals process with the "them" that maintain the Row and want him dead, nor does he say how some of "them" are protective and some are malevolent. The difference is unambiguous and situational: the abstract processes are friendly, the individuals are not; the abstract processes protect and keep one alive, the individuals do not protect but wait to deliver death.

It is difficult to believe that most of these men would be on Death Row if they had first-rate legal representation at their trials. Their court-appointed lawyers are rarely as experienced as the prosecutors, and they rarely had the money to hire their own investigators or medical experts. A really competent defense to a capital charge is an expensive affair, and there are no wealthy men on Death Row.

Most people don't have the thousands of dollars to hire an attorney to represent them in court. If they were suddenly pulled in on something, they don't have the $15,000 or $20,000 or $30,000 it takes to hire a good criminal lawyer. The state appoints these wet-behind-the-ears kids, just out of law school, and they are handling life-and-death cases. There's one lawyer who was appointed to represent four of us down here on Death Row right now, all different cases.

My lawyer, I just found out who he was. They told me his name in court. I've been down here since July of last year and I have never seen my appeals attorney. I just recently got his name and address and I had to get it through another inmate.

I've studied these law books. I've worked on these laws. I've worked and written and checked and done everything that I possibly could, but I can only do so much from here and they ignore you in these courts. These lawyers, if they want to write you they will. If they want to come and see you they will. Ninety percent of the time they won't. They'll say, "Look, I'll come see you when I can, if I want to." The judges will not answer letters. They will not try and help you. They don't want to help you. They've got you here, they want you to stay here. It makes you wonder sometimes how these men can sleep at night, but apparently they do, 'cause they're still out there doing it.

My lawyer didn't even let me know when the transcript was finished. He filed it in the Court of Criminal Appeals and sent me a copy because I kept after him about it. I got my copy of the transcript and it was complete. Nothing changed. It was exactly the way it was supposed to be about what I remembered. And I remembered everything.

When I got through with it, I gave it to my parents and then they said, "Well, my God, you are innocent."

They weren't in the courtroom. They weren't allowed in the courtroom because they were sworn in as witnesses. They were to be character witnesses and later I found out that they could have been in the courtroom.

I'll give you an example of how money matters from my own case.

Cullen Davis,[2] in his case, could call in specialists, psychologists, sociologists, whatever he wanted from all over the world. I asked for two expert witnesses on identification. One of them was in Brooklyn, New York, the other was in Washington State. I asked for both, and it would have cost less than $1,500. The fee was $500 a day for testimony plus travel expenses. The judge said, "No. I've got to watch the taxpayers' money. You can have your choice of one of the two."

If I had $2,000 of my own, I could have had both of them there. The judge was bitching about this little ole $1,500 or $3,000 expense, when they've already spent probably $150,000 because the prosecutor screwed up the first trial. The prosecutor isn't restricted. He can call in anybody he wants from anywhere in the world.

I've seen people that look me right in the eye that were supposed to be my friends and lied about me. And know they were lying. Like this lady, she looked me right in my face in that courtroom and lied. And then she came down here to visit me. She does visit me. She come down here and set right there and cried and told me to my face, "I wish I hadn't lied about you."

Why did she do it?

Because the DA told her that if she didn't do it, he was going to give her husband the death penalty.

That's her picture. That's the lady that got up on the stand and testified against me. Then she comes down here with my wife to visit me.

Do you hate her?

No, I don't hate her at all. That's just like I told her when she sat there crying. "I wished you hadn't done it, but I'm not going to do nothing to you for it. You acted under pressure. I don't blame anybody for acting under pressure. Because I've had to act under pressure."

I'm not going to blame anybody for something they were forced to do. But now her husband—I'd like to punch him in the eye a time or two. I wouldn't kill him, but I'd like to whip on him a little while. Same with that district attorney. I'd like to whip him. Oh, but I'd like to whip

2. In two separate trials, Texas millionaire T. Cullen Davis was charged with the murder of his ex-wife's lover and daughter, and with the attempt to have the judge in his divorce case shot by a contract killer. Davis was not convicted in either case. His legal fees are reported to have been over $4 million.

him. I wouldn't want to kill him, I just want to beat him up a little bit. And the judge too. I'll beat him up too if I had a chance. I don't want to do anything violent to them, I just want to dot their eye. It's aggravating.

The judge told me in his chambers—my lawyer was there, they called me in there and my lawyer read me my rights. I didn't like that. Then the DA started laughing. I told him, "Hey," and I showed the judge all this evidence, physical evidence, and I said, "I didn't do this."

And he says, "Oh, I know you didn't do it. But that don't mean you're not going to get convicted for it, now does it?"

I turned to my lawyer, the one that just read me my rights, and I said, "What are you going to do about this?"

He said, "Do about what? What do you want me to do?"

And then I knew what it was.

If you ain't paying no lawyer no money to come up with a case, they just sit on it. They ain't gonna down the state for nobody. They say they law and justice, but they not law and justice. One told me, "I got to make a living in that courtroom. I can't do some things. You're just going to have to face the consequences."

When you ain't got no money to fight your case, your ass is down.

I couldn't blame them. That judge told my lawyer two or three times, "You sit down. You be quiet. All of this is not necessary." And that lawyer sit down. This was the first death penalty case he ever tried, the first criminal case he ever tried. The other lawyer I had, he was a alcoholic.

Only thing that pissed me off, if they got me investigated like I asked to be investigated, I'd been all right. But those lawyers told me, "We're gonna investigate your case. We get money out of our own pocket because the judge don't want to grant no motion for an investigation in this case. It's too much money being spent on it now. You're guilty and that's it. We're gonna do our investigation." That's it.

This old man got killed. He was supposed to have been a good citizen in the neighborhood. They wanted to see justice did for this. They was going to see that I got the death penalty.

All my mail that was going out, they just was taking it and putting it on the side. They mailed it after I got the death penalty. Whole lot of people I had written to for legal advice and stuff, but I never heard from them yet.

The federal judge who answered me, the only reason he got his mail was because I had certified it. I had to send it out certified. They must have signed the little green slip and brought it back to me.

I talked to that preacher at the county jail and I asked him about getting in touch with people. He gave me a real funny look. He looked up at my name over the door and give me a real funny look.

I started learning not to trust anybody. Telling nobody nothing. The preachers over here and all of them are working with the system. They ain't going against this. A man just got to forget about it, if he want to go along with their little thing, laugh and grin in their face and say, "Yes, sir, no, sir," and this and that. You'll make it that way. You mind your own business, you'll make it over here. You get to going a bit too far, they'll do something to you.

There's some things about this justice system that is so farfetched. It's so one-sided. I'm going to give you an example. It can be documented.

The lawyer that handled my case was court-appointed the first time. I got a reversal, and after I got a reversal I went back. The judge called for an informal hearing. I went before the judge. He said that he was removing my attorney because he was a big-city attorney and I didn't need him. He was gonna appoint a local boy. See, I got busted in a small town.

I objected. The attorney wrote a letter stating that he wanted to continue representing me. The judge refused. He appointed me an attorney that had no experience in capital cases. All right. Now they turn around and hire a special prosecutor out of San Antonio, a criminal law specialist to prosecute the case. And they think he won't stack the deck on you!

I filed a writ of mandamus to the Court of Criminal Appeals in Texas. They refused to hear it. Then I filed a restraining order and a writ of mandamus with the federal district court. In June of this year, the DC court of appeals—federal—ruled that a judge could not arbitrarily remove an attorney over the defendant's objection and the attorney's objections. So I've got that case and my attorney is working on that aspect of it.

Did you ever hear of a judge sleeping during a trial when they're trying to take your life? Well, I've got a whole family, all my sisters and brother-in-law all sitting in the courtroom, and this judge was asleep. They had to wake him up to rule on things. And I'm sitting up there and they want to take my life.

You know, sometimes, if you don't control yourself, you can sit back and think of these things and you can get so bitter. So bitter. It's important for a person to find something so he can control his mind, because if you don't, it's going to get the best of you sooner or later.

There's one dude up there, he's all the time gonna pull my arms off. Pull my arms off and beat me with them. Teasing.

There's a lot of good people there, people that don't deserve to die. But then, there's some that need to. And there's some that if I ever met them on the street, I would kill. Even though I'm not a violent person. Because they're flaky, you know, just strange. I heard a man say one time that if he got in a situation where there was an individual that he was robbing and there was kids there, that he would tell the man that he was going to kill him and, not only that, he was going to kill the kids too. If a man come in my house and told me something like that and I had the means, I would shoot him right there. And then I would call the police and tell them he burglarized. Because there are certain situations that you get into where you've got to do something whether or not it's right by the public or not. A man that is going to do something like that, I don't want him in my house, I don't want him around my kids. It's bad.

Then there's others. I'll call one Fatbelly. You know who I'm talking about. I won't use his name because he don't want his name used. That man don't belong here. No way. He made a mistake, he admits it, but he don't belong here. And he's just getting a terribly rotten deal. His lawyer is making money and that's all that's going on. He may die.

His lawyer is court-appointed, but he run his parents into debt collecting money from them and collecting money from the court. This is illegal. But the people think that the lawyer is going to help their son. The lawyer got him the death penalty, the lawyer got the case affirmed in Austin, and now the lawyer's going to the Supreme Court. And all this time, the lawyer has made about $60,000 from the people plus what he's made off the court. And the one that's going to lose is Fatbelly.

I've tried to talk to him. I've showed him different laws, but he is the type of person that doesn't want his parents to worry, so he won't do anything. And it's going to cost him.

He shouldn't be here. He readily admits that he did what they said he did. Okay, that's a man. A man that made a mistake, a man that turned himself in whenever he found out that they were looking for him, a man that went back, a man that whenever he was sentenced to death blessed the judge and the DA.

Should that man die? He may need to do some time. I don't think if they turned him loose right today, right now, this minute, he would ever be in trouble again. Because he's learned a lesson. So now the state wants to kill him.

Why? What good will it do? He would be less a problem to the state of Texas than just about anybody you can point to out there. He doesn't drink. He doesn't cuss. He reads his Bible all day long and says he wants to be a preacher. And by talking to him, you believe him.

Many men, such as myself, don't deserve to be here. We no more constitute a threat than Mickey Mouse. We're considered to be some kind of animal and there's continuously that pressure on us. We have not the money to get the lawyers.

I could have had my family go into hock up to their ears to buy the lawyers, to hire the lawyers, to buy the defense to get me, possibly, out of here or not to even end up here. But I would not do that to my family. That is what I am fighting against. The state says I'm guilty. The police said that I was guilty. I am not guilty. I have fought it tooth and nail and I refuse to let thousands and thousands, $75,000 and more, be used to buy these lawyers, to hire these lawyers to defend me. I feel it's the state's responsibility to give me a lawyer, and when they didn't, I had to get help elsewhere, but I still refuse to let my family, who's worked hard all their lives to have what they have, pay for it.

There's men here whose families had homes before this happened to them. They had homes, they had property, they had land, they had stocks, they had bonds. They have that no longer. They're living in apartments while they're trying to get their sons off of Death Row. Just to get them into where they're serving life or to prove their innocence to get them out of here.

I'm not saying that everybody here is innocent or meek as a lamb, but there are many men here that are that don't deserve what they've got. They're here because of politics, because of the DAs that wanted to get reelected, the sheriff who wanted to get reelected.

It's many things that happen in courts that the public does not know about. People do not realize that it can happen to them until it does. Whether you have a record or not you could end up here.

My case has been in the federal district court a year with no action whatsoever. I feel and think with good reason that the district court will reverse my case.

I'm going to have a hell of a fight on my hands trying to convince the jury again that I'm not guilty of murder, but after six years of sitting and thinking, I have come up with a defense for myself, and I'm not talking of a dreamed-up defense. I mean one based on what really happened.

See, a person like me, I couldn't think for a year. They say you're competent to stand trial. You're not legally insane by any means, but I was in such a state of depression and sickness at what happened—I don't mean about the man's death, I mean at what happened to me and how it happened—that I really couldn't think. And I think my lawyer made a lot of mistakes. If you ever read my brief, you'll see that he did.

Was he court-appointed?

Not at first. I hired him. But my money run out pretty quick, pretty dang quick. Then he was appointed from that point on because it just took everything I had. It wasn't a hell of a lot, but it was some.

He could have had a lot more if he had paid attention to his business. For instance, my boat, my automobile, and everything were repossessed. There was equity in those things, and he could have had that too, but he didn't fool with it.

They repossessed my car before I even had a payment due on it. And they sold it two days after a payment was due. I had traded a '70 Buick in on a '74 and I had already made one payment, so there was still some equity. I had the boat for over a year and had plenty of equity in it. It was a sixteen-foot Bass boat with a sixty-five-horse Johnson on it, and all the accessories that go with it. And there was the personal property. My apartment manager robbed me.

My mother got over to the apartment along with my attorney on a Saturday. This thing had happened on Wednesday. People were there cleaning out my apartment. They took all my camping equipment and jewelry, none of that ever did show up again. They took my TV set and my rifles. My mother got the rifles and the TV set 'cause she called the police and the police came out and said, "We can't do anything about it." That kind of made me sick. The attorney was there, he could have got the stuff back. There was several thousand dollars' worth of stuff there. It is surprising how a man accumulates things.

But, nonetheless, I ran out of money and he was eventually appointed by the court to handle my case. That was talked about when I hired him. He knew I had run out of money and he promised that he would carry it all the way through.

I don't mean to be detrimental to him, but he's really not a very good attorney. I don't say that maliciously, but here's an example. The Witherspoon decision handed down in 1969 states that a man cannot be dismissed from jury service simply because he doesn't believe in the death penalty. He must state unequivocally that he will not let his personal feelings interfere with the fact decisions of the case is what it amounts to. You cannot get him up on the witness stand and say, "Do you believe in the death penalty?" and dismiss him just because he says no. That's not cause. But twenty people in my case, they did that to. "Do you believe in the death penalty?"

"No, I don't."

"You're excused."

No objection by my attorney. One objection is all he's got to do to protect me and he does not do it.

That's just one thing that was ignorance on his part. I don't mean stupidity now, I just mean ignorance of the law. I asked him when I hired him, "Are you a criminal attorney?" and he said, "Yes." To me, a criminal attorney would know about Witherspoon.

But attorneys are, I guess, like everyone else. They learn what they practice, and he had never had a death penalty case.

I told him, "I'll eventually file incompetency against you if I have to, not to be malicious about it, but to protect my life." He seemed to understand that and he didn't seem to be too worried about it.

The lawyers mess them around. They say, "If I take this case and I take it all the way to the Supreme Court, two or three years of fighting, that's automatic money in my pocket. If I want to leave this part out of the transcript, I'm the lawyer." The longer he keeps the case, the more money he makes. There's nothing you can do about it.

Some guys think the DAs are smarter than some lawyers and the judges are smarter than the DAs. It's just a law dictionary that they have. They take and get words out of a law dictionary and use them. They use them to make people think they're highly intelligent.

It's just another way of making a living, you know. If they didn't get anybody prosecuted, they wouldn't get paid.

They had that psychiatrist come to see me. I was in the old county jail in Dallas. I had sent out to see the doctor and they called me out. They said it was a doctor, so I goes out and when I realized who it is, I tell him, "I don't want to talk to you."

You thought he was the doctor you had asked for?

At first. But then, he was sitting in the interview room, so I knew it couldn't be a MD doctor. So I told him I didn't want to talk to him. But then the officer told me, "You're going to talk to him whether you want to or not." I just turned around and didn't pay him any attention.

He got up and he testified in my trial that I was a sociopath. He said he wouldn't be in the same room with me if he didn't have a shotgun.

Two doctors testified in my trial. One of them, I hadn't even seen him before the day in prison. He got up there and testified that I was a sociopath. My lawyer objected to it and the judge interrupted and he said I could talk to one of them if I wanted to. My lawyer went and talked to one and my lawyer said, he said that if he talked to me it wouldn't make any difference because he wouldn't change his testimony, regardless.

I don't know all that much about him, except for what I heard. I heard that the state pays him to do that. I'm not sure how much, but it was way up in the thousands and thousands of dollars. Just for him to testify. He gets up there and he testifies the same in all death penalty cases.

I haven't heard but once that I know of where he testified in the defense's behalf. And the defendant happened to be a lawyer. He was being tried in Dallas for killing his daughter. That's the only one that I know of.

That psychiatrist, I feel he's more of a criminal than anybody in TDC. Because he gets up there and he lies. He don't have to see your record, he don't have to talk to you or nothing. He lies. He's the type of person, he's being paid for what he's doing. He's being paid to put a person here.

He gets up there and says things. They go off into a person's juvenile record. It's really nothing wrong with a person's record, but they'll make something out of it. They use a person's juvenile record and it has nothing to do with a person being grown up, how he is now. He'll say, "He's been to reformatory. He's a sociopath."

I don't really understand the man because he talks and everything he says will be a lie. Everything, I think. Personally, I dislike the man. But then, he has a job.[3]

You know in the punishment phase, Texas has been using a lot of psychiatrists to testify against the guys, to evaluate them. When they came to our punishment phase, they didn't have a psychiatrist, so they called the medical examiner. He got on the stand to testify in the place of a psychiatrist. He got up there and predicted our future behavior.

My attorney asked him, "Do you have a degree in psychiatry?"

He said, "Well, no, but I've been in school for twenty-eight years. I had to learn something."

And the judge said, "Well, I think he's qualified."

My attorney said, "Did you interview either one of these defendants?"

He said, "No, I didn't have to."

Does that help you with Texas justice? It's in the record. And I'll put a little icing on the cake for you. My family sued this particular doctor back in 1972. So my attorney said, "Are you doing this to get back at the defendant's family?"

"Oh, no. No."

The judge still said he was qualified.

They watch you. The jury looks at you, whether you know it or not. They're looking at you. And that is more determining whether you get the

3. US District Court Judge Robert W. Porter's opinion in Ernest Benjamin Smith's lawsuit (445 F. Supp. 647) and the Fifth Circuit Court's affirming decision written by Judge Goldberg (Smith v. Estelle, 602 *Federal Reporter* 2nd, at 694) support the inmates' contentions about the character of some psychiatric testimony during the punishment phases of capital trials.

death penalty than anything else. I didn't say anything in my trial. I was drugged in my trial. I didn't say nothing. What hung me was the fact that I sat there impassive.

The jury thought I was a cold-blooded killer. They didn't know that I was drugged. When they took me to the courtroom, I passed out a couple of times. They had to drag me in there.

Sure I was unemotional. Sure was. At that time, I wouldn't have cared if the whole world fell apart.

Then here's my court-appointed defense attorney who said he had no comment on the verdict. When asked if I received a fair trial, he said, "I couldn't say it was fair. I couldn't say he did it." This is the man that looked at the medical records and found out that I was drugged and he refused to do anything about it.

Now he was really protecting his client. He's one of them I'm going to sue. I'm going to sue that doctor, too. I had my wife look up Melaril in the PDR [*Physician's Desk Reference*] and it clearly stated that the normal dosage is ten to twenty-five milligrams a day, and they had me on four hundred milligrams a day.

I do not have any type of prison record to speak of or police record either in the state of Texas. I was busted for fishing on an expired license. I paid $27.50. And I was busted for riding a motorcycle without a motorcycle stamp and I paid $27.50. And I was busted for being drunk in public because I was speeding. That's what my record consists of in the state of Texas. And I'm a bad individual and should be put to death, right? So the law says. And beyond that, I can prove I didn't kill nobody. But I'm still here.

They bring a juvenile record in the courtroom. I have a juvenile record.

I thought they weren't supposed to introduce that.

They bring it up in the punishment phase. I can name the cases that I had: three runaways, a loitering, and a burglary.

I went to Gatesville for it. But they bring the folder in there and it's about four inches thick. My record. And the records of my three brothers. This is enough to inflame anybody, you know. They look at that. I looked at that box, that's the record, and I say, "Oh man, I sure had a long juvenile record."

Then the judge say, "I instruct the jury to disregard that."

If I tell you something, you can't disregard that, regardless. If I say something—

I'd probably remember it better.

That's right. Because they're going to feel that there is something that you are hiding in some way.

It's not any justice. If I tell you something, it's not any way in the world that you'll just forget that. You're going to think about that later on.

This is the way I would do it if I was TDC or the people that dictated what was going to come down.

First, I'd get rid of the juries in the trials. I would make the district attorney prepare his case, the defense prepare their case. This is not on speculation, this is on fact, proven fact. Now, as far as the facts go, the juries could be there to determine fact because that's what they're supposed to do.

Once they get these two piles of evidence accumulated and refined, put it in a computer. Have a computer decide what the odds are that this individual with this information actually committed this crime. A man makes mistakes, but this machinery, through thousands of people, geniuses over the years who built it, there is a better chance that you're going to get the man that's guilty than with all the jury trials put together.

A computer cannot be swayed. A computer cannot be swayed by a district attorney getting up there and letting tears run out of his eyes. A computer cannot be swayed by witnesses that may have something against the defendant. It would be 99 percent sure that the person convicted would actually be the person that did the crime. I've thought about it quite a bit.

But a computer has to be programmed by a human being.

But these human beings that program these computers—let's not take one, let's take twelve good men and program this computer.

You think twelve good men who know how to run computers are better than twelve good men you just get off the street?

Yeah. This is their job. They've got computers that can tell you the odds on anything you want. And with the background and the knowledge, this would be more effective than the sentiment we have now.

I read one law book where it said that this one lawyer would take a piece of wire and put it in a cigar and he would light this cigar and be smoking it, but he would light it in time for the ash to get up about an inch, inch and a half long before the district attorney started presenting his case, so instead of the jury paying attention to the district attorney, they're waiting for the ash to fall off the cigar. It's gonna fall off, they're thinking. And all this old stuff about sitting there, playing with something, moving their hands and the jury will catch the motion. He'll jerk his hands up and the jury will wait and see what he's jerking his hands away from. And they're not listening to no DA. And the DA does this the same way.

Do you ever sit in the courtroom and watch the DA? After he gets his point made and the defense gets up and starts talking, he'll go over there and start twirling a pencil, shuffling papers, coughing. All this is to distract the jury away from what the defense is saying.

Trials, as they are now most of the time, are nothing but who is the slickest, who can distract the people the best way. But this computer, it would be pretty well sure that the man committed the crime.

I've got all the records I need to get out on. I've got my first trial transcript. The law states that any time the judge, without manifest necessity, declares a mistrial, then double jeopardy attaches, and further retrial is prevented. But the judge refused to give us this.

My wife stole it, is how I got it. The copies were delivered and she was talking to my lawyer and the lady come back to get them and he gave the lady one and told my wife to take the other one. He had two copies and the lady didn't remember if he had one or two. And that's how I got mine. And when they found out I had one, they got very upset. When they found out I had it, they liked to went through the roof because they didn't want me to have anything.

I write everybody I can. I got a book of addresses: TSU Law School, Stanford Law School. I correspond with Amsterdam, Stanford, and Joel Berger. And my lawyer—he's with the ACLU.

He just graduated from law school in '76. But I like him 'cause he's young and he's really enthusiastic. When he was first assigned to my case he came down and talked to me. He told me, "I just came out of law school. If you don't want me, tell me. I have no experience in this whatsoever."

I said, "Well, hey. If you got desire, that's what counts to me."

And he's really enthusiastic about it.

That's what counts. In a case like this, all that experience that some have, if you got plenty of experience and you're not willing to get down and look for the errors, you haven't got any win. I believe that enthusiasm counts for a whole lot. At least, I think it does. Hopefully, I'm not wrong.

There's some people on Death Row that shouldn't be there because they're crazy, incompetent, whatever you want to call it. I don't know if they were when they were tried. Some of them were. But they're not supposed to be there. You're not supposed to kill a mental patient. These people are mental patients, there's things wrong with them. They don't go deeply into that.

That's because Death Row is the garbage can for the state of Texas. They got everything in there.

There's old lawyer H——. I'm going to talk about him because he's funny. He had several cases on him. He's deranged. I've talked to him and you can't tell it unless you talk to him for very long. He was gonna be his own lawyer. He's going to defend himself in his capital murder case. He don't want no court lawyer. So he goes out there and they tell him, "Okay. You defend yourself." And they say, "How do you plead?"

He said, "Not guilty by reason of insanity."

He got two or three more life sentences, a couple of death penalties. They just took him on a tour of the state. He had about fourteen cases on him. He came down with one and after his tour of the state, he come back with four or five. They even put him on TV.

I begged that man—he was in my group—I begged him not to go down there and do that. I said, "If you do that, that DA is gonna laugh and pat himself on the back and just take you everywhere in the state."

"I'll beat it, I'll beat it."

See, a prosecutor wants a death penalty case because it makes him look good. They all pat each other on the back, feed each other. "Hey, I got a guy down here that's going to cop in your county and he's going to defend himself and get up there and plead not guilty by reason of insanity." "Well, bring him on down."

And that's what happened. I talked to him for two or three weeks. I begged him not to do that.

What did he say when he came back? Did he say you were right?

I haven't talked to him since he's been back. They put him on the other side [J-21]. But one guy I knew who was beside me, he's on the other side, he say, "Hey, man, there's a guy over here that's as good in the law as you are and maybe better."

I said, "Oh, yeah?"

He says, "Yeah."

I said, "What's his name?"

He said, "H——."

I said, "You better get away from him." I told him who he was. "That's him? That's him? That's the guy that did that?"

"Yeah."

"Man, I'm getting his stuff out of my cell. He's jinkie."

The dude I was talking to is a black dude, he's pretty funny. They call different people "jinkie," you know. Homosexuals are jinkies. Certain people been busted a lot of times, they're jinkie—you know, bad luck. Voodoo and whatnot. He told me, "Wait a minute." He went over there and took the papers that H—— gave him and throwed them out on the floor and said, "I'm getting them out of my cell, man. They're jinkie."

I've seen some men get off the Row.

One was a fella out of Fort Worth. They had tried him for conspiracy. He supposedly hired a security guard to kill his girlfriend. He got the death sentence and came down with it. They tried his fall partner afterwards, the one that supposedly done the killing, and they acquitted him. But the first man stayed on Death Row about two and a half or three years. But he had money, so now he's out on the streets.

Hard to prove a conspiracy if the one supposed to have done the killing is innocent. They went through numerous court appeals and rehearings and, after a while, he was finally acquitted.

Another one, his case was reversed and he received a ten-year sentence. Another one out of Houston had a twenty-five-to-fifty-year sentence. He had pled guilty and then he put in an appeal and the DA got mad and reindicted him and asked the death sentence, which he wouldn't have done had he just copped out to the twenty-five-to-fifty. They reversed his case because it was just retribution on the DA's part. One out of Commanche got a life sentence. Two out of San Antonio—one received a forty-year sentence, the other a life sentence.

Whether it's reversed in a higher court or not, if you are convicted, you still lose time. Appeals take time. Any time that you lose, it's time that you'll never get back. If you spend four years fighting something on appeal, that's four years gone.

Once you are brought here from the county, you cannot communicate. I'm from Houston and to communicate with my lawyer is almost impossible. It takes a week by mail. You're not allowed to use the telephone. In the county jails, you are allowed a telephone call to your attorneys. Here, you can't even in an emergency. Not even if your son or daughter died, they wouldn't let you make a phone call.

Law books are too hard to come by. The library doesn't have all the lawbooks that we need. When we reach a point where they don't have these books, then we have to depend on Austin's library. Have to buy the law. It costs us a nickel a sheet. And if you send to the county, it's around a dollar a sheet. If you are a poor person that don't have no family and you're depending on a court-appointed lawyer, then you're just up a hill unless you can get a stamp to write him and ask him to look it up for you. And the majority of the court-appointed lawyers, they're not going out of their way. They only get so much to represent you.

If the person remains in the county, then he stands a better chance. Like the law library in the Harris County jail. They've got typewriters and they furnish the paper, the carbon paper, tapes, staplers, everything that a person would need, they furnish it. The law library there is unbelievable. It's got everything a man needs. If they should stumble across something they don't have, then immediately the officer that's in charge there will get on the teletype downtown and have them bring it out there. And they'll either Xerox copies or have it typed up and put in a special book where they know where it's at. Sometimes books get tore up, but they make sure that it's all there.

Here, they don't. And they don't care.

You have people from all walks of life. You have everything from the ghetto people to the street people to the upper middle class. Crime and punishment respect no boundaries as far as class is concerned.

There aren't a lot of rich men on Death Row.

The people that are rich are the ones that can afford not to be caught. But if they are caught and if they are prosecuted, they go in with the same ground rules. It just depends on whether or not they can buy the officials.

Or the lawyers.

Or whatever.

Do you think they can very often?

Yes, I do. Case in point: T. Cullen Davis. If it were not for the fact that T. Cullen Davis was a very wealthy man, respected in the community and able to employ Richard Haynes, I'm afraid Mr. Davis would not have secured a mistrial. The state of Texas is vindictive when it comes to prosecution and they will make a case if there's any way possible. It all boils down to respect. They had to respect Davis because he's a prominent man. And they had to respect Haynes, who's a prominent attorney. And they know that they can't snowball either one of those men, they're too powerful.

Every man on Death Row has been snowballed. He got caught up in the system. The system has a way of making a loser where a loser was not there. If you don't have all the chinks filled in the wall, the wind will blow.

I may not have got the death penalty if I hadn't pled guilty. I pled guilty 'cause the judge wouldn't separate me from my fall partner, he was going to try us together, and to try us together, we'd just hurt each other.

My fall partner got a life sentence. After I went to trial and pled guilty, they gave him a change of venue, 190 miles from Amarillo to Lubbock. He got a life sentence over there. So he'll come up for parole in 1988. Twelve calendar years, he'll come up. That don't mean he'll make it.

He was my best friend and his sister was my girlfriend. His sister got pregnant and she was just seventeen and we were going to be married in September. She turned eighteen and I got arrested in August. She had the baby and two months ago I heard she got married. I don't hear from her no more.

I've been here twenty-two months. My attorneys said the court was supposed to rule on my case in eight months. I was convicted April 15, 1977, and they filed my appeal brief November 15 of 1977. The court argued it March 15 of 1978, and that's all. They haven't ruled on it. They generally rule on one in six to eight weeks after they argue it, but it's been thirteen months and they still haven't ruled on it. I wrote them a letter and they just said it's pending.

It's in Austin. That's really the first court you go to besides the county judge, and then you go before him and ask for a new trial and then Austin is the next step and I can't do nothing until he rules. There's some that's been waiting longer than mine.

One of the reasons it might have taken so long is I pled guilty of capital murder and received the death penalty. And the US Constitution says you can't do that, you can't plead guilty where the death penalty is imminent. I did. That didn't do much. I still got the death penalty.

I was never even in jail before. Well, I got arrested once for being drunk in public, but the next day I didn't even remember what jail was like. Had I known what it was like, I would never have been back.

I was eight months in the county jail waiting on a trial, and then two months after that I come down here. You look out the window and see the streets you used to run around on, people you know driving up and down. There's a lot of people thrown together in there—blacks and whites, Chicanos, young and old, people been down and done a lot of time. The county jail really can be harder than this place.

They had a lot of rapes and beating on each other. It's pretty hard sometimes. Because of my size, I can keep people from bothering me most of the time. Just threaten them, talk loud. Don't have to do nothing. I enjoy that privilege a lot. But then you try to use it down here and you have to fight.

I had one fight the two years I've been here just because a boy was talking crazy and I tried to get him to be quiet and he wouldn't do it. So I went down to his cell and jumped on him and dragged him out in the hall and he cut me across the eye. He had a razor blade melted off onto a toothbrush.

How were you able to go to his cell?

The cells are all in a line. They opened all of ours for recreation. I got put on indefinite restriction; he didn't get anything. To them, I started it because I threw the first punch, but to us, I didn't start it. It don't make any difference. I didn't really care about seeing him punished. I wanted to punish him myself.

It's pretty hard, you know. When I come down here, I didn't want to fight nobody. I've never enjoyed hitting people. I didn't never even enjoy killing rats. But the longer you stay here, the more you notice what them people are doing to you.

I'm still on restriction. This fight happened January sixteenth. It will probably be over after six months, unless I get in trouble again, then they'll let me off at Christmas. They let everybody off at Christmas unless you've just done something. Some inmates have stabbed one another and they get off at Christmas.

Then the time to make vengeance is the twenty-third of December.

That wouldn't work. Have to do it in November.

Here is what the law is. Nixon stole from the whole United States. He hasn't done one day. And I just got a article out of the paper: he's being paid $800,000. And he stole from everybody in the United States. You know, we talks about the law all the time on the tank.

How does a man on trial do anything, just say a man of my standards? I have never went to law school and there's very little that I knew about the law. Suppose you object to something. How can I win that? You know, all over in different countries, they talking about the rights of those people. What about these people here? They say the law is there to protect society. Who's gonna protect the law?

When the law make a mistake, it's just written off. It's just written off.

"I knew that you all would be upset by the murder of Spenkelink—or should I say legal murder by some very coldblooded SOBs. It was very quiet and upsetting here when we heard the news. They don't like to turn the TV on early any more and a bunch of the nuts here started. I myself was listening to the radio and getting the reports, as were many of the men. About 15 minutes before they did kill him, the TV was turned on. Surprised me that they allowed it. Anyway, myself and my family was sure a stay would come from someplace somehow. The good old U.S. of A. took a giant step—backwards into the dark ages. No more bullshit for me about our redneck President and his human rights. My mother for one is very, very sick and upset over it all. Mom is worrying about the dead man's mother, her health and heart condition.

"The reason I am a little rattled by this letter is that I have had an execution date set. Yeah: me too!

"It happened Thursday the 7th. They pulled me out with no forewarning and took me to Bay City for a date in the court where I was tried. . . . Even the same lawyer that set me up, the same one that has put three other men down here besides myself, was there as my lawyer. I was so mad I could have kicked the walls down in the courtroom and jail. I didn't know what was up or who was to be there as my lawyer until 5 minutes before the judge gave me the date.

"On Thursday, mid-morning, I was working away and suddenly I am told to pack all my stuff, for the guards were waiting to take me out. A bench warrant had been issued from Bay City. No one could or would tell me what was up. As I told you earlier, I had been told that it wasn't going to happen, so I was relaxing a bit.

"So, Friday, June 8th, I was standing before the judge at about 1:40 in the afternoon, facing a judge without a friend in the world there. I couldn't get my parents and Lauri was in Oregon. It was like a party there—for them, the DAs, law and others. When I was asked if I had anything to say, I just said, 'Your Honor, it wouldn't make a bit of difference.' He asked if I had anything to say as to why I shouldn't die.

"I was so mad and upset that they had done it to me again. I had hoped someone from the ACLU or someone from the law firm that is supposed to be helping me would be there. No. The judge had requested that the trial lawyer be there. It was planned and worked that way so I would be off guard. I was!

"My mother did get word to me this morning through the chaplain that she had talked to lawyers and that a stay was to be in the works Monday morning—tomorrow. I know I will get a stay, but the fact that the state has that blood thirst, it gets me down.

"They moved me to Bay City real quick. I sat in the county jail the night of June 7th and then went to court the next afternoon. After court and the paperwork was ready, I was moved back here that day, but it was real late by the time I got here.

"And you know what? No one here said a mean word to me. Most of the officers that know me asked how it went, were sad to hear about the date. No one knew for sure, that is, why I went to Bay City until I got back and the papers were with me. Officers, guards and then the inmates were glad to see me back safe and sound, but not that I had to come back. It sure surprised me. Everyone sure has been nice since I got back.

"Oh yes! Before I forget: the judge at the first, when reading my death warrant, set my execution for June 9. Yes, the next day after I was before him. I had to stop and ask him, in the middle, if he was setting me to die June 9, the next day. He said, 'What?' And someone did speak up and say that was tomorrow—Saturday then, this past Saturday. Before I could say anything else, the judge then corrected the typing and set the date for July 9.

"It didn't upset me. Just made me mad that they took it so lightly as not to check the typing or have it correct. The whole thing was an act. They know I won't die then. Just a waste of money."

"The county authorities came and got me Friday morning, May 11. I was worried about the ride, but there were two other men from Ellis Unit (not from the Row) and I was glad I was not alone. We rode in a small Ford van with windows. I realized just how weak my eyes have become while I was on Death Row. I can't see things that are too far away. The ride was beautiful, no problems. When I got to the county jail I called my mother-in-law and told her I was here. I tried to call my lawyer but he was not in. He came to see me Saturday and told me I was the first man to 'snap his fingers and get off Death Row.' He said the district attorney was worried about some of the things I filed in federal court. I said I was glad and he had reason to be worried. I was offered a cop-out deal and I turned it down. My wife and in-laws came to see me and I saw my oldest son. Yesterday (Monday) my lawyer came to see me again and we talked awhile. I showed him some of the work I have done and discussed some legal moves we plan to make at the hearing Thursday. I told him of some new laws he didn't or hadn't known about. He asked me if I enjoyed the ride and I said yes and I liked being in the county jail again. He told me again the district attorney said they would have the death penalty taken off me if I would 'plea right.' I asked what they had in mind and he said, something beneficial to me and the state, and I said no. My lawyer is going to subpoena the district attorney because that is the only way he would come. I can't go into much detail about my plans until after I go to court. But I will keep you informed by mail as it unfolds. There is a pretty good chance I won't go back to Death Row. I have many legal moves to make and I am sure part or all of them will work. The federal writ was on the things I talked to you about. The federal court issued a 'show cause order.' That is an order telling the state to give reasons why the federal court should not order my release on the grounds of my original complaint. If the state answers and gives reasons, the federal court can say the reasons are not good enough and order my release anyway. Or they can set the matter down for a hearing, and then the state and I present our evidence, me for release and the state for why I should not be released. My evidence is much stronger, therefore I have a better chance of being released than the state does of keeping me locked up. Personally, I don't think the state will push the issue in federal court because they also know the way things look. The only chance they have is to try to get me to cop out for something before the federal court deadline is up. They have about three weeks left. I have always been told I was stubborn. Can I help it the state made the mistake of teaching me to be patient? So what it comes down to is this, they can let me go now or they can let me go in a month or two. I can wait. This place is like a vacation house to me. The food is excellent compared to what I have had to eat in the past couple of years. I do miss the ice cream I could buy down there but I can get along without it. I have felt like a kid on Christmas morning ever since I got out of that hole on the Row. I guess the inmates here at the jail think I am crazy because I laugh all the time here. My wife, in-laws, and my lawyer have all said they had not seen me this happy since before I was arrested. Everything looks so beautiful to me I can't help being happy. On the ride down here the trees and grass were so green. It rained part of the way down here and even that was beautiful. In one of the towns we stopped at a service station and I saw a small boy about eighteen months or two years old run to the bathroom. I started to laugh and they looked at me like I was nuts. I had a chain around my waist with handcuffs through the chain, and my left leg was chained to another prisoner's right leg. But I didn't care. I knew I was on my way out. I have worked so hard for so long and for a while it looked like everything I tried to do was no good. I know now that I had caught some interest of some people. Here my name is well known by all who work in the courthouse, and most every lawyer in the county knows me. What can I say? I am happy."

Adjusting

The first thing you see when you come in the steel gate of J-23 is a large chrome and red leather barber chair. If it is late afternoon, the guard or one of the porters might be sitting in that chair, watching television or drinking coffee. It is usually positioned in front of 2 or 3 cell of one-row.

Texas now kills by lethal injection, but, oddly, some men coming to the Row are not aware of that, or they are so shaken by their rapid shipment from the county through Diagnostic and out to Ellis that they forget.

They look at the barber chair and think it is The Chair. Sometimes, other inmates nearby will watch for a new man's reaction.

The older hands carefully size a new man up. It's not just a matter of curiosity: there are some truly violent people who come to the Row, there are some men who haven't learned that the violence of the streets has no place in this tight community. The old men watch the new men to decide if they're safe to be near, if they're worth helping. Some new men get a lot of advice, they get cigarettes and envelopes with which to write home. Some get nothing.

Some rules are never uttered. No one bothers to say, "Hey, kid, make sure you don't snitch on people. The guys don't like that." If you're the kind of person who has to be told that, telling you isn't going to do any good.

The advice is most often about psychological matters: *Hang on, I was as scared as you are, nobody's going to hurt you, you'll get used to it, just don't let yourself go crazy before you do get used to it.*

Life is very spare on the Row. Not much happens, there isn't much to do. Nonetheless, there is a terrifying range of things with which a new inmate must come to terms. First, and most difficult, is the meaning of the new residence. It isn't the jail where one is fighting one's case and where the family is nearby and can visit regularly, where the lawyer stops by to say, "Hello, here's what we'll do today." It is a place where one is surrounded by perhaps fearful people, where communication is difficult, where there is no direct contact with the agents and agencies deciding whether one will live or die. It is a place where one must face the fact that one will spend years in a very small room.

In a short period of time, some of them age decades. They show you photographs of themselves taken during their trials or just before their trials, and only because you accept their word do you believe they are really showing you their own photographs. Others remain in remarkably good physical condition; their changes are deeper, darker. On the Row, you don't only adjust to where you are now but to what has happened to you while you're there.

They took me in that gate at Diagnostic and wished me luck. The sheriff had done me real dirty, but he still wished me luck. He didn't care, I wasn't from his county, he didn't know my family or nothing, I was from out of state, a little twenty-four-year-old guy.

They took me in there and took the handcuffs and belt off. I stood there in tennis shoes, a Levi jacket, Levi shirt, and Levi pants. It was really a jacket, but I was using it as a shirt. I didn't know what I could keep. I only had money with me. I didn't have no watch, no rings, nothing that if it was taken from me I would really miss. Money, I only took thirty dollars. I let everything else go back with my family. I came in without a Bible or nothing. I came in with nothing.

They had me strip. I was expecting that. They never done it to me in the county jail, but they said strip and there was men all over the place, inmates and guards and everything. I stripped.

Then they go through the search routine. Then they took me over and cut all my hair off. I didn't mind that. They were trying to egg me on to find out if I was a troublemaker or not. Then they sent me into the shower, which was right there where the haircut was taken, still completely naked and everybody all over the place, but all of them were wearing clothes. I soaked down real good and I came out and they sprayed me with something like DDT or some bug spray in case I had anything on me, some parasite or amoeba or pet spider I was trying to smuggle in. They tried to kill everything. Hair, arms, everyplace.

They had me put on some overalls and took me upstairs where I was fingerprinted and photographed. I did everything they told me to do—they were in uniforms and I was the inmate. I had already set my mind to that: I wasn't going to cause no trouble. Never have been one to cause trouble.

So they found out who I was and they cussed me a little bit.

How? What did they say?

"You're that sonofabitch that did that," or "You're that asshole."

Were they hostile all the time?

All the time. But it was because I was supposed to have killed that officer. I told them, "I didn't do it." I still say I didn't do it, and I will always. "You're saying this because you don't know," I said, "you don't know me any better. You weren't there. I was there and even I don't know what happened. I can't tell you exactly what happened, so I don't hold it against you. You say what you think. You might change your mind later on."

They shackled me and handcuffed me with a chain around my waist and they loaded me in a white van. I thought I was going to be in the Diagnostic Center. I had been told by my lawyer that I was going to be in the Diagnostic Center for a bunch of physical tests. He lied to me. He said, "You'll be there for a bunch of tests and then you will be taken someplace else." I didn't know where. He said I'd have those tests and I would be able to go to the movies, the gym, to be in population. He lied to me all the way down the line.

Did he lie or didn't he know?

He had two other men on Death Row. He knew. He had been here to see them, he had been told by them what happens when you come in, but he lied to me. And he lied to my parents all the way down the line.

I tried to get him fired afterwards, but the judge would not dismiss him and put another lawyer on my appeal.

I was loaded on that van and I was already shook and upset about what had happened to me the day before. It was happening so fast. They had already processed me through, fingerprinted me again, loaded me in that van. I said, "Where are you taking me? I thought I was going to be here."

They said, "Oh, no. You're going to Ellis."

I had never heard of Ellis before. Not from this small, county jail, not being from Texas. I knew nothing.

So we drove and drove and drove and drove and drove and they finally got me out here. And they brought me in that back gate and I was looking around and you know what I realized? It clicked, I'd seen it before.

I worked for a while as a projectionist and I've run many a movie and I watched movies. I recognized this as from a movie, *The Getaway*. This is the same visiting room. It clicked on me: "I recognize this."

They brought me in that back gate and I was met by a captain. Captain Brosher. He's a pretty good captain. I've talked to him. Matter of fact, he came down once about some life insurance my mother had on me before this happened. If I don't keep it, I'll lose it, and even if I get out of here, who's going to give me life insurance again? So we have to keep it. I had to sign some papers on it and they sent it to be certified and I said to him, "Isn't this funny? Here I am on Death Row getting life insurance." He kind of snickered.

The captain brought me in here with two other guards. They knew what I was charged with and they had the papers and knew I was coming. They brought me through the gate, through the washroom, and brought me down in those overalls. They said, "Keep walking, keep going."

I said, "I don't even know where I'm going."

They said, "Turn right, turn left." They were trying to provoke me to see if I was a badass, as the saying goes. It's a system they go through to see how easily provoked the person is, if the person is a hothead. They can't really handle that kind of person with kid gloves, though they have to try and not actually be physical with them. It was the inmate that was physical with me later. They want to find out if you will explode or take a swing at them, they want to know how dangerous you are.

I knew this, so I had to play along. I'm not easily provoked anyway.

They brought me to Death Row and turned me over to the guard that was inside. The captain stayed, a guard stayed, and there was three inmates. They said, "Strip." Checked me again for anything on me. "Take your overalls off. In the shower." I went in the shower and they said, "Wash good."

One of them opened the door when I was showering. I just about went through the wall. A big old black opened the door and looked at me and he says, "Wash your head and all your parts real good 'cause you got that stuff on you and if you don't, it's going to burn you." He was decent to me, at least about that, because I didn't know. I was scrubbing as best I could.

Then they said, "Come out." I put on a pair of shorts, men's regular boxer shorts, and they took me upstairs to three-row.

I could see men and they were watching me to see what I looked like. When I first came here there was only a little bit over thirty Death Row men. They have grown since I've been here. I'm almost considered an old-timer now.

They put me in that cell. I walked in part of the way and turned around by my toilet and was looking and an inmate walked in and looked at me and said, "Now we're not going to tolerate no shit, no screwing up, no fucking around."

I says, "Yes, sir." I looked at him and I said, "Yes, sir."

He didn't know how to react to that. So he reared back with his right hand—

Were the officers there?

They saw it. He reared back and I saw it coming so I just said, "Well, here it comes." I stood there and I was waiting for something to the stomach also, but it was just a slap in the face. He popped me and I come back. It did irritate me and it was stinging. But I had to freeze my face so I wouldn't squint an evil, mean look at him. My eyes were almost watering.

I wanted to, you know. Damned if you do, damned if you don't, but more damned if you do. They were all standing outside that door looking at me.

It was two inmates running Death Row then. They were running it. They said what came, what went, what went on. That's how it was when I first came here. Cecil and Guinea.

Okay. I didn't do nothing. I just stood there.

Cecil was hated so bad he could not live in population. He had to stay on Death Row or sleep where he could be locked away and nobody could get to him to throw hot water or something on him. He was that hated. He had that bad a reputation. A snitch and all this. He was a notorious backstabber.

Are the present guys like that?

Not in the least. There's some people here you don't want to know your business, but nothing like that. It's still bad here, but back then they had blackjacks, they had sticks. They beat up one man and scalded another with hot water. They took food away from others. They had their special pets. Someone who would order them a bunch of commissary to make sure they got extra food off the tray, they'd put on TV what that person wanted to watch. That's the way it was. It's not that way now.

While I was waiting to go to trial, they put me in the county Rehab Center. When I got to the Rehab Center in the chain wagon, they took me in there and gave me some good clothes, some nice clothes to wear. They took me down to the chow hall and they fed me. Then they took us—there was quite a few of us, ten or fifteen of us altogether—down to the first floor and they gave us a haircut, cut our hair real short. Then they started sorting us out, what floors we were going to go to.

They got me up to the third floor. When they got me up to the third floor, they set me over by the first-degree-murder tank. They sent me down there and I set there for about ten, fifteen minutes, and then all of a sudden the boss on that floor, he called my name and said, "Come over here." So I came over to him and he said, "You don't belong in the first-degree-murder tank. You belong in the capital-murder tank."

They only had one capital murder tank there and that was tank 3C-1. They opened the door and they put me in there.

When I walked in there, about ten or eleven of the guys there were in the dayroom. I walked in the dayroom and the building tender, he asked me what my name was and where I was from and a bunch of questions. He wanted to know if I had money and I said, "Yeah, I got some money from when I was arrested."

He said, "There's an empty cell down the hall—cell 9. You go down there and move into cell 9. That's where you gonna be livin'."

I said all right. I went on down there and got in my cell and him and another guy come down to my cell and they sit on the bunk talking to me and they asked me some questions about my case and stuff like that. Then they walked off and went on down the hallway and didn't bother me anymore for the rest of that day.

The next day when they turned the TVs on about ten in the morning, I went down in the dayroom and I sat there watching TV and one of the Mexican guys in there, he come up to me and he asked me a question. I must have said something wrong, I don't know. He hit me and knocked me down. When he did, he knocked me out. When I regained consciousness—I was knocked out about two minutes, maybe not quite two minutes, about a minute or something like that—I got up and I started fighting him back.

That's when the other capital murder guys jumped on me and brought me down on the floor and started kicking me in the ribs and kicking me in the stomach, in the face and everything. Beating on me.

Then four or five of the guys picked me up off the floor, carried me down the hallway to cell 9, they laid me down on the bed and they said they were gonna have sexual acts. And I said no. And they said, "Yes, you are, or you're gonna die. We're gonna hang you or we're gonna do something worse than that to you."

And I said, "Well, I don't want to die 'cause I have too much to look forward to out there, my people and everything." And I thought, "It won't last long 'cause sooner or later I'll get out of this tank and then word will get out."

And they raped me. They forced me into sexual acts with them. They got out razor blades that you shave with. They shaved my legs and my butt. And then they raped me. Seventeen of them.

Two of them held my legs and the other two held my arms and one of them got on top of me and raped me and he got off and another one got on top of me and raped me. This went on for two hours straight. For two hours straight it went on.

When they got through, two guys stayed in the cell and made sure I didn't tell the boss that comes down the corridor way checking to see if anybody's hurt, anybody got in a fight or what's going on in the tank. They made sure I kept my mouth shut.

For one week. I was in that tank a whole week and all this went on for a whole week.

Two days later, after they done this to me, the guy that started the fight with me in the tank told me to come down in the shower. Made me get in the shower with him and have sexual acts with him. He raped me and had sexual acts in the shower with me. Some of the guys were throwing water over the shower on top of us.

It was a living hell, a nightmare that I went through that week.

After the week was about up, one Monday morning, they called my name to go to court. They pulled me out of the tank and put me downstairs in the holdover tank on the first floor. They got me down there and some of the guys that were involved in the rape were telling other prisoners there in the holdover that was going to court from other tanks.

They were giving me go-to-hell looks and spread the word all through the Rehab Center what they done to me.

When I was through with court and I got a lawyer and went back to the Rehab Center, Lieutenant Knight was out there. He knows me from the few times I was out there before. I had been a trusty at the Rehab Center on misdemeanor charges. He put me in a safe place out there after I told him what happened to me. They had doctors examine me and everything.

When the doctor examined me there in his office, I was a nervous wreck. I was shaking so bad I couldn't hold a cigarette in my hand. I was so bad, I didn't know what to do. They put me in a safe place there by the hospital and I stayed there for seven months. In that cell by myself, away from those animals that done that to me.

When they sentenced me to die, they was fixing to transport me out here and they had to put me in a separate car with two officers. They had a paddy wagon with other prisoners that were coming here to the Ellis Unit and they had to put me in a separate car so that the other inmates wouldn't kill me, do bodily harm to me in the paddy wagon coming down here from Houston. That was because of snitching I did on the breakout at the Rehab Center hospital.

When they got me out here, they had one Death Row man, a Chicano, they had both of us handcuffed together. He wasn't one of my enemies. He was an all-right dude. He didn't know anything about me and I didn't know anything about him. They brought us out here to the Ellis Unit.

Major Steele met us out at the gate and brought us in here. They brought us into the dayroom. Cecil Reinhart was the trusty working here at the time. This was February 23, 1976, the day I arrived here.

They brought me in here with my belongings. They laid all my belongings out on the table. Cecil Reinhart [a building tender] made me get up against the wall. They made me take all my clothes off, strip naked. They checked me over to make sure I wasn't smuggling anything in here. They gave me some different clothes.

They wouldn't let me have certain things that I brought down here with me. They tore them up and threw them in the garbage. Cecil Reinhart slapped me in my face, told me I better watch myself and I better not cause no trouble here or he's gonna use that billy club on me. He threatened me two or three times after that.

The word got down here, somehow the word got on Death Row, spreaded around about what happened to me at the Rehab Center. And it's been a living hell ever since.

The only thing I have is the TVs to watch, my soap operas. I've been watching three soap operas for three years and one month now, and that's the only thing I care about because I can't recreate because some of these Death Row men want to get me. I have to stay in my cell for my protection. The TVs and the radio is the only thing I have for recreation or entertainment. The majority of the time, they don't let me watch anything I want to watch on the TV here.

I've snitched on a bunch of people here 'cause they were treating me like dirt and I wanted to get back at them, and stop them from treating me so bad. They made me so mad I wanted to get back at them so I snitched on a few of them here and now they all want to get even. They all want to get me if they could.

What do you think is going to happen to you?

The Supreme Court turned my appeal down four weeks ago. All I know right now is my lawyer is going to send a request for a hearing back to the Supreme Court and if they turn it down again, a second time, then he's going to use the lower federal courts, and if they deny it, turn me down, then I'll probably be the first man to be executed here on Death Row.

Don't you think it's a little odd to be in a position of having to be protected on Death Row?

Yeah, it is. It's been a living hell through the county jail, and here on Death Row. It's been a nightmare. This is living hell here.

If they execute me or if they put me out in the population with a life sentence, if they commute my sentence to life, I'll die out in population because of all these enemies I have.

What they done to me, it's not my fault. It's their fault what they done to me. They done that just to be mean and hateful. Just to have something to do.

I wouldn't live five minutes out there in population doing a life sentence or doing any other kind of time. I need a new trial to prove my innocence. I'm scared every day here, 'cause I have no friends here. My next-door neighbors, the other Death Row tank next door, all of them are my enemies over there. They want to get to me just as bad as the ones over here. I have no friends here. They hate me so bad it hurts.

I stay in my cell twenty-four hours around the clock. The only time I come out of my cell is to shower and when I have a visit. That's the only safe time I have, the only time it's safe for me to come out of my cell. And that's bad. That's worse than dying. Living through hell here on Death Row.

Bellville is where the courthouse is at and they treated me decently there. It was a very old jail built about 1893 or something like that.

As soon as I was convicted, they immediately brought me down here. No motion for a new trial or nothing. They got me convicted and then they brought me down here immediately the next day.

I was taken to the Diagnostic Center. It was all new to me. I had no idea where I was going or what the different colored uniforms meant or where I was or anything. I knew I had to do a lot of looking because it was probably going to be the last thing I was going to see for a long time, if ever again. You know, cars and things.

I'd cry terribly, not because of what they done to me, but my family. I could see what it was doing to my mother and father. They were there and I knew I just touched my mother and father for the last time for a long time. I knew that much about how it was up here.

I haven't touched any of my family or kissed anybody in two and a half years. Actually, it's two years, eight months now.

The Diagnostic Center had big fences and a red brick building. It's all I've seen except when I went to Huntsville once and saw that prison with the wall they have there. I went in the back way and I didn't know I was in prison till the gate opened and I said, "Well I'll be. Prison."

That's the only time I've been out since I've been here. I went in there with a sheriff's deputy and the sheriff. I was only handcuffed and belted at the waist, no shackles on. I said, "Look, if you all get tired, I'll drive."

It takes six weeks for a regular inmate to go through Diagnostic. It takes forty-five minutes for a Death Row inmate.

They made me take a shower with handcuffs on. I had just got a haircut and it was awful. Got that bug spray, you're fingerprinted and have your picture took.

I never heard of someone showering with handcuffs on.

There was a pretty bloody killer in Texas with the same name as me on Death Row. But that's been fifteen years ago. Anyway, they put all them chains, leg irons, belly chain, handcuffs on. They brought me over here to the back door. They wouldn't even let me help them take the chains off, like from around my middle, they wouldn't let me take it out of the belt loops. They made me stand still.

They had a boss get a shotgun out of the gun tower before they even opened the van. He gets a shotgun out and there's a warden and another boss and another boss. You've seen these Dodge vans that they drive around here. There's about a foot of chain between my ankles—how in the hell am I going to step down out? And I ain't wearing shoes. I had to jump.

And this sonofabitch over here, one of them college boys with a twelve-gauge shotgun, I had to jump and make sure I didn't take two steps. I was scared. Why did they need that shotgun? Shit. They could have beat me up. I couldn't fight back.

I jumped down out of there and they took all of this stuff off of me. Handcuffed me and brought me in. First thing the warden says is, "You ever been in prison before, boy?"

I said, "No."

"That's no, *sir*."

"Yes, sir."

And he said, "You're on the Ellis Unit now, boy!" Goddamn, I got in a heap of trouble. I couldn't keep from laughing. I've been in trouble ever since. He sounded so much like Kenny Price: "You're in a heap of trouble. You're on the Ellis Unit now, boy!"

The first day I come out to recreation, I was scared. Didn't know what to expect. Didn't know anybody on Death Row except one guy and he was a cop before he come to Death Row. I was going to play like I didn't even know that sonofabitch.

Come out to recreate and everybody's just like me: they're scared of the new guy 'cause they don't know what he's going to be.

Pretty soon, I was just one of them. And then I went back to my cell and thought of it: I'm one of them, and what are they?

The biggest fear is when you walk onto this place. I've seen one man walk out there and he stood right there and he broke down and cried. I've seen more come in here and live three days and start praying. I've seen them come in here and cuss the day they was born because of fear. I've seen grown men come in here and get down and pray like kids. And cry.

I came here August 26, 1974. Four o'clock one afternoon I arrived here. I came here and the gloom—wasn't nothing on here but just emptiness. One barber chair and two men out there in the hall where we entered out there. I was warned not to speak out or be loud or anything. If I did, I'd have to pay the consequences. The consequences then was a good beating because of the floor men that was here. However, now it's different.

I spent the first year on one-row. Next year and since then, I've been on two-row. In 8 cell and the cell I'm in now.

And it's been more or less filled with loneliness, I guess is what you'd put on it. My first three years here, I never even got a visit. Never had nobody to write or nothing.

When I first got here, I was scared. I mean, I was so scared I threw up at night. And I couldn't eat and they thought the reason I wasn't eating was because I was trying to be a hardass. I was just scared, sick to death in my stomach. And when I would go out to shower, my legs would wobble because of fright. I didn't know what to expect. I didn't know if I would be knocked in the head or what. It was just a scary feeling.

This is a whole new world. This place is an entirely different new world. I made my mistake and I tried to talk to the officers. I said, "Look officer, I need this and that." That's where I made my first mistake. When you need something, you tell the floor boy, you don't tell the officer. The floor boy tells the officer.

I really believe that my age has had a lot to do with my mental anguish because I've never been exposed to this type of life before. I was born in Germany. I'm an American citizen, but my father was in the service and I was pretty much babied all my life. Mother's baby. Well, I am the baby of the family. I have an older brother. I was pretty much pampered.

It was hard to be on my own. You've got to watch what you do and the things you say. And the worst thing you can do is fight them. You can't fight them.

I didn't know anything about law. I do know now because I've studied it since I've been here. They have a library. But I didn't know anything about law. And I didn't know if I'd be taken out and executed a month from now, a week from now. I didn't know, I had no idea. All I could do was show my ignorance and ask my next-door neighbor. I didn't know what would happen from one day to the next. It was really scary.

It's the type of fright you can't understand because here you take a person, he's been told he's going to have to die, and it's entirely different from the person who's been on the street and he gets hit by a car, because he didn't know that was going to happen. Here, you are told in advance you're going to die.

And every night you lay awake. You think about it. You say, "Wow, will it really happen?" And you say, "What will I do? How will I react when the time comes? Will I go crazy? Just how will I react?"

I've tried to comprehend this, but it would take more than the human mind to try and understand and comprehend it, because I can't. It's scary to be told you're going to die and you don't know when and you don't know how.

I let the pressure build up on me so strong—I've always considered myself a strong person, but I let it build up so strong on me that I tried to end my life. I cut my wrists. I was discovered about twenty minutes later and I was put downstairs in 2 cell, in an observation cell where they kept an eye on me.

And as ridiculous as it may sound, instead of trying to help me, I was placed on what they call restriction. They took my privilege to go downstairs to a little room with a few other inmates and talk and smoke cigarettes. They took that privilege and said that I had to be locked down. Locked down means that I can't leave this cell unless it's for a shower, and the shower is about ten feet to the right here. So I don't never leave this cell. I'm locked down twenty-four hours a day, seven days a week.

When I was in 2 cell, I was having problems and I felt I wanted help, but there was no one that could help me because they don't come down here. They don't come down here unless somebody has tried to end their life or if a fight breaks out, which is rare. If a fight breaks out in the dayroom, they'll call the major or the warden, but other than that they don't come down here. And if anybody tells you they do, they're lying 'cause they don't. 'Cause I stayed in 2 cell on one-row for three months. Out of the three months it would really be hard to remember once if I ever seen them.

The once that I did get them down, I wrote several letters, what they call 1-127 forms. You have to fill those out and it's a request to see them. It's kind of like filing a complaint. That's what they are.

Finally they came down and I said, "Look, I'm having a hard time."

They really don't want to hear it because it casts heat on them. Like when I cut my wrists, they said, "Look, man, you put a lot of heat on us doing this. I've got to protect myself." So they took all my things from me.

It was enough hell after being locked up like that, but then they took everything: my letters, my stamped envelopes. I had nothing.

When you come down here, they take your pride and your dignity, but then once they get you down here they take everything. And that's physically and that's mentally. They break you down and they break you where you don't know anything.

And that's the way they like it.

I've been here two and a half years. I came here in 1976.

I wasn't even expecting the death penalty when they brought me down here. I was convicted one day and brought the next. I was totally terrified. I didn't know what to expect or where I was going to be coming. Next thing I know, when they bring me in the door down here, I see the barber chair down there and thought I was seeing the electric chair.

It just about freaked my mind out.

This, where I am right now, has been my second home since I've been here. The first time I ever had a house here in prison was up on three-row.

They brought me in and put me up there and read me my rights and told me what to do and what not to do and what I should expect and what I shouldn't expect. In other words, they put the fear of the Lord into me. I was fed that day and it was the first time I was able to see TV again in five months. I was really picking up on a lot that wasn't going on that happened while I was locked up, that wasn't going on when I was free. They cut all my hair off, they checked me, they took some medicine and gave it to me. They also took blood and swelled up my arm for a long time.

When I said our rights were read to us when we first came in here, it was what was going to be happening to our heads, to our bodies, to our total being if we did something that they didn't like. But they weren't going to tell us what we could do and what we couldn't do that they liked or disliked.

We were totally in the dark, so the man next to you had to kind of become your brother no matter what color he was, to help you to understand what was going on around here—when you were going to recreate, when you were going to eat, when you were going to shower, when you could buy your commissary and get things you need. You didn't even know when the mail went out or how it came in, or what you could seal or what you could open, what you could keep in here and what you couldn't keep.

We were totally in the dark. I have to keep saying that because it was just like coming into a whole new world. What we might have known out there in the free world and what was happening to us before we were even arrested, before we were charged with something, it's a totally different atmosphere here where murdering and killing goes on all the time, or plotting or even drugs and things that you wouldn't want to expect or look for in jail or prison.

The frustration is so intense, the pressure on you continues from all sides. Even if we don't see or hear from any of the officials, see any guards, we know it's there.

Of course, one little mistake and there'll be thirty men running in here, some of them with clubs, some of them with just bare hands. I'm talking about the inmates that are trusties or helpers as well as the guards.

Most of them are scared and apprehensive when they first get here. No friends, they don't know really what it is. They hear so many rumors. A lot of them haven't been in any prison environment before, and there's the thought of prison alone and then the thought of being on Death Row where supposedly they are all vicious killers and whatnot. Naturally, you're going to be scared and apprehensive of what's coming and what it's going to be.

Some act tough. They're actually scared, but their way of dealing with it is, "If I portray this tough image, well, then, I can keep the world away and nobody will bother me." Some of them talk constantly.

Paul hasn't been here that long. He has cussed officials and he's gotten onto them about some things. I'd call him over and I'd say, "Paul, you've got to go at this from a different angle because you're just being hard-nosed at them."

At one time, they cut off his showers completely because he was being so hard-nosed about something. He cussed somebody out. I said, "Paul, you're just hurting yourself. They can say you can't shower and by the time you get them to reverse that, you've been sitting there stinking for a long time."

He did. He sat there for over a week before they'd let him shower. They can do those things to you. And by the time they say, "Well, we didn't realize we were doing that," they've already messed him around. They can play mind games. I called Paul over and I said, "Paul, I hate to lecture you, but you got to see what's going on around here. They're too big. You're like one ant trying to stop a railroad train speeding down the track."

They bring all these rules about having haircuts. You got to shave every day. They have these rules that they bring down here. I read the rule book where it says this is for the people that are doing time, the population. We're not doing time. We're not serving time.

I don't like the idea of getting my hair cut by somebody that don't have no experience. He don't have no experience to cut my hair the way I have it. He might have a license, but there's black dudes and white dudes and us Chicano dudes and we wear our hair different, and the way they cut it is supposed to be different. You can't have just one man and say, "You go over there and cut his hair."

Who are we here to please? We're here to die.

For the type of haircut that I have under TDC policy, it is definitely prohibited. The type of haircut that I have, if the building major would come in here now, he would give me fifteen days in solitary, cut off my recreation and stuff like this, just for a simple haircut like I have.

My hair's really not that long.

The policy's for black guys, brothers, to wear their hair about [one or two inches] long and the policy for white guys is to wear their hair basically the same length. In other words, they want you to look like a kid. They don't want you to wear beards or mustaches or anything.

The reason why they want you to wear short hair is because, they say, if your hair grow long you get bugs in it. But this is not true. People in here shower every day. The doctor comes around two, three times a day, and at night. If a inmate got bugs, I'm sure he'd have enough sense to report it.

The haircuts. I think if a man is going to die, if they gonna kill him, let him go with his hair the way he wants. You know, I can understand if a person won't comb his hair. I can understand them talking about full beards because you can't recognize the people if they've got a full beard. But if a man says, "I'm going to grow my mustache, I'm going to grow me an Afro," they should be able to do this here. They're doing it everywhere else in the state.

Most of the penitentiaries I have read or heard about are growing long hair. I'm talking about mostly up north. And I'm talking about places like Angola, Louisiana. I feel that an individual should be able to grow his hair and things the way he wants to.

They want you to wear your hair something like a Marine would wear in boot camp, you know. I don't understand it. The white guys, they really do their hair bad. They skim it up the back of the neck, just a little top in the front. It looks terrible. What puzzles me about that is how they love one guy with long hair and hate the next one 'cause he wear the same long hair. They go to church on Sundays and they worship this picture of Jesus and they portray him with the beard and the long hair coming halfway down the back. They love this image. But they hate somebody else like that. They usually tell you, "Well, he's the son of God." Well, ain't we all?

I was talking to an officer yesterday and I asked him about that. I said, "Don't you love the picture of Jesus? Well, why come you-all don't let the white guys wear long hair?"

It mocks individualism. A man should be able to carry his own identity if nothing else.

The only thing I can see is they try to keep you in the frame of mind of being a kid. They don't want you to be yourself. They want everybody to look like little robots, you know. Everybody dressed the same, haircuts the same.

They slide the food trays under the door. One of them is a real big, heavyset fellow and he's bald-headed and when he bends over, the sweat just rolls off into the tray. You can't eat that. You see that and it just turns you.

The eggs are sometimes so cold and greasy, they slide back and forth across the tray. I don't like to complain about it, but they're not doing the best job they could.

It's monotonous in the kitchen. Same menu every three days, just about the same menu. I believe a good percentage of the trouble is the inmates who fix it down there. They don't care. I hear stories about what goes on down there because some people on Death Row now used to work down there. You know, they got paroled or got out and committed a crime and came back to Death Row. They tell about what used to happen in other units and this one as well, about rats and cockroaches and bugs and worms. The inmates there might see it, but they don't care: "We're not going to eat it so let's send it on." They don't care. They don't have enough supervisors standing over each one's shoulders to see what's going on.

And the cart comes down there with nobody with plastic gloves handling the food. The bread is picked up, it's sitting out. Some men are notorious scratchers while they're serving food. If I was sitting there where I could see them as they prepare the trays, I know I would not eat at all.

Sometimes you put your mirror out and watch them down there and see what's going on. Some of the guys watch to see who prepares their tray and who's bringing the tray before they'll even accept it because of the things that can be found there. One man found a big old beetle in his greens one day. He sent the whole tray back and they brought him another one. Some would eat it or they'd eat around that beetle. Some people like it. They really do like the way they're living now. They don't have to work. They're being fed. They're being clothed. They watch TV. They get their mail. Their family is sending them money. So they are happy.

It is hard to believe, but there are men like that. They are living better now than they did in the free world. And some of them are completely turned off to sex and they don't care, it doesn't faze them at all.

Instead of cutting little tray holes in the bars, where you can slide the tray through, they'll slide the trays on the floor. It's like you're feeding a dog. You set his food on the floor. Those doors on the bottom are extremely filthy. Sometimes they might have rolls or something piled up on the tray and when you slide the tray, the rolls fall off. They get stuck under the door. You tell the floor boys, the ones that serve us, "Man, the rolls fell on the floor. I need some rolls."

"Catch me later, man, I'm busy right now," or "I ain't got no time. Tell the boss."

Some guys sit back and accept it and other guys complain about it. They rattle the bars and stuff like that. Kick up sand. I do it. I don't never just sit back and take it.

Some men get three or four letters a night and some men do not get one single letter. Do not get any visits at all. And something like that at Christmas can be bad.

At Christmas, as long as I've been here, I send something to the guys that don't get anything. Coffee or tobacco, things like that. This year, me and another man that's down there sent coffee, apples and oranges, things we can only get in the wintertime, to a lot of the guys. I put a little card in there with a horsehead on it, telling who it's from. There's no church organizations come down here at Christmas to see the guys. The only really super meals we get is at Christmas or New Year's and Thanksgiving.

How about Easter?

We might get a colored egg.

One year they gave us a colored egg with some little chocolate candy in it. Everybody thought they had died and gone to heaven.

The hardest part for most people is accepting that you are actually here and accepting that you're going to be here. A bunch of the new guys—I've been hearing this for years—they say, "Well, I'll be going home in six months."

You try to explain to them, "It don't work like that." But they don't want to hear that. And when it comes around like you tell them—"It's going to take six months for you to get your transcript," and they say, "Oh, no, no, no"—and when it comes down like that, they're disillusioned.

I believe it actually takes the average guy that comes here at least six months to adjust. Sometimes they feel like they're going to get their transcripts done, they're gonna get their brief into the Court of Criminal Appeals and they're going to get a reversal. That's one out of thirty, it's not very many at all.

After they get into the court, after they see them take so long to get into the Court of Criminal Appeals, and then they have their hopes up and then they get them dashed, I believe that's when all their illusions are finally gone and they start to settle down.

Everybody takes it different.

I've changed so much as far as physical appearance. I've lost so much weight in my face. My face, it looks unreal. I look in the mirror and I see a face that's not mine. I say, "Where did that come from? Is that mine?" And it is mine, but I don't recognize it. I don't recognize it because of the changes it's went through.

That is a picture of me taken in '73, six years ago. That is how I have aged within that time. You don't realize, day by day, that you're aging. You do it so gradually that you don't realize it and then all of a sudden, one day you pick up a mirror and you look in the mirror and "Wow. Is that me?" You say, "Wow. I can't look like that."

The way it happened to me, a friend of mine down the run, we were talking one day and he said, "Man, how old are you?"

I think this was last year. I said, "I'm twenty-seven."

"No, you're not twenty-seven."

"Yes, I am."

"No, man. You got to be at least thirty-five or forty."

"No."

And I took a real close look at myself and said, "Gee, I really do look that old. I really do."

It's hard to believe that one can age so swiftly in that amount of time.

I guess it's all to do with the mental pressures. There's a lot of mental pressure, but you don't let yourself go. You try to suppress it. You keep something going with the fellas along the row, jokes going and so forth, to more or less keep the position that you're in off your mind. But it's steady there, it's constantly there anyway. You might not realize it, but it's there and it's working on you. You know, day by day. Regardless of what you do, it's always there in the back of your mind. "Hey, you're on Death Row. You could be executed. They could kill you."

I've been here four years, a couple months, a few days now, and this has a tremendous mental effect and physical effect on one that most people don't realize. I'm twenty-eight years old and I look a whole lot older than I did when I first came here. I can talk to some of the fellas around here and it's almost impossible for them to believe that I'm only twenty-eight. And there's a number of others here who have been here as long as I have, and some longer, and when they came here, you could just see the visible effect of the aging, what this has had on them.

It's mentally hard to cope with this. It has much more pressure on you than, say, one that's out in regular population that moves around from day to day. Most of the time, we're confined to these cells, with the exception of the recreation periods and showers, and there's just virtually nothing to do but think about the position you're in.

You're kind of in more or less of a limbo here, not knowing what will happen to you and whether you will ever see next month, next year, whatever. You never can tell. Mostly, I just sit around, watch TV, radio, read books, anything to help keep my mind off my position, and I try to cope with what I find myself in.

The hardest part of being here is not knowing. Just sitting here and not knowing what's going to happen to me. One day you get a ray of hope and the next day you're down again. It's just you never can tell.

It's a mental torture. Everyone else, regardless, whether they are on a life sentence or not, they know that it's a possibility that one day they will get out. Here, you don't. You don't know if you'll be with your friends, families, and loved ones again or not. It's just day-to-day mental agony.

Every man here, when he comes here, comes here humble, but when he leaves here, they leave hard.

That's right. This is no recruiting place, no correction place. TDC is known as the Texas Department of Corrections. They're supposed to correct people, train people, to pay for your crime. But what it is, it's a place to harden a man up.

Death Row isn't a place to correct people. It's for people they don't want to correct.

Death Row. You ain't gonna find no ease on Death Row whatsoever.

A man can walk by my cell any time of the night and I can hear him when he comes and I can hear him when he goes by. I never miss it.

You might have noticed my pillow at the far end of the bunk there. I got a reason for it. Because I don't trust no one on these walkways. And all the old hands that's here, you've probably seen them sleeping at the other end, too. 'Cause they've heard men scream out at night, they've heard 'em "Ahhhh." Hear 'em gagging and choking for breath.

Every bit of that is fear, man, it works on you every way.

I've been here five years. These five years to me has been like fifteen in the outside world. And I've aged more than two of that on the mental-wise side. But physically, I'm physically in good shape. But mentally it hurts you.

All right. When he comes here from a judge, he's considered an outcast.

Then his people, first thing you know his people start leaving him one by one. I'm not talking about his aunts and uncles and girlfriends, something like that. I'm talking about his mother, father, sister, and brother. That's his people. Even your children.

I'm the father of five children. Not one of them writes me. Not one of them writes. I got a boy finishing school this year.

And then he comes down here and he reaches out to people—with no success. First thing he knows, he's down here and he takes life for what it's worth, and he makes it any way he can. He learns to hustle. This is a school, more or less, than anything else here, but it's a school for the criminal mind, not the good mind.

A man sits down there and he learns how to connive people on the outside. Me up there, I can write one letter and get a ten-dollar bill every time I write it.

But without that, he don't make it.

If a man depended solely on what TDC gots here, he don't make it at all. The TDC don't give you nothing. They say they give you towels, food, and things like that. Sure they give you that, but what about your toothpaste, toothbrushes, hair cream, deodorant, things like that? What a man really needs. Shoe polish. They don't give you shoe polish. You buy it. Things like just the small things a man needs. Writing paper, envelopes—they don't give you that.

If you was a man on the outside, that may seem like nothing, but in here, a writing tablet and ten envelopes is worth a ten-dollar bill to a man. That's right. Even though they don't cost him but $1.60 for the envelopes and sixty cents for the writing tablet. But it's worth a ten-dollar bill. A bag of coffee is valued to a man a five-dollar bill. He gives [the commissary] $1.75 for it. But on the outside, people take it for granted. Something like this is just a everyday thing. Here, it's necessity. A man needs it to survive.

And without it, without these little things I've just told you, you'll sit in that cell and you'll crack completely up.

I've seen men walk that cell up there and it'll get their heads and they'll run up to them bars and shake it and they'll scream out just to break the monotony of that cell. And then some boss come up there and say, "Shut up," or some floor man walk up there and threaten him or cuss him out. If that don't do it, he's liable to be pulled out and carried down to deep-six, which is another punishment here. That's one good meal every other day, just have restricted diet, and on top of that, chances are when he gets down there he gets a little "exercise."

That's where Death Row is at.

If I do walk out of Death Row and I do become a free man again, I try to wonder, I say to myself, "What are they gonna say?" Are they gonna say, "We're sorry. We're sorry that this happened to you, man. We thought that you was guilty"?

But it's too late. The damage is done.

What kind of life am I to live? What lays in the future for me? Right now, it looks bleak. I don't know what will happen.

This place here is a nightmare and you don't never wake up. You keep hoping that you'll wake up but you don't.

I'm twenty-one. That's what's really hard about it. Holidays, they come and they go and they don't mean anything. For me, it's been very difficult because I haven't been locked up that much in my lifetime. I've been put in jail for drinking and things like that, but it's very difficult to come in here and just be in a world all your own. It's difficult to try and understand how it works here 'cause you have to learn on your own. Nobody is going to help you. Nobody is going to give you a kind word. Nobody is going to ask you, "How's it going, how's your day? Is everything coming out okay?" You're totally ignored.

Death Row is totally ignored and anybody tells you it's not here in Texas is lying.

I've changed drastically since I've been here. My attitude and my way of life. I've had to change my way of life to adjust to jail and Death Row.

Here you have to take the kindness out of you because kindness is not going to be given to you in return. You would think the officers around here would, because you're sentenced to death, would be nice, but that's not the way it is. A lot of them resent you for that reason.

A lot of them resent the fact that you're here all day long and don't get out of your cell and that you don't work. They want so bad to have you out in those fields working so hard and this upsets them.

If you tell them you're innocent, that's worse. Like when I tried to take my life, as hard as this may sound, they laughed at me. They laughed at me. They said, "He's crazy. He's a crazy sonofabitch." And I couldn't believe this because I've never been done this way. I've never been shown or exposed to this type of hatred. It's a deep-seated hatred. It's something that you would not believe exists. You would have to be here, you'd have to sit in my cell. You'd have to be in my shoes and I hope to God you never are.

My main worry is that I'm going to come out of here and be the kind of people that I've met in the county jail, the kind of people who steal their mama's TV set, sell it for a jug of wine. I don't want to be that kind of person. But that's the kind of person that this place breeds. That's my biggest fear of being in the penitentiary. This Death Row thing or some man threatening to kill me, that don't scare me, 'cause that's all happened before. But being the kind of person that would hurt my family, that scares me.

There's a lot of things that should be changed. Especially when they have a young offender, first time he's arrested for any kind of crime, he has never experienced anything like this before. And when they put you in the cell for twenty-four hours a day without any communication from the free world, you're not used to it. You can't get adjusted in one day. I don't like the idea of having somebody being locked up for five years in a cell.

Your mind sometimes plays games with you. If you're not capable of handling them, you're liable to maybe lose your mind a little bit. Start getting paranoid. They have some guys like that.

Being so long locked up in a cell, it does get to you. You get nervous. You worry about what is going to happen. It's bad enough having the death penalty, and then to turn around and here on Death Row, you're locked up, and if you do something wrong against the rules, they go and lock you up for fifteen days.

You think about your people, how they're reacting, how it's affecting them. Your people are suffering as much as you are suffering, maybe more. They have never experienced this thing before.

If you went to school and learned about loneliness, or how you will feel being locked away from the ones you care for or the ones you love, it would help. It does get to you.

See: we are humans, you know? And the people that build these prisons, they know what kind of life it can lead to. They know that if they put a man in a concrete box or a steel box and then throw the key away and just look at him and laugh at him, it's going to have some kind of effect on him. He'll start wondering if that's the way it's supposed to be or if he's human, too.

I'm not saying that it's wrong for them to put a man behind bars and then lock him away. I guess if he do something wrong, he should, like they say in the law, he should be punished for it. But I don't like the idea of this way. They should treat him better.

The first poem I ever wrote was "Why Me?" That was back in '74. I'm a mechanic and I like to work on cars. I come down here and there was nothing else to do to pass the time, so I started writing poems. At the same time, I wrote poems about how I felt about me and about some of the people that I cared about. I found it very hard to say, "Well, I can't do what I want to do." I don't like writing, but if I didn't put my mind to work at something, I knew that I wasn't going to last long inside my head. I might lose my mind just being in one little cell doing nothing.

I'm a loner. I don't talk much. I don't laugh much. But I always try to be honest with myself. This is not what I like, but I have to adjust. If I don't like it, I have to do it. I don't like the idea of being locked up. There ain't nothing I can do except wait my time and hope for the better.

It could get worse, being on Death Row, but I've always got it in my mind that it might get better, too.

I don't get very much mail. Maybe one letter a week. If I get a letter, I sit down and answer it back.

But it's hard. Some guys here on Death Row don't got no families and it does get to them.

Your mind plays games. If you're not capable of handling that kind of pressure, it's gonna get to you. I've seen quite a few people lost their mind, or at least they were not them anymore. They were just a different kind of person. They changed all the way around.

I have a good friend of mine, his nerves started getting to him. His nerves were so bad and he couldn't get no medication at all. He didn't know what else to do. He say, "I need some medication, I need some nerve pills." They won't give him none. Finally, he set himself on fire. He thought that—I don't know what he thought, I couldn't speak for him, but from what I've seen, I thought myself that he was doing what he thought was best. If he was hurting himself to get medication, if he was going to hurt himself and it might cost him his life, he was trying to show them that, some say, he was trying to tell them that he needed help.

I don't think they care. Because if they did, they would prevent something that might happen to you before it happens.

He set himself on fire. They took him to the hospital, brought him back again and locked him up.

Was he badly hurt in the fire?

No. He just burned his arm, part of the head, and one side of him. It was nothing serious.

I always felt that if you wanted to commit suicide, why not do something right. Instead of just trying to show them.

He wasn't trying to kill himself. The few times he talked to me, he says, "Hey, I'm tired of it. I don't know what else to do." And he couldn't find no other way but to hurt himself to show them that he was not right, that something was wrong with him.

He was so paranoid that his nerves was so bad, and then he got paranoid and he was scared to himself. Not that he was scared of what might happen to him, but his mind was playing games from being locked up for so long.

I was always told that if you have a dog and you treat that dog wrong, sooner or later, that dog will bite you back. So that, I guess, is what happened to him. They treated him so wrong that he just got tired of it. And there was no other way that he could strike back but trying to hurt himself. To make them look.

They cage me up like an animal and whenever you get out of line to get your rights that they've taken away from you and you try to get them back, they say, "Oh, you're acting like an animal."

Well, let me ask you this: what is human behavior under these conditions? What is normal for a man to react when he's told he's gonna have to die? When everything is taken from him? His life, your mail is censored. They read your mail. Take a visit, they're standing over your shoulder. They know everything you're saying. You shower and they're watching you. At night they're shining flashlights in your cell. You never have a free moment. And I ask you, what is normal behavior?

Whatever it is, I don't know it. All I know is what's happening now, the present. And it's a nightmare for me.

When I first came in here, I knew things was going to be pretty bad when I heard this guy screaming up there. He was in administrative segregation. Old Cecil would go upstairs there with a high-pressure water hose and spray water in his cell to get him to shut up. The old boy was crazy, you know, and he'd talk all night and keep everybody awake. Cecil would get mad and run that hot water or cold water in there.

I got here in June 1975 and you never knew what kind of mood Cecil was going to be in in the morning. Of course, I got along. I kept my mouth shut.

Cecil was a building tender and so was another big black guy by the name of Lawrence Guinea Smith. They run it on this side. If they want to whip somebody, they just tell the man to open the door and they run in and whip him.

Cecil was a psychopath. He liked to whip people. I've seen him whip a bunch of them.

The people they whipped mostly were writ writers, the people the administration wanted it done to. Now this is my viewpoint: I don't think anybody got whipped around here unless the administration wanted them whipped.

They would catch these people either going down to get their haircut or going to get a shower. When you'd come out by yourself to take a shower, there Cecil and Guinea would be waiting on you. I've heard a guy would be getting a haircut downstairs and they would start ribbing the guy, you know, calling him nasty names and everything, trying to get him to jump in a fight. If they couldn't do it that way, they'd just catch him in the shower up here and beat the hell out of him. This went on as long as Cecil was here.

Then Guinea went in the hospital and died. He has a stomach disorder and he died. And Cecil, we heard—I don't know if this is true, this is a rumor—that they paroled Cecil to a New Mexico prison where he had a life sentence. He escaped from there. They said it wasn't a few months after that they found him hanging in a shower with his guts cut out. Well, it made everybody very happy around here.

Don't know whether it's true or not.

I was never whipped myself. Like I say, I kept my mouth shut.

It has changed. The head-strumming has stopped. When I first got here, it was a daily occurrence.

Just troublemakers or just—

Not necessarily. They picked the ones they think they can get by on.

I'm the type of person, I don't put my mirror out the bars to see what's going on. No. Because I know who I am. I know what I am. And I mind my own business. So I don't have any problems in that aspect.

So you didn't used to get beaten up?

No. I have been to the penitentiary before. When I first come in, they knew that.

They knew you knew how to pull your time.

Right. So, like I said, they would pick only on the weaker people that they knew they could get by with.

Do some people still get picked on?

Oh, yes. Sure.

What kind?

The weaker people. They always do. And always will as long as they're in the penitentiary. That will never change. That's one of the facts of penitentiary life. The strong prey on the weak. Day in and day out, twenty-four hours a day.

When I first came here, in March of '75, it was a totally different place than it is now.

Adjustment wasn't that hard because I had been in jail for quite a while.

Back then, they didn't tell you anything. You just came through Diagnostic, got showered, shaved, sprayed, haircut, and they brought you right over here. Bring you in through the back gate and put you in a cell.

They had an officer working from about eight in the morning, got off about five. That was the only officer they had working here then. The building tender that was in here, anything you wanted to know, you had to ask him. If he felt like telling you, he did, if he didn't, he didn't. That's the way it was.

It was only nine people here when I got here. I was number nine. Everybody was on one-row here then. If you wanted to find out the address so you could write letters, you ask the guy next door to you. And if he didn't know, you didn't find out.

If you get locked between two morons, you're in a world of trouble.

Right. The fella that was next door to me when I first came, he just got here the day before me. But the guy on the other side had been here a couple of months, so we would get information from him.

It wasn't too bad. You have this mental thing about what you think it's going to be like, and I don't know about everybody else, but with me, things weren't quite as bad as I thought they were going to be. I felt like, "Okay, you're on your way to Death Row. They're going to drag you in there, throw you in a little hole or something. They might feed you, might not." It was just a mental thing.

The building tenders, well, they weren't what you call good and they weren't bad. With some people, it was an extortion thing. Some people here had to pay their way, but it wasn't like that for me. I had a bunch of home boys out in the population. So I didn't have any real problems.

But then again, I couldn't afford to pay anybody. There were a number of people who came in with a lot of money and they paid their way through. It was in a sense pretty bad.

It's gotten somewhat better. Like they got officers working all three shifts now. Back then, you only had that one from eight in the morning until five in the afternoon, and then it was just the building tender. And he did what he wanted to do. If he wanted to do something for you, you could get it done.

Now it is practically impossible to get things done for you here. It's not because the officers don't want to do it, but there are so many of them that's only been working here a couple of months and they know less about it than you do. You want to know something and you ask the officer. He'll give you a blank look. "Well, I don't know."

"Could you find out?"

"I'll try."

But it's getting better. The officer here now, Summerville. He's been here a couple of years. He's the only one working here now that has been here for some time. And he knows things pretty good. He gets things taken care of for you.

When I first came here, I came with the attitude, "Hey, you're going to die. So what? What the hell. You know you got nothing to lose. Whatever goes down, you know you've got nothing to lose."

I wasn't more or less scared, I couldn't say that. When I first came in I was nervous about some things. I had this thing in my mind, I didn't fully understand the appeal process then. I thought, "I'll be down here a couple of months and then they'll execute me or something and it will be over with."

I've talked with a lot of guys and they thought that too.

The barber chair wasn't up there then, but I talked to some of the other guys that came here since it's been put in here and they said that they thought that was The Chair.

It was a period of adjustment. I would imagine it's much easier to adjust then than it is now because then there was only about nine or ten of us here. We used to go out every day. They used to open the cells in the morning for shower. They just open all ten cells and one would go to shower. When he came back, another would go. At that time, everybody be standing out on the run and we be talking back and forth to each other. And everybody went to the dayroom every day. So it wasn't too hard to adjust like that.

But it was a hell of a mental strain.

When I first came here, I tried to cut all ties with the outside world, like with my parents and brothers and sisters. I'd write my mother and my wife and that would be just about it. Everybody else, they'd write and I wouldn't answer. I was more or less cutting ties because I didn't want anyone out there to feel that they had any type of responsibility toward me. I felt that the more ties I could cut, when I was executed, the people I have known wouldn't feel the effect of it as if they were steady communicating with me day in and day out.

Since then, I have changed. I'm writing a lot of people that I knew.

Like I said, when I first came here, I was more or less resigned: "Hey, you gonna be gone in a couple of months. So what? Big deal."

I don't know whether everybody feels that way. But I'm sure that there's a lot of guys here that knew more about the workings of the justice system than I did. They knew that they were going to be here for a number of years. I didn't know this.

Anything else I ought to know about this place and the way people pull through?

Well, it sucks.

I determined that.

It's better than it was when I first came here. You only had the building tenders in here from five in the afternoon until eight in the morning.

Old Reinhart. I kind of draw back from calling him a complete animal because he did have his human side. Most people didn't realize it. I was one of the very few people that he would talk to.

He was building tender, he was flunky for the Man, but he was still human. He needed human companionship just like anybody else. And on the whole Row, I guess I was just about the only one that would talk to him. Sometimes he come down and sit in front of the cell and we would talk.

But he was still an animal, you know? I guess after a while, being in a place like this, it happens. And he had been here for a while. He was one of those old-timers. I guess after you been here and you play the Man's game for so long, it rubs off on you. I don't know.

It might sound weird to you, coming from a dude who's setting on Death Row. But actually, believe it or not, Bruce, I am actually into nonviolence. Believe it or not. It's really hard to accept.

I have told some people that. "Oh, really?" Yeah.

See, I'm on Death Row. I have a murder-robbery case, shot a dude in a robbery. Well, okay. Any time you kill anybody, it doesn't sound good, and it most definitely doesn't sound nonviolent.

Matter of fact, it sounds downright stupid.

Family Affairs

In the early evening, when the guard sorts the day's mail on a large wooden table on one-row, many inmates stand quietly at their bars, watching the envelopes. Some can spot from twenty feet away a letter they're looking for. "My girlfriend uses orange envelopes," one man told us. "That way, I can see right away if I got anything coming up." "I always know when you or Diane are writing somebody on the Row," another wrote us, "because I see those envelopes of yours on the table."

Mail is the primary link with the outside world. The television sets on the walls are there to be watched, but they don't listen, they don't care. The officials are concerned with the running of the wing. Mail brings you to your family, your lawyer; mail lets you pretend you're still a part of life.

Many of the men anguish over changes in their families. They talk about what happens to the children in their absence, about their sense of impotence when they hear of problems, the impossibility of attending even a mother's funeral. Changes in the family, perhaps more than anything else, mark their own separation from life, signal the fact that they are not of our world.

Pass by a cell and a man will be sitting on a bunk staring at a massive array of snapshots arranged atop the small bookcase; he may sit there for hours. Pass by another time and none of the photographs is in sight. "I just couldn't stand looking at them," he says.

Personal friends drift away early. Some stop writing because they are repulsed by anyone who might be a murderer; more stop writing because they are embarrassed or don't know what to say. What do you say to a man who is waiting to die? "We had a swell time at the beach, wish you were here." The lawyers write rarely, if at all.

The relationship with the family keeps some of those men sane; the fragility of those relationships puts them in the most terror.

I hate Sunday. I hate Sunday so bad. I hate it because you can't get no letter. The most important thing to anybody, I guess, down on Death Row is the letters. It's a rarity to some folks. When I don't get some mail, I immediately get upset. I really get upset. I withdraw into my Bible. I say, "You done a job on me, Lord. Here I am, I'm trying, and you done me like this." Then when I get a letter, it will make it all better. It'll come just in time, every time, on time, all the time, just when I need it. I never have a whole bunch of it. But I always have exactly as much as I'm going to need.

You write your letters and you stick 'em in your bars at night. You lay there awake. And this is all mental strain and fear—whether you're going to get anything out or not. This is all working up here, it's not working down here on your body.

And you lay there and your eyes get heavy. After a while, somebody comes along. You look up, your mail's gone. You jump up. You ask that boss, "You seen my mail?"

"I ain't seen none a your letters."

And he's telling you the truth, he told you the truth. What happened was, that night a floor man went by there and *whish*, took 'em down, and he'll read them. If they're okay, he'll put 'em back in the mail slot.

I came here in November of last year. What was wearing me and hurt my heart was my mom. I thought all kinds of bad things about her—that she would have a nervous breakdown or maybe she'd just give up.

She stayed away for about three weeks before she came down here to see me. When she came, she had bags under her eyes. She was looking bad and it just killed my heart. It really killed my heart. I thought I wasn't going to be able to take it.

I told her, I said, "Streak, you're going to have to get a hold of yourself because you're really in bad shape. Don't you see how I'm doing here? I'm smiling. These people ain't going to do nothing. They ain't killed nobody in a long time."

She was worried, real worried, and that was my worry: how she was taking it all.

Since then, I had other things hit me. My oldest daughter got pregnant and she ain't married. She's only sixteen. And my son got throwed out of school.

But I look through on the other side and there's still sunshine on the other side. It just can't be bad. I keep getting richer and richer.

My dad, he don't come over here and see me. He sent $1,000 to them state-appointed lawyers and told them to help me where I needed it. He's never wrote me a letter since I've been here. I have never seen him in eight and a half years.

The last words that my dad said to me was, "You are the sorriest, piss-poor excuse of a man that I have ever seen and I should have pulled your head off when your mammy had you."

I said, "Dad, I sure hate you think that."

I turned and walked out. I had just gotten out of jail from a six-month term for a DWI. That's the last words my dad ever told me personally. I called him up while I was in Wyoming and I had been doing dope and I was sick. I had a wreck. I called him up for fifty dollars. I really didn't want the fifty dollars, I just wanted him to tell me hello and I love you, I need you or something. And I said, "Dad, could you send me fifty dollars?"

He said, "Son, it wouldn't hurt me a bit to send you that money. I've got loads of it. But it wouldn't do you a damn bit of good." And he hung up.

I've had him go as high as three weeks at a time when I worked for him and seen him every day and he never told me hello. The people that were working out there with me—I was just working as a common laborer too—they found out one day that he was my dad and they said, "I don't believe it. I couldn't never believe he was your daddy. I wouldn't even thought the man knowed you the way he acted. He's really your daddy?"

I said, "He sure is."

I feel sorry because I know how his heart's hurting now.

You know, I hated that man for years. I hated him and I hated him enough that I even planned to kill him if I had time to do it. I really did. I had it in my mind. I said, "I wish I could." I wished I could just kill him.

I don't know if I would have went through with it or not, but there's a few times I just kept wishing, wishing that I could.

I didn't know why I wanted to kill him. I just wanted him to straighten up and let me in on something. He'd never commend me. Never say "Hey, you done a good job" or anything. If I did do a good job, he'd say, "Shit, anybody could do that."

He whipped me—the last time he whipped me, I was seventeen years old and I told him, "I hope you don't never do that no more." 'Cause I wasn't going to take no more of it. I had my mind made up.

The only families that stick with a person is trusty, dedicated Christian people. I mean people that are Christians. The rest of them will drift.

I've got a sister I haven't heard from in four years. That's right. To today, I'm still trying to run her down. I know where she's at, and people saw her, but she won't write to me. She done washed her hands.

The day my mother died, that's the day she left. My mother died in November of '74, right after I got here. These people wouldn't let me go to her funeral—that's something you don't do.

I was lucky. I got to talk to the chaplain out there.

It destroys the relationships that you've had with people that you may have known for years. Just for the simple fact that you have been adjudged to be a murderer. It makes it difficult to maintain relationships. There's always a doubt in the other people's mind that they don't really know. It makes it hard to communicate.

You have a life here, they have a life on the outside, and they're totally different. A person who hasn't been in a penitentiary cannot identify with penitentiary life. There's so many changes. There is no individualism. You have no opportunity to express yourself in the ways that you may have been used to expressing yourself. It's hard to maintain a close relationship with anyone.

There's no way that a man can be incarcerated on Death Row without encountering some of the ostracism. The relationships you've had with casual friends dissolve. You lose contact with them. And understandably so, because it's not physically possible for you to write or maintain communications with people that you've known for so long. Relationships that have been nurtured over the years, they vanish. And there's nothing that can be done about it.

It's a sense of loss. It's a loss that can never be recouped. The relationships that you lose can never be rekindled because there's always that doubt.

What if one is overturned and gets out again? Do you think it will always be there because of the conviction?

There's always the stigma. The person on the outside, unless it was a relationship that was very intimate, a long-time relationship—the casual relationship, there's going to be a doubt there. They're not going to know in their own mind and they won't be able to identify with you in the same way that they were. There will always be the doubt: Is he or is he not a murderer?

There are a lot of families that accept it. But you have to look at it from the family's viewpoint. They can either accept it or they can reject it. If they reject it, they lose a family member.

And that happens.

It does. I was showing Bruce, before I came out of my cell this morning at six, that I received notification that I was being sued for divorce.

Did you know this was going to happen?

I had expected it. You can't be isolated from someone for eighteen months without it happening. People on the outside, their life goes on just as ours does. They have to make adjustments, just as we do. And it follows that their adjustments will not necessarily include us.

Even though it wasn't a tremendous shock, it can't help but make you think. You're ending a relationship with someone, it's something that's gone. Even though there was no animosity there, it's another thing that you have to accept. Something that you have no control over.

The death penalty don't scare me because I don't think they're going to kill me. And if they did, I think I would go to a better place than this. I'm not worried about myself.

But when my mother comes down here and I see her, I know she wants to cry 'cause she's scared to death of this place. My dad, he's scared. Boy, that's the only part that makes Death Row hard on me.

Of course, I get depressed. My girlfriend got married and moved to Wisconsin and I didn't even know. I had to get it from the grapevine. I get depressed about things like that. My sister's having a kid, getting married and all that.

Somewhere in the back of my mind, I always know there's going to be a tomorrow when I'm out there. Even if they make me do fifteen years down here, I think there'll be a tomorrow out there somewhere.

But the way I've been acting, when I get depressed I write home. It shows in my letters and I hurt a lot of feelings and I bring them down to being as depressed as me. And that's gonna make it hard for them to stand close by me through all of this, especially now that they don't know how long it's going to be.

Every year, my mother and my sisters write me better letters. I mean letters like they miss me. I think I get better in their eyes or in their memories every year that I'm down here. I write my sisters poems for their birthday presents. I don't guess their boyfriends ever done it. They sure do go hog wild with the thank yous and all.

Some people don't have much family, or they don't seem to stand by them.

I see that a lot and I can't understand it because mine have always been there. If they wasn't there and if they affirmed my case, I'd make them execute me. You know, if they affirm my case, then I don't have to appeal it any further. I have to appeal it to the level it's at right now. That's mandatory in Texas law. But I don't have to go any further than that if they affirm my case. If they reverse it, I get a new trial, but if they affirm it, I don't have to. If I didn't have my family, I wouldn't. 'Cause that's a long road I'm looking at. I don't know what's up there. There's going to be five or six more years down here. Lots of people that's been down for five or six years. Lots of people that's been down here for a lot of years. They're the kind of people I don't want to be. Some people say they're institutionalized, but I think it's something else. They just get harder and meaner and they see everything different.

Lots of people live on fantasies, live on memories. I just keep looking for tomorrow. Every Wednesday the Texas Court of Criminal Appeals releases their decision for the week. That's what my mother waits for. Every Wednesday. So every Friday or Saturday I get a letter, "Well, they didn't say nothing this week. Maybe next week." She's trying to build my hopes up, and then I know she's just about had all she can take, waiting, 'cause everybody said they were going to rule within two months, three months at most.

Do you know why they haven't?

Have no idea. Just because of my guilty plea, that's the only thing I can think of.

What does your lawyer say?

He says he don't know either. He's not real cooperative.

The thing that bothers me most is my family. They're the ones that's really hurt by me being here. I've been through two trials. It really tears them up. It hurts them. I can handle it better than they can. They're beginning to be able to cope with it a little better, but they don't understand the legal process. When you say, "death penalty," they think it's coming. This hurts me more than having the death penalty, to know that my family is suffering.

Have they stuck by you?

The greatest. Fantastic. We're all from Houston, so it's kind of close by, and it's unbelievable how great they have been. After all the hurt that I've caused them. It kind of renews your faith.

Without them, I don't know what I'd have done. I wouldn't have the art supplies that I'm working with now if it wasn't for them. And I wouldn't have the attitude that I have if it wasn't for my family.

I don't get a lot of visits because most of my family works. It's hard for them to take off. That doesn't bother me 'cause I know they'd be here if they could. Usually, during the holidays they come. But they keep me with the mails. The last seven days in a row, I've had mail every day. It's kind of unusual to get mail every day.

I have a guy lives next door, last night he said, "How come you're getting so much? Give me some of it."

It's great. Of course, I just had a birthday, so that counted for some of it. Birthday cards.

It hurt me to be here, but there's nothing I can do about it because of the law. I can't go home when I get ready. I'm used to eating when I get ready. I have little kids, two kids that I'd do anything in the world for. I miss them more than I miss anything. They just turned three and four in October. What is it now, April?

I miss them more than I miss anything, but this is something I can't do anything about. Just accept it. I wouldn't want them to know where I'm at. Have them say, "Where's dad?" and their mama say, "He on Death Row." I wouldn't want that.

They don't know?

I don't want them to know.

So they never come to see you?

It's something I'm not used to even though I've been here before. I don't like the bars. I would just like to hold my kids. My real mother's dead, but my stepmother, I'd like to hold her. It's something that I guess comes natural, you know. But we can't do that, so I don't see any reason for them to come down here. It's not going to hurt me and I feel that it would hurt them.

The single worst part, I think, would be just being away from the family. Not being able to watch the kids grow up. That's something that I believe every man and woman would like to share, that his children is growing up. That's something special. I mean the little things, like the baby's first step, his first day in school or something like that. To me, that's something that's very special and I really miss that.

Sure, the old lady writes, she tells me, "Robert did this today." Well, that's great, but I really can't truly appreciate it because I'm not there able to see it. And it makes a difference.

I sit back sometimes and say, "Six years from now, if I'm still here, my oldest child will be graduating from high school, and I won't be able to be there."

It's probably all a mental thing, but you have this feeling that all your children, they're growing away from you. In the process of growing up, they're growing away from you. I mean, they know you exist, but when you're not there, they can't feel the influence a father would have over a child. The little everyday things that they might ask you. You're not there for that, so they have to turn somewhere else and ask this question. And that really hurts you.

We are under the death penalty. We don't belong to the state, we belong to the county. I feel they should leave us out there in the county until all our appeals are finished.

We are here to die. We are under the death penalty. They should leave us over there where your people can be close to you and they can see you more often. Especially with the economy now, everything's so high, you can't expect to have a visit but every few months. Who knows when anybody will get a visit? Some of our families don't have anything. They're poor. It's just no good the way everything is.

I didn't give a shit. I didn't think I was good or bad, I didn't have nothing in my mind about that. Then I got to thinking about it down here. Well, I've done this and that's bad, and I've done that and that's good. Shit, the bad outweighs the good. There ain't no hope. I died over here, I done give it up.

If my daughter hadn't a wrote me that letter and told me, "Daddy, we all love you and we need you," I wouldn't be here now. I know I wouldn't. I would have hung it up. I'd a made somebody kill me. I wouldn't have done it myself. I'd a made somebody.

I'd have jumped on him and I'd a forced him to do it. If I hadn't got that letter. It said, "Daddy, I love you and I miss you and we know you're gonna get out."

Hell, I'm on Death Row. They done told me I'm gonna die. But you know what? They just give me hope. I said, "I can't leave them. I can't." And I couldn't. I didn't have no chance anyway, it was stupid for me to think there was, but that's the only thing it was. Hope.

The barber chair and television sets, cellblock J, Row 23, Death Row. Ellis prison farm, Huntsville, Texas. Billy Hughes, who arrived on Death Row before Texas started using lethal injections, said, "I see the barber chair down there and thought I was seeing the electric chair. It just about freaked my mind out."

Excell White. Executed March 30, 1999. “I’ve had a death day set on me three different times. And each time, facing death wasn’t no problem. It was the up, the stay of execution, the kickback on it. That’s what really hurts you. My last time, I got within three days of execution. I was ready to go on. It didn’t bother me a bit. And turned around, come up with a stay of execution. That’s what hurt. Like to put me in a state of shock. As far as that goes, a man just lives and survives on Death Row.”

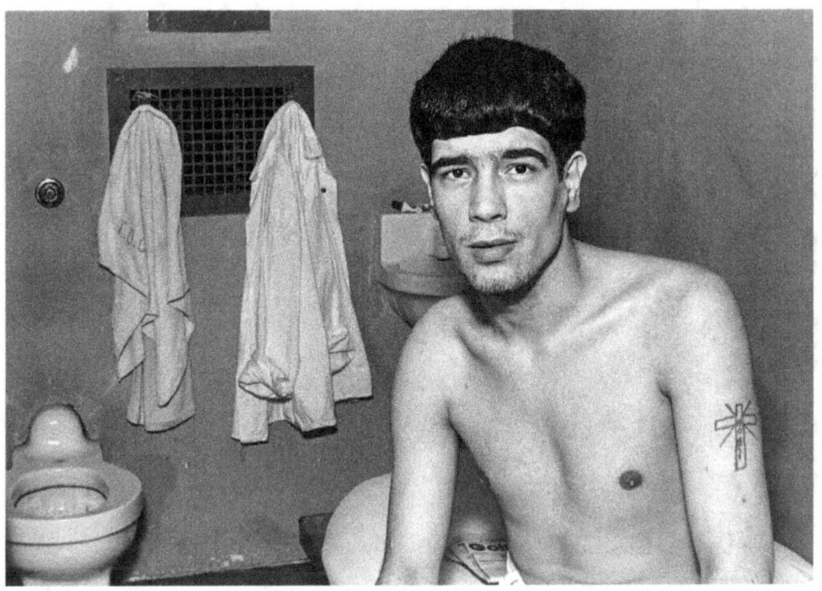

Kerry Max Cook. "Sentence overturned August 6, 1997; pled no contest and sentenced to time served. Released"; subsequently cleared by DNA evidence. "This place here is a nightmare and you don't never wake up. You keep hoping you'll wake up, but you don't." In a 2009 telephone conversation, Kerry told Bruce that people often ask him how he kept from going crazy during two decades on Death Row for a crime he hadn't done. He'd reply, "I'm not sure I didn't."

Murriel "Donny" Crawford. Sentence reduced to life November 27, 1987; paroled April 2, 1991. "If they start executing, it could just snowball and everybody could go faster and faster. But we don't know. Maybe they won't, and maybe they will. The execution could start next month or they could start next year or they could never start at all. We have no idea of knowing. We're just waiting. And day after day, seeing the pain it puts your people through to have to see you wait . . . I can wait. I think I can wait here for ten years. And be all right. But the pain it's putting my people through makes you want to do something about it, and there's nothing I can do. Just sit here and wait."

James Russell. Executed September 19, 1991. “TDC has constantly refused to give me a simple set of teeth. I have offered to pay for the teeth myself out of my own money, to have my own doctor come down here. TDC has refused my doctor to come down and also has refused for me to pay for the teeth. They say, ‘Well, you don’t need no teeth. You gonna die anyway.’”

Harry Jack Smith. Died in the prison hospital, April 8, 2016; he had arrived on the Row October 10, 1978. "The library doesn't have all the lawbooks that we need. When we reach a point where they don't have these books, then we have to depend on Austin's library. Have to buy the law. It costs us a nickel a sheet. And if you send to the county, it's around a dollar a sheet. If you are a poor person that don't have no family and you're depending on a court-appointed lawyer, then you're just up a hill unless you can get a stamp to write him and ask him to look it up for you."

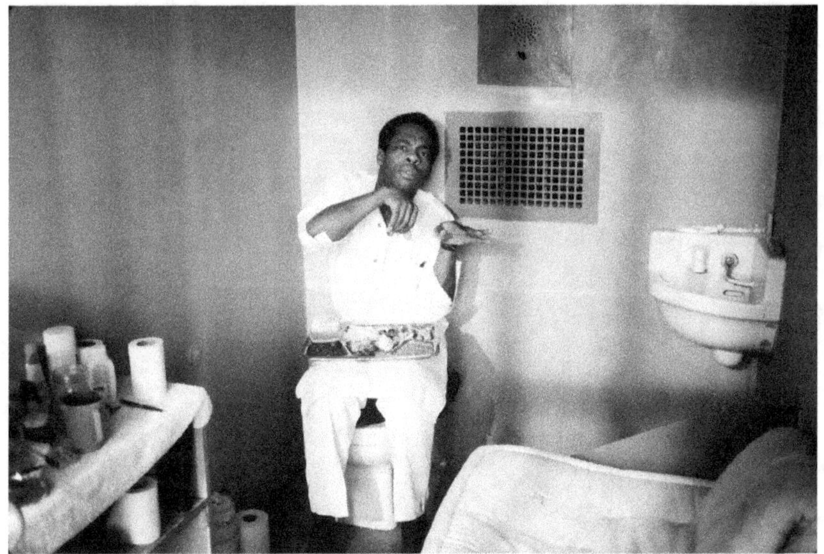

Thelette Brandon. Conviction reduced to murder with a deadly weapon; sentenced to life, July 28, 1982. "Understanding the real language that is being, is being spoken."

Emery Harvey, porter. "Physical work, then clean-up, that's just part of prison life. Everybody has to work. The difference on this job is not just the work, but you have to be a social worker or a psychologist. Just a good listener at times. You come down the run with a mop, they'll stop you for just any little thing. An article in the newspaper, ask you questions just to stop you to have somebody to talk to. The guys in their cells, they're all alone."

Jerry Jurek. Sentenced reduced to life, January 29, 1982.

Billy Hughes. Executed January 24, 2000. "We know that we are going to get out of here one way or another. Either we're going to walk away free; we're going to walk away into population, serve a life term or some sort of term; or we're going to leave here feet first in a box."

Billy Hughes and Diane Christian in Ellis visiting room.

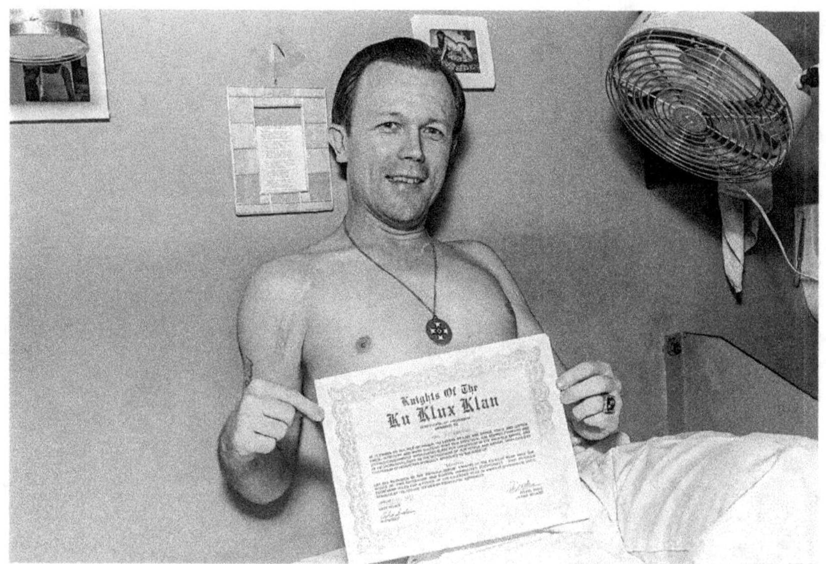

Fred Durrough with his new KKK membership certificate signed by David Duke. Conviction reduced to murder, July 14, 1982; sentenced to life. "I published an article in the *South Africa Citizen* newspaper and I got over a hundred letters from the people over there. . . . I support South Africa. I think that this country is really screwing them around, you know, asking those people to commit national suicide. The one man, one vote thing, that's a bunch of bullshit over there."

Pedro "Lobo" Muniz. Executed May 19, 1996. Every morning, when he cleaned his cell, he'd find bugs that he would feed to his two wolf spiders; afternoons, he watched *Days of Our Lives* and *As the World Turns*.

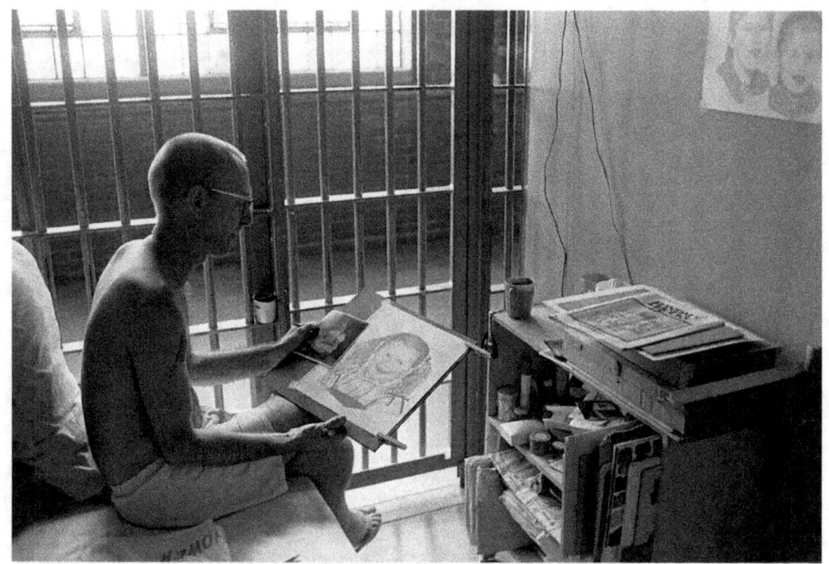

Doyle "Skeet" Skillern. Executed January 16, 1985. "If there's anything good that's come out of receiving the death penalty, it's that I've discovered I have a little talent in art. So I can be thankful for that."

Thomas Andrew Barefoot in Ellis visiting room. His mother stepped away from her chair the other side of the glass, saying, "Make sure they can't see my face." Back in the cell, Andy said, "I have shot heroin to the point where I was beamed so far out of my head I'd nod. And before I could get the rig out, I was knocked plumb out. When I'd come to myself, the rig would still be in my arm. I was more higher when the Spirit come on me than I have ever been on any kind of drug. I tried to do that again and I can't. I'm happy, but I don't have that flush like I had. I don't know if you ever get that high again or not. Or maybe that's how heaven is going to be, because it was close to heaven. It was real close. It really was. But maybe you don't get that no more."

Executed
10-30-84

THOMAS ANDY BAREFOOT

EXECUTION #621 <u>SCHEDULED FOR EXECUTION OCTOBER 30, 1984</u>

DATE OF BIRTH: 02/23/45 (39)

COUNTY OF CONVICTION: BELL

DATE RECEIVED: 11/21/78

RACE: WHITE

CONVICTED OF CAPITAL MURDER FOR THE AUGUST 7, 1978 SHOOTING DEATH OF POLICE OFFICER CARL LEVIN, AGE 31, OF HARKER HEIGHTS, NEAR KILEEN, TEXAS. BAREFOOT, AN OILFIELD ROUGHNECK FROM NEW IBERIA, LOUISIANA WANTED IN NEW MEXICO ON CHARGES OF RAPE TO A 3-YEAR-OLD GIRL, KILLED OFFICER LEVIN TO AVOID ARREST.

BAREFOOT HAS PREVIOUS PRISON RECORDS IN LOUISIANA AND OKLAHOMA.

<u>PRIOR ARREST INCLUDE:</u> AGGRAVATED ASSAULT, BURGLARY, HIT AND RUN, D.W.I., LEWD MOLESTATION, THEFT, ESCAPE, POSSESSION OF MARIJUANA, POSSESSION OF AMPHETAMINES, POSSESSION OF A SAWED OFF SHOTGUN, POSSESSION OF AN UNREGISTERED FIREARM WEAPON, ATTEMPTED RAPE, ARMED ROBBERY, ASSAULT AND BATTERY, BREAKING AND ENTERING.

BAREFOOT HAS HAD **4 PREVIOUS EXECUTION DATES:**

09/17/80	STAYED, SUPREME COURT JUSTICE POWELL
10/13/81	STAYED, 10/09/81, CT. OF CRIM. APPEALS
01/25/83	STAYED, 01/24/83
12/14/83	STAYED, 11/20/83 U.S. DIST JUDGE LUCIUS BUNTON
10/30/84	

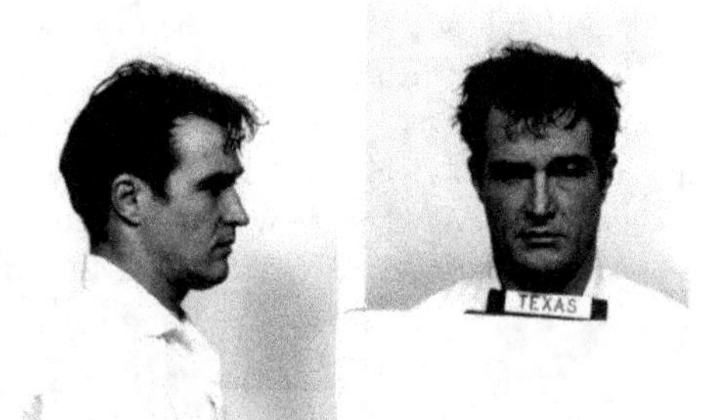

Barefoot's Death Row fact sheet and death date.

Paul Rougeau. Executed May 3, 1994. "All of it hard to me. It's just all hard. Just being away from life is hard."

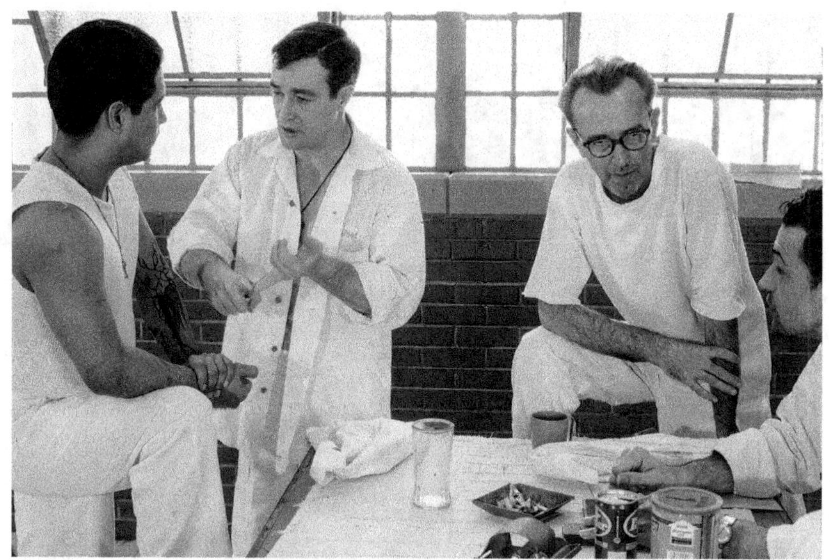

Four dead men: Pedro Muniz, Thomas Andrew Barefoot, Doyle Skillern, and Paul Rougeau in the day room during one of their three weekly ninety-minute recreation periods.

Chess on the Row. John Thompson (executed July 8, 1978) and Emmett Holloway (conviction reduced to murder with a deadly weapon; resentenced to life).

Wilbur "Wolf" Collins. Sentence reduced to life, February 1, 1983. "I've been here four years, a couple months, a few days now and this has a tremendous mental effect and physical effect on one that most people don't realize. I'm twenty-eight years old and I look a whole lot older than I did when I first came here. I can talk to some of the fellas around here and it's almost impossible for them to believe that I'm only twenty-eight."

Correctional officer Scott Summerfield handing out razors, which he will take back in a few minutes. Barefoot said, "They got Dr Pepper cans and Coke cans, which is made out of all aluminum. They allow us to have glasses and everything in there, but they won't let us have no razor. You can take our mirrors, which I'd say are six or eight inches around, and you could take it and break it if you wanted to kill anybody. I have been in the life of crime all my life and I would know how to harm somebody if you wanted to. Or the wire around the notebook papers. You can cut a man's neck completely off with it. But they won't let you have a little ole razor, which, if anybody came at me with a little old razor, I'd laugh at him. It's crazy. It wouldn't even hurt nothing."

Kenneth Davis folding Marlboro and Camels wrappers and blue Bugler tobacco bag labels to make picture frames. Sentence reduced to life, November 13, 1981.

Billy McMahon with some of Davis's wrapper frames. Conviction reduced to murder, September 22, 1983; sentenced to eighty years.

Three in the air during volleyball in exercise yard. There were six volleyball players that day. Three were later executed: Kenneth Ganviel (February 27, 1996), Billy "Steel Bill" White (April 23, 1992), and Jerry Bird (June 17, 1991). One, Jessie Jones, had his capital conviction reduced to ordinary murder (March 27, 1986); he was resentenced to life and died in prison January 10, 1994). Two had their sentences reduced to life and are still doing time: Larry Ross (August 5, 1982) and Alton Byrd (January 3, 1984).

Ronald "Candyman" O'Brian (executed May 31, 1984) and Raymond Riles ("sentence reformed from death to life," June 16, 2021). Riles had arrived at the Row thirty-seven years earlier, on February 4, 1976. Candyman got his nickname because he murdered his son with cyanide-laced Halloween candy for the insurance. Riles's death sentence was "reformed" because an appellate court found he never should have been sentenced to death in the first place.

Porter Charles Grigsby sliding a food tray into a cell. Doyle Skillern said, "Instead of cutting little tray holes in the bars, where you can slide the tray through, they'll slide the trays on the floor. It's like you're feeding a dog. You set his food on the floor. These doors on the bottom are extremely filthy. Sometimes they might have rolls or something piled up on the tray, the rolls fall off. They get stuck under the door. You tell the floor boys, the ones that serve us, 'Man, the rolls fell on the floor. I need some rolls.' 'Catch me later, man, I'm busy right now,' or 'I ain't got no time. Tell the boss.'"

Hands outside cells: Moses Garcia (cell 10), Murriel Crawford (cell 11), and Clarence Jordan (cell 14). Jordan is still on Death Row.

Bruce talking to Billy Hughes on J-23.

Diane talking to Fred Durrough on J-21 after screening of *Death Row*, December, 1979.

Diane, porters, guards, and prisoners on J-23 watching first screening of *Death Row*.

Kenneth Davis, looking out with his broken mirror.

Dominoes on the two-row of J-23: Billy White (executed April 23, 1992) and Jerry Bird (executed June 17, 1991).

2. Surviving

Have you ever thought of what it's like to live on Death Row?
Do you care? Do you really want to know?
We're kinda like an idling Car Slowly running out of Gas
We really don't know how much time We will have to pass
Do you know what it's like to cry inside
or to wake up in the dark of night Afraid you'll die without a fight?
We all live with one fear or another
Mine is how this hurts my mother
To see the pain behind her eyes She just can't hide it no matter how hard she tries.
What makes this time so hard to bear, Is knowing so so many people
just don't care.
You all know we're here to die
We ask for help but you won't try
You just don't care about us men
you think your killing ain't a sin
So we go on in this timeless time
And the law makes our people the victims of our crime.

—Donnie Crawford, execution number 569, April 13, 1979

Community

Everyone is aware of the continuing potential for violence on the Row: nerves fray, tempers flare, punches or glass jars are thrown. Men try to get by, to establish their own rules for what they will or will not accept from others. The goal is to get by with as little trouble as possible, while at the same time preserving some sense of one's own self, one's own boundaries.

Some violence on the Row is seems irrational. The problem is, there are no alternatives on the Row. There is no way one can get away or avoid every situation. Some men on the Row go crazy, some hide or create for themselves envelopes in their cells so they never have to come out. Most do come out, most do socialize, and most do work out some kind of relationship with their fellows.

They gossip here worse than old ladies. Way worse than them. Men is worse than old ladies. I used to think ladies gossip. The men, they start messing,

messing, messing. They become unreal. Ladies don't gossip as much as men. I noticed in the free world how men gossip a lot. They talk about each other. But over here, it's worser because that's all they got to do is down each other talking, start messing, everything.

Each man is on his own on Death Row. Ain't nobody—you can call a person a friend, but when it comes down to hard fact and you need a friend to stand up for you, ain't nobody stand up for you but yourself. That's right. That's the way it is. Nobody tries to butt in nobody else's business. Each person's supposed to pull his own time. It's just a rule of Death Row. That's a rule all over the prison system, I imagine.

There's plenty of rules on Death Row, but they're suited only to the people that runs Death Row. I was given a rule book here, what a man's supposed to do, but soon I found that rule book didn't qualify to me, it qualified only to the people that runs the prison. You pull that rule book out and quote some. "Uh uh"—they push it aside—"we ain't gonna pay no mind. We make our rules here."

You get people one way, then you get people another way. You get people who look at you and be straight with you all the way through and you get 'em that will cut you in half. And there's people here I wouldn't trust 'em with two bits—because they'd kill you for it. There's some people in here I wouldn't even sit there at that table with.

Fighting in a penitentiary doesn't go by the Marquis of Queensberry Rules. You have to assume that when you get in a fight in the penitentiary, it's gonna be the best man walks away and the man that's not quite good enough is gonna be laying there. It's just understood. It's not usually done in the sense of camaraderie. It's not something that's done as a pastime, in a ring with a pair of twelve-ounce pillow cushions on your hands. If you get mad enough to fight, you're usually mad enough to hurt somebody.

I haven't gotten that mad. There may be some—I'm sure there are some—that are more antagonistic towards people than I am and in general would attempt to bully. I don't attempt to bully. I'd rather be left strictly alone. I don't try to prove my superiority. I'd just as soon you not try to test me because if you do try to test me, then I'll try to prove it.

I'm acid-tongued. I'm antagonistic. And there's a purpose to it.

Protection?

Preservation. You don't walk up and fondle a cactus because you know the cactus is going to get you. And if a man is deliberately antagonistic and he has a sharp tongue, one of two things is going to happen: he's either going to be left alone or he's going to get knots on his head. I've never been opposed to scrapping, so either way, it's all right with me.

The way you usually get somebody here is you heat up some water boiling hot and when he comes by your cell, you scald him. Or take a mayonnaise jar and throw it through the bars and let it cut people up. I got cut over there yesterday when someone threw a glass through the bars at the floor boy. That glass, hitting the bar, it's got a lot of momentum and it will cut you bad.

Why did it get thrown?

Someone thought he didn't get what he thought he should have. He was mad because this one over here got a little more than he did. It's like a game down there.

I come in one time and they didn't have nothing but one kind of lighter. I brung one in and it didn't have enough butane in it to last a day, but I sold it for four brand-new ones. Four brand-new ones because there was no other ones like it here. Anything that's different, you know. They got all that money and it's of no value.

You won't believe how freaky things is. Like a rock. If I could get me a rock in here, why I could sell it for three or four packs. Just a regular old rock. Really. Ain't nobody got a rock in here. Don't you know I could sell that rock!

Or a different kind of plastic cup. You can buy good plastic cups in the commissary for twenty-five cents. I've seen them pay three dollars, four dollars, even five dollars for a plastic cup that wasn't worth twenty-five cents because it was a different color or a different kind than they had in here. And the fool would say, "Look at my new cup." He'd bring it out there in the dayroom, he'd drink his coffee in it, and why, shit, it ain't no better than no other cup. But he got it in his mind that it is because it's different and ain't nobody else here got one like it.

You revert down from being intelligent to the childish ways.

I'm not a violent person, you know. I don't believe in violent crimes or anything like that. It was just a freak thing, the way I got busted. I shouldn't even be sitting in here right now. Somebody else should. It was all because I didn't take the stand and testify.

But like I told my nephew out there, criminals live by a code, and if you're going to make it in the penitentiary, you can't snitch on nobody. That's the worst thing you can come down to the penitentiary with—a snitch-jacket.

There's one man on Death Row now who's known as a snitch.

Yes.

Would people like to kill him?

Oh, yeah. Sure.

Because he's a snitch or because they're the people that got snitched on?

Just because he's a snitch.

There's three people that took the stand in my trial, were put under oath, and got up there and told out-and-out lies.

If I would have had any sense, I would have took the stand myself and run down to them what really went down.

And you didn't because of the code?

Yeah. I just don't believe in snitches, you know. I don't believe in snitching on somebody.

But they snitched on you.

If I saw somebody just pull out a gun and murder somebody in cold blood and the police put me on the stand, I wouldn't open my mouth. I don't believe in that.

Is there anything you would do it for?

No, I don't think I would.

What if somebody did something to someone in your family?

I think I'd take care of it myself. I couldn't take the stand. I know it may seem strange to you, but I just don't believe in it.

I'm not saying that I don't believe in law and order. I do. If there wasn't any law and order at all, it would just be a killing ground out there.

Just think about it. If it wasn't any law and order, somebody would get in an argument and just kill somebody. Nobody would be there to do anything about it. I wouldn't want to live in a world like that. There has to be some law and order.

But not the law and order that we have, the corrupt system that we have. It's ridiculous. I don't believe that the president of the United States runs the country. I believe other people run the country. And I believe that he's told what to say in his press conferences and things like that. I believe he gets up there and tells the people what he's been told to say. I really do.

I think he's real weak. He was raised in an all-woman family. I'm not saying that he's queer or anything like that.

The calmest, the most easiest going people that I've ever seen in any penitentiary is the murderers.

Everybody that I mingle with now, other than the floor boys, is killers, or convicted for killing. They don't let us associate with nobody that's in population.

The murderers are more calmer, don't bother nobody, they're carefree people. Whereas your drug addicts, your sex offenders, or your robbers—those people are crazy, really bad crazy.

For a lot of the murderers, it's a first-time deal. He comes in here and this guy catches him doing it and then he kills him. Or you're liable to get mad at your daughter and then just jump up and slap the heart out of her and then say, "Hey, I wished I didn't do that." Or you pull that trigger.

If you pull that trigger, you don't bring nothing back. It's gone. The anger is what it is.

I would be a whole lot more afraider fooling with robbers and armed robbers and drug abusers and stuff like that than I would a murderer. I love to stay with a murderer because I know where I stand. I know how much he will and how much he won't take.

In the free world, if someone insults you or bothers you, you can just walk away. In here, these things build and build because usually the fools are doing the abusing, and when you try to just get away from them they take this as a sign of weakness and bother you even more. Then, when you have to do something to their ass, you are a vicious criminal.

Take this little black that killed the big one here the other day. He weighs about 115 pounds and the dead one weighs 175 or 185 pounds. It is my understanding that the big one had threatened to kill the little one (I heard this). What was the little one to do? Wait and see if he tried? Hell, everyone here is convicted of capital murder, so a threat cannot be taken lightly. I personally feel that the little black did exactly what he had to do. I don't think he intended to kill the guy, he just got lucky (or unlucky, depending on your viewpoint).

The point is that in prison you cannot let things slide in some situations as you could in the free world. Also, some (hell, quite a few) of these men have a very strong "macho" attitude, which is really silly, but it is there and they are quick to take offense to things that really are unimportant. I used to be the same way, but I have grown out of it. I know what I am capable of, I know I am a man, so I don't have to go around proving it to every fool that bothers me. Only if he keeps on bothering me is he endangering himself. I will always walk away that first time, and if possible, even the second, but I won't be pushed too far. I don't want trouble, so I go out of my way to avoid it. I don't even play dominoes with aggressive individuals because I have seen their attitudes lead to nasty words and fights over a silly game. Fight over a game? How silly can grown men get?

There's been two glass-throwings over here in the last two or three days.

Bruce saw one.

That's right, he was in there when it happened.

They had whipped this one guy in the dayroom. He'd been hollering and raising all kinds of Cain and everything. You know what that's like on the guys living right next to him. Your cell is four feet wide and it's seven feet deep. You're in a cage and you got another cage on the next side of you. If this guy poops over there, you can smell it over here. And this guy is raising Cain. They had told him a bunch of times, "Cool it, give us a break."

You know, there's no quietness over there. You got every TV going in there. You got a speaker in the back of your cell that's running the whole day from six in the morning till ten-thirty, eleven at night. And you got three stations that you can select out of all the stations. But there are cells back-to-back there. Our cells back on 21. You hear all the other speakers from all the other cells on your row and on the other row. You don't know which one you're listening to.

You're trying to think and this guy is hollering over here, and this guy is blowing one of them paper things here, and there's a nut over here. So that guy that was hollering, they whipped him pretty good. So he says he's gonna get them back. They secluded him and wouldn't let him recreate with the rest of them.

They got to let them out to shower. When he came out to get his towel, he run up to the guy that done it to him and said, "You sonofabitch," and throwed the glass.

This guy, he's not really dangerous. He's not going to hurt nobody. Oh, it scared a lot of them in there when he threw the glass and they thought he really was dangerous. But if he really wanted to do something he'd have acted calm and said, "Hey man, I'm really sorry, I didn't mean to bother anybody." And then when they let him out, then he would do something to the guy. If you want to get someone, don't act crazy about it.

Does it ever happen?

Sure. I have never seen it on Death Row. I seen seven killings when I was in El Reno, the federal joint. They killed a bunch of them. One of them stabbed another one with a lawn mower blade. Stabbed him sixteen, seventeen times through and through.

One guy told me he didn't like the way I joked. He came up to me and said, "I don't like the way you joke. I don't like the way you talk. I don't like the way you look."

I said, "Are you willing to change it for me?"

He says, "What do you mean?"

I said, "Well, I've always been a little dissatisfied with the way my face is arranged. Want to help me with it? I love pain. I'm a masochist." He didn't know whether to laugh, get mad or hit me.

What did he do?

He walked off. I play with their minds so bad sometimes, you know. I can talk above them or I come down to their level and just cuss like one of them. I will get mad if provoked long enough. But I don't stay mad.

They trust no guard, they trust hardly anybody else.

I have a few people that I will talk to that I might confide a little in, but I have none that I call an actual friend. I am friendly with them, but I have no actual friend. I will not establish a friendship. Especially when I know the man is guilty.

I mean, I can forgive the man if he's really truly sorry, but if he don't care and he says, "I'm going to do it again," I say to myself, I won't associate with that person.

You run across that?

Yes. There's one man now that's got the death penalty now and five sentences on him and he don't care. He tells exactly how he did it, blowing the brains out and the whole works. There's other men that's come down there, as you know, and have been finding God. I've had my exposure to that and I can only say to them, and I do say it, "It's fine and dandy, but there's somebody dead in the ground now. They don't have a chance. And you want to be forgiven. Fine. But why didn't you think about this before you did it to that person?"

The ones that get on the God trip, in my opinion, are guilty, because their conscience is eating at them. Plus they got caught. And they don't think they have any help in the courts, or have any hope, and it's like a primitive caveman. They don't understand it, but they got to ask for help from someplace.

I've been in that cell two years now. I don't like any of the cells. There's no preferred cells: closer to the front, closer to the back.

I don't consider this my home. I almost consider this like a giant, extralarge, overdue camping trip because it is so cold in the winter and so hot in the summer. You only got that little fan going.

I don't turn on my fan until I am so hot I can almost not breathe, and that's the only time I'll turn the fan on because then it's a relief. If I had the fan going all the time and I get used to it, then when it gets even hotter, then I'm not going to have any relief.

Mostly, I only run my fan at night when I would be real super hot.

It gets terribly hot down there. The windows are facing north and they only open from the top and they open to the inside. When the wind blows, if it blows at all, it blows up, not at us. Maybe it hits three-row or the top of two-row.

There's one guy who's a drug addict. He beat an old man to death with a pool cue and raped the girl. When I first saw him, I knew I wasn't going to like him too well, so to pick at him I said, "Oh, you're the one that raped the old man and beat the girl to death with the pool cue."

He says, "No, no, no." He thought I actually had the story backwards. He got upset.

It's a lot easier getting along on Death Row because out in the population you have more racial conflict going on between the blacks and the whites and the Mexicans.

I live right next door to a black dude here. I was a pretty headstrong dude in the world. I didn't get along with blacks. I never have. I don't know why, I guess I was just raised that way. But in here, we go to the day room together, we play dominoes together. I play dominoes with the dude next door and it's pretty easy.

I haven't seen a fight since I've been here. I came last September. I've heard fights, but we've never had one in our group.

There's a lot of hollering, cussing each other out. But I think a lot of that is just a put-on. We've got three rows, three tiers. Someone down on one-row will holler at somebody up on three-row, and that is because they don't go out in the same group. They know they're not going to be fighting.

The noise sometimes drives me crazy. Like when I'm trying to sleep. I stay up most of the night and read after the TV goes off. There's a little light, it doesn't go completely black, they have to keep some hall lights on. There's a light down the run that shines in my cell.

I know it's bad on my eyes. I've been trying to get glasses. I've been put on the eye doctor list four times, but they still haven't taken me to get glasses.

It's a lot easier in population getting things like that done because you can walk around and talk to the bosses and the warden. Here, you're in the cell, you've got to send out notes, and a lot of notes don't make it to where they're going. You tell a boss that works on the row up there and he just forgets about it.

There are some pretty good bosses down there. Some of them are just lazy, but some are pretty good.

A lot of the problems, you got to look at the convicts, because there's some convicts on Death Row that never been to the penitentiary before and they're always hollering at the bosses, calling them names—now this isn't everybody, this is just some of them. And it gets on them bosses' nerves, you know.

If you want them to treat you right, you've got to treat them right. A lot of them don't do that. They just holler and tell him to get his ass down the run. "Bring the fucking mail," and things like that. It's just this hollering at the top of their lungs. They call them bitches and whores and things like that.

A man doesn't have to stand for that kind of treatment. And a lot of these people don't understand why these bosses screw them around. If you want them to treat you right, you got to treat them right. A lot of these old convicts know this, they've been down here before. But a lot of these young dudes down there—seventeen, eighteen, nineteen years old—they don't understand that. They just don't give a shit.

There's more protection on Death Row, a lot more protection. On Death Row, you've got a big screen where nobody can get throwed off the run. In population, I don't know if it's like that here, but it wasn't on the other farms that I was on. When I was on Ferguson, we had a young kid that got throwed off three-row and landed flat on his face. It didn't kill him, but it broke all his limbs, it broke his arms and his legs and knocked all his teeth out, broke his nose. He got in a fight up there on three-row, the highest tier there is. Got in a fight up there and got throwed off. I imagine that's why they keep those wire cages up on Death Row, because they think we're all crazy.

I'm watching that one. If he comes near me, I'm going to climb up them windows and set on the top and holler. He's too big for me to mess with. If they get too big, I can always run. Can't run very far on Death Row, but I can sure climb up them three stories of windows and holler. Holler down the row.

Sometimes when there's a fight in the recreation room, the key gets lost. Mysteriously, it gets lost. When W—— was beating on Dancer a couple of weeks ago, they found the key quick and the boss came in there. But one of the bosses told the dude the next day, "Well, if I'd been here, I'd a lost my key bigger than shit."

Every time you come out, like when you come out for a shower, you're just about blind. You have to squint so you can see. I wouldn't be surprised if everybody along here was suffering from nearsightedness.

People that have been down for a long time, they know how to act. They know how to stay out of other people's business and keep to themselves, how to stay out of trouble.

The newer people don't?

No. There's a lot of them that have never been to the penitentiary before. They just come off the streets and they think that they can act any way they want to. But penitentiary is a different world.

A lot of people are institutionalized. They feel comfortable. That is one thing I could never do. It's nerve-racking up there. I like my freedom, I like to move around, and staying in that little cell up there . . .

I have a hard time. I stay up most of the night and read, and then I have a hard time sleeping during the day. I guess I sleep about three or four hours out of every twenty-four hours. But I never get tired.

I don't do no exercise or anything and I always stay in shape. I don't know why that is. It might be mind power or something like that. I never gain weight. I can eat all the food I want. A lot of people, they'll just lay around and get listless. Let their bodies deteriorate. But that's one thing that's never happened to me. I never get flabby or listless or anything like that. I always feel pretty good physically.

There's a few I don't like because of their actions. And there's a few others that they could never put me around because I would jump on them.

These are the ones that are down here for crimes to children. That's my number-one pet peeve and I can't stand it.

That's what everybody hates the most, isn't it? Aren't those guys on the very bottom?

No. There's a couple of weirdos in there. There's a couple of them in there that have been busted for child offenses and they talk about it. It's all they talk about. *They're* on the bottom.

They say, "Boy, that's what I want to do most in the world." I can't stand them. They pretty well know that most of these people in here have kids. For their own safety, they'll be quiet as far as yelling out, but if they're around small groups, they'll talk about it. They'll see a child on TV and say, "Oh, look at that."

Death Row inmates, everybody down there has got a capital murder case, everybody's got the same sentence. We all have to live together. There's no reason in the world we can't all be friends. It should be that everybody is tight as they can be, but no. These people create anarchy down there. Sometimes we don't see a ranking officer for a month or two months. Everywhere else they make their rounds every day. They go to every wing except Death Row.

And the medicine. They carry a little bitty pillbox down there. "Take aspirin and walk slow and you'll make it." That's Death Row. I live on Alka-Seltzer and Rolaids.

Three Specimen Days

Changes in the routine of the Row are rare. Food carts come and go, the radios and TVs maintain their curtain of noise, the medical attendant makes his routine passages with aspirin and prescribed medication, the recreation groups get their turns in the small room and the caged yard, the men are sent one by one to the showers, the mail comes, the radios and TVs and lights go off, and the next day it starts all over again. The control is so neat and efficient that a man on three-row may spend years without ever seeing the faces of any men on two- or one-row but for those in cells very close to the steel stairway.

We asked three men on J-21 and J-23 to write for us what went on in the course of a specific day.

August 27, 1979

4:00 a.m. The lights come on in the cells. If you left yours on, you don't have to get up at that time. Matter-of-fact, you don't really have to get up at all.

5:30 a.m. The radio comes on in all the cells and this is about the time I like to get up, if I have had six to eight hours sleep. Today I get up and start reading the *New York Times* and finish a book I started.

6:05 a.m. The chow cart comes at this time because it was on the other side, the other wing of Death Row inmates. One week the cart comes to 21 wing first and then 23 the next. They switch from week to week. The breakfast this morning was pancakes, coffee, pork gravy, rolls (called catheads), yellow grits, butter. I ate . . . and almost regretted it . . . as always.

7:12 a.m. Showers start on two- and three-row. During this time I am reading and working on my outgoing material.

8:30 a.m. First group goes out to the day room. This is my recreation group and I went out for the hour and a half that we were to be there. Sometimes we get to go in the yard, which is a wire enclosed area that is about twenty yards by forty yards. This is with a volleyball net and ball, the only exercise. But today we only went to the day room and everyone talked and played dominoes.

10:02 a.m. First group comes back in and we are put back in our cells and doors locked. There were twelve out of the sixteen men that could have gone out to recreation in the day room. The ones that didn't come out were asleep.

10:37 a.m. Lunch chow cart comes. What is served is almost always the same. Corn bread, white bread, cathead rolls, tea, beans, greens, noodles, and cake.

11:37 a.m. Second group goes out to recreation.

11:40 a.m. TV is turned on for the day. *Tic-Tac-Dough* is on the ABC station, channel 9. This is where we start watching for the day, or rather the soap freaks do, which come on next.

12:01 p.m. *Days of Our Lives* come on. This is an NBC soap opera, but is shown on the ABC station.

1:01 p.m. Doctors, another soap opera comes on, also an NBC show.

1:03 p.m. Second group brought back in from recreation and put back in their cells.

1:31 p.m. *Another World*, another NBC soap opera on the ABC station.

1:36 p.m. Third group goes on to recreation.

1:57 p.m. One-row showers at this end first. I shower at this time.

3:01 p.m. Movie comes on. *Run Stranger Run*. This is on the NBC station, channel 2. The TV was changed to it.

3:15 p.m. Third and last recreation group comes in. This is all the groups that will get out of their cells. This is one more group, fourth. It gets to come out last tomorrow and then moves to second group to get out on Thursday, and fourth group gets to come out first on Friday. Then it doesn't come out again until next Tuesday, last again. All groups are rotated like that.

3:44 p.m. Chow cart comes. Supper. Meat loaf, corn bread, white bread, pudding, greens, potatoes (mashed), and water with ice.

5:01 p.m. Local news comes on TV. *The Ron Stone Scene* at 5.

5:31 p.m. National NBC news. The same Houston, Texas station, channel 2.

6:02 p.m. More local news on the same station.

6:30 p.m. *Sha Na Na* comes on the same station. Sick-silly show. . . . This one I watch, as well as the news, none of the others.

7:01 p.m. *Monday Night Baseball* on ABC. TVs were changed to channel 9 again. Houston and Montreal playing in Montreal.

7:26 p.m. Mail comes in and is handed out by officer on duty. I got newspapers and mail as well as a letter and note from a friend about an attorney in Dallas.

10:06 p.m. Baseball game over and the news comes on. Houston won 3 to 0 over Montreal.

10:37 p.m. News goes off and Johnny Carson comes on. Both of these shows shown on the ABC station. Guess they buy or use what they want.

11:02 p.m. Lights, radio, and TV cut off. (Weekends the TV can stay on later, like Friday and Saturday.) I remain up and do a little reading by bright light outside the building that shines into my cell. I am up to around 11:45 and then retire. Until it starts all over again tomorrow.

During the day, when I wasn't out in the dayroom at recreation and then the minutes I was showering, I have been in my cell like any other Death Row inmate. This is unless someone had a visit and went to the visiting room, which I didn't, so I was reading, drawing, and working all day. Many of the men will sleep late and then nap again at the time soap operas come on. Many others read or write letters and study law books. Just a few do the law books. This day was also LBJ's birthday, so the library books were not run. The outside field hands and turnrows did not have to work. The fields were empty except for the milk cows moving in to be milked.

This was a very typical day on Death Row.

September 11, 1979

6:00 a.m. Wake up as radio is turned on in control room. Each cell contains a speaker in the back wall with three channels to choose from. The radio "control" operator usually tunes in two rock stations and one country and western station. I only listen to the country and western station. I prefer semiclassical, but that is just not tuned in here. I get up and put on my coffee water to heat while I wash my face and comb my hair. Then I make up my bed and get down my *Dallas Morning News* newspaper that came in the mail the night before. I make my coffee. I have a seat made from folded-up newspapers and I sit down facing my bed and spread out my paper to read as I drink my first cup of coffee.

6:30 a.m. Finish newspaper and can hear the food cart being wheeled to the wing. Breakfast is served by floor boy sliding the food tray under my door. Today it's one egg fried hard (it's easier to serve them fried that way; I personally prefer mine "over easy"), gravy, syrup, oatmeal, and rolls. Food is usually served cold or at least cool.

6:45 a.m. Finish breakfast and brush teeth.

7:00 a.m. Listen to national news on radio and make second cup of coffee. I get out letters received last night and go over them before getting out typewriter to respond. I usually spend from one to two hours answering my mail or writing a woman I hope to marry.

7:30–8:30 a.m. On most mornings, the second row, where I am at, gets to shower first. I shower. If today were Tuesday, I would be going out to the exercise yard at 8:30 a.m. for one and a half hours.

We are allowed to go the day room in groups of approximately fifteen men per group. The groups are divided by cells. The first group is first floor cell number 4 through number 16. Second group is first floor cell number 17 through second floor cell number 10, and so on. We get to go out in this order. Monday, group number 1 8:30–10:00 a.m., second group 11:30–1:00 p.m., number 3 group 1:30 p.m.–3:00 p.m., Tuesday second group 8:30 a.m.–10:00 a.m., number 3 group 11:30 a.m.–1:00 p.m., number 4 group 1:30 p.m.–3:00 p.m. Wednesday is haircut day and reporter day—no exercise. Thursday number 3 group 8:30 a.m.–10:00 a.m., number 4 group 11:30 a.m.–l:00 p.m., number 1 group 1:30 p.m.–3:00 p.m., Friday number 4 group 11:30 a.m.–1:00 p.m., number 1 group 11:30 a.m.–l:00 p.m., number 2 group 1:30 p.m.–3:00 p.m. Saturday and Sunday—no exercise period. The day room consists of four tables of heavy metal and we can play dominoes or chess. There is also a yard area that is screened in and we get to go out there on some days. We are given a maximum of four and a half hours a week of exercise time. Three one-and-a-half periods a week.

10:30 a.m. Time to get ready for our noon meal. The food is not too bad, but not too good. I eat very little of the bread and substitute crackers, which I buy from the commissary. I try to not eat very much from the tray, since it is heavy in starches. If one notices the men when they arrive and then a few months later, you would notice that they put on weight from too much starch. I am not fat and intend to see that I don't get that way.

11:a.m. The TVs on the wall are turned on. There are approximately eight TVs on the walls outside the cells spaced in a way that no matter what cell you are in, you can view a TV. The TVs are all put on the same channels. The programs beginning at 11:00 a.m. are *Family Feud.* Since I cannot stand the MC who kisses every female that comes on the show, I do not watch it. At noon, the soaps come on. These are *Another World, The Doctors,* and *Days of Our Lives.* I do not watch soaps, but was a victim of this disease when I first arrived here in 1974. For one and a half years I was hooked on them all until I woke up one day that they never had an ending and were quite dull.

Actually, the TVs are a pain in the ass. You can't get away from them, and you have no choice in the selection process. The "children" here determine what we watch. The programs we watch will always be the most stupid, the silliest (not necessarily the funniest), the ones with the most violence (they seem to thrive on sirens and police), and of course if there is any "T&A" (tits and ass) programs they are also a must. Any educational program or newsworthy program is something to be booed at until the guard changes the channel to the "kiddy" shows. If the news didn't come on all three channels at one time, we would never get to see the news. We have never seen a movie such as *The Sound of Music, Cabaret, Cat on a Hot Tin Roof, Love Story,* et cetera. Only the movies of Clint Eastwood or the various made-for-TV shows where there are lots of tires squealing and girls giggling. Put simply, to anyone with a mentality of over a fourth-grade level, the TVs are a form of mental torture. I would like nothing more than to push the TVs off their stands onto the cement floor below.

12:30 p.m. I lay down to take an hour to two-hour nap. I try to do this every day, seven days a week.

2:30 p.m. Get up from nap and put on hot water for coffee and read if I happen to have anything decent to read. Usually, I have the Houston papers other inmates have passed to me as they came by to shower. I read the *Dallas Times Herald*, the *Houston Post,* the *Houston Chronicle*, and the

New York Times (which I only read to see what my enemies the liberals are up to).

3:30 p.m. Time to get ready for supper. We eat pretty early around here. Finish supper and throw out most of it. Brush my teeth, and if I need it, I shave. (I have an electric razor.)

If today had happened to be a Wednesday, it would be commissary day and I would be looking for it to be delivered. I always order a pint of ice cream each week. We only get to order one time a week.

4:30 p.m. Lay back on my bed (under my fan) and relax until news time.

5:30 p.m. Get up and make last cup of coffee for day and watch NBC News. (If we are lucky. If not, we have to watch ABC *World News Tonight.*)

6:00 p.m. I watch a little of the local news, but am pretty pessimistic concerning the news media in general. I have found that they suppress more news than they give us. All establishment media is too far left to suit my taste. Also start looking for the mail to come in to be sorted out and passed out. This can occur from 6:00 to 9:00 p.m. Lately, it's been around 6:30 p.m. As I am right over the table where it's sorted, I can watch to see if I receive a letter from Suzanne. She puts her letters in a brown envelope and I can spot it easily, since it's oversized and has a red sticker on it.

7:30 p.m. If mail has come, I read my mail (assuming I receive some) and if there is a letter that needs to go out in the next day's mail, I respond to it. Our mail is picked up about 5:00 a.m. each morning but Sunday and is delivered every day but Sunday or holidays.

8:30 p.m. If the mail has run, I go to bed before 9:00 p.m. each night. There are no exceptions. The only thing that keeps me out of my bed past 8:30 p.m. is the mail being late. I can never go to bed before the mail is delivered.

The TVs are turned off (and the radio) at 11:00 p.m. each night but Friday and Saturday or the night before a holiday. The lights are turned off as well. I usually wake up when the silence hits me, but I go right back to sleep unless some fool is talking after it gets quiet. There has been much trouble over this problem of some "very few" inmates being so inconsiderate as to keep us awake with their talking. It's a standard procedure that when the TV and lights go off, that you are to shut up. Some people don't know this or just don't give a damn.

This is my daily schedule seven days a week. I never change it. I enjoy the silence of the mornings best. This is the only time when you can have some peace and quiet here. Most of the inmates sleep late as they are the TV addicts or just like to stay up late.

One incident a few weeks ago broke the dullness around here. At 8:30 a.m. on Tuesday, the 28th of August, as my group was leaving our cells to go to the day room, one black inmate of about 115 pounds walked up to another black inmate of about 175 pounds and drove a knife into his heart and killed him. It happened about ten to fifteen feet from me, but of course I didn't see anything and went on down to the day room to play dominoes. In a few minutes, the guards came running past the day room up the stairs, and in a few more minutes they were carrying the black guy down the stairs. I could see his wound and knew he was hurt pretty seriously. We went on about our domino game until we were locked up at 10:00 a.m. At 11:30 a.m. the major came back and sent several of us back into the day room so they could search our cells. It seems they never did find the knife that was used. We also learned at that time that the guy was dead. We got extra day room time anyway. The next morning, I sent a floor boy down to the dead guy's cell to get his pillow. Mine was without any stuffing and he had a good one. I knew he didn't need it anymore, so I got it. I had been trying to get one for four months. I told one of the guards that it was a hell of a thing for someone to have to get killed around here for another to get a pillow. We were concerned that we would be locked down, but the prison officials let us have our exercise periods on schedule. We were glad of this. Actually, the killing was no big deal. These things happen when people are thrown together and have no way to vent their frustrations over long periods of time. Little things become big things and before you know it, the situation is out of control or reason. That day room and yard set there seven days a week and we can only use it for four and a half hours a week. So much for common sense around this place.

Friday, September 21, 1979

At 4:05 a.m., Hayter is in front of my cell, collecting sheets. I didn't have to get up, the general procedure being to put your bedclothes in the bars before turning in on Thursday night. Linen is picked up every Friday morning.

I get up to enjoy the rejuvenating quiet and stillness. I give Hayter my glass for hot water, dress and wash up, put my linen out, then make a glass of coffee. After sitting and sipping for a moment, I reach for a pen and paper. It's time to work, write, read, before population wakes up. Then banging of doors, water running, and yelling starts: at about 4:45. By then I'll be ready, willing, and able to endure another day.

The radio of the cells behind and around me blast on—one rock, one country, one Spanish, with static! My meditation is shattered. It's 5:50. I do some kinhin (walking meditation) and some serious thinking: Who'll understand this? Will this end. . . . Pots and pans and metal pitchers begin clanging downstairs. The chow wagon is here: 6:25 a.m. Coffee comes first, a one-armed floor boy carrying three pitchers! I ask about the milk. "No milk this moan'n." The spoons come, are placed in the bars. Then the trays: oatmeal with sugar, pork gravy, three pancakes, "syrup," two rolls and butter: virtually the same meal as four and a half years ago. I pass on it and munch several peanut butter cookies. Those who do take a tray toss them out quickly. A floor boy comes for them, using a wet towel pushed with a dust broom to "clean" the floor. The spoons are picked up.

For a while it is quiet, the radios tuned somewhat, everybody back in bed. Then doors began to slam open. Shower time: 6:55.

Group four recreates first, so they shower first on three-row. I live on three-row too, but am in the third recreation group. We don't recreate today, or Saturday or Sunday, so we shower whenever they get to us. No hurry. We recreate Monday at 1:30 p.m., hopefully. A long wait before going out of here again. The thought depresses. I grab a book, later a pen and paper.

Not quite finished showering—fourteen of them showered. Group four goes out to recreate at 8:45, late. Sixteen men in their group, thirteen in my group. Only three men left on three-row now: two are asleep. I sit alone.

The sheets come at 9:30. So do two guards to shake down group four cells while they're recreating.

I'm immersed from time to time in my actions. Surfacing a moment ago, I realized there's a tremendous lag outside of actions. From breakfast till now, I've been for the most part absorbed. Still there's nothing to do, still I'm nowhere, still it's not chow time—action time! I wonder, if from 7 a.m. to 10:40 a.m. is eternity, what is a life sentence?

No one seems to know, no one seems to care.

Turn the television down! (I'm yelling!) Inevitably, they're on: 10:45. And they won't go off before 1:30 a.m. Saturday morning. I have at least fourteen hours of it.

They're archenemies: should be in the dayroom like they are on every other wing except here and 21, not a mere ten feet from one's bed, blasting, whether or not one cares for it. And I don't care for them other than for news, sports, and documentaries. Certainly not for a morning of game shows and an afternoon of soap operas.

Nonetheless, we have TV and lunch, the chow wagon arriving at 11 a.m. The tea comes first, then the spoons. When they come, I note the trays: chili and rice, beans and sauerkraut, cake, roll, and cornbread. Again I pass.

Few others do, however. The recreation group is back in, everyone's up, shucking and jiving. Trays, pots, and pans are being thrown around: the radios and TVs blast!

It's a storm that gradually subsides. By 11:40 it's past.

A few words with a neighbor, then I read in *A Manual of Zen Training* by Jiyu Kennett. I realize I'm on the wrong road and level spiritually, make true contrition, do zazen, change shoes, and begin running, shadowboxing, kicking . . . huffing and puffing. It's almost time to shower, so I must exercise. I get enough to perspire and burn away the . . .

Everything is bright as I march to the shower. It's 12:15. Returning, I rest till 1:30 p.m.

It's a long day. I read and write. Pillowcases come at 3. Meditate until 3:45. Chow comes again. They have water it seems. The spoons come. The trays: cornbread, corn, beans and potatoes, a meat gravy. . . . I pass and eat a few cookies. I'm tired of them now, however.

Did some reading and writing until 5:30. Listened to NBC evening news and the Houston channel 2 news. Read until 7:15. I discover it's relatively quiet. I make a cup of coffee and quiet sit, realizing one must show gratitude for the opportunity to have this human body and hear and practice dharma.

7:55, mail comes. I get two letters, one from Oral Roberts. He wants a twenty-five-dollar donation! The other from a sister at Goree. She's ill. But aren't all prisoners, if only in spirit?

9:05, another cup of coffee. I've been trying to read, tempted to lie down, anxious to do something, read more, write, anything: to pass the time.

I listen to the radio, the ball game. At 11:05 the Astros have won! I'm exhausted from pulling them through. It's bedtime now.

Porters

Prison officials rarely visit the Row. Some, like the chaplain or the psychologist, make occasional perfunctory tours. Others, like the wardens or the doctor, come down for specific reasons, in response to specific problems. A guard is on the Row constantly, but it is not the same guard every day. None of the guards on duty in August 1979 had worked the Row in April. Guards have days off, they transfer to other jobs in the prison, they quit and take jobs in the free world. Even when guards are on the job awhile, most of their time is taken with the mechanics of operating the Row. They lock and unlock the Row door when special visitors come, when someone has a visit, when the doctor or priest or warden descends; they lock and unlock the cells for showers and recreation; they shake down inmates in and out of the recreation room or when they're going to or coming from a visit; they sort and deliver the Row's mail. Inmates on the Row, unless they've been moved around a lot, rarely know many other men on the Row. They can talk with other men in their recreation groups, but conversation with anyone in any other recreation group in their wing is rare and unlikely, and conversation with someone on the other side is impossible. Some men who have been on the Row for three years have never seen other men who have been on the Row the same length of time.

The men who have the most contact with Death Row inmates, the men who know all of them, are the porters (also called hall boys, floor boys, or building tenders). The porters serve the food. The porters bring hot water to the men without stingers. The porters clean the runs. The porters carry notes or newspapers or commissary from one part of the Row to another.

The porters talk to them. And they study them. That is not done without self-interest. If fights break out, the porters are likely to be involved in breaking them up; if someone attempts suicide, the porters, who are constantly moving about the rows, are likely to discover it. For their own safety, and to make their jobs as uncomplicated as possible, they work hard at knowing what is happening in each of those lonely cells.

The porters are all convicts who have done a lot of time. Naive new inmates don't get those jobs on Death Row or on any other Ellis row. Some of them are surprisingly kind and sympathetic; some of them are coldly cynical.

They used to be called building tenders, and for a long time they have been a central part of Texas prison administration. In the old days, they functioned as administrative aides; they would run a wing. If convicts got out of line, they would administer beatings. In some of the prisons, they ran various hustles and controlled homosexual encounters. Most of those functions have been curtailed in recent years, in part because of the development of a more professional prison staff and in part because of pressure from outside lawsuits. The porters/floor boys/building tenders still function in all units of the TDC as bearers of information. Some people defined their role with hostility, as "institutionalized snitches," but prison officials—and the porters—argue that there are many things an inmate would discuss with another inmate that he would never discuss with a guard or other official.

The convict workers live as marginal men within the prison and serve as critical interface agents.

Their role is more important on Death Row than anywhere else in the prison because Death Row inmates have less mobility and fewer options than any other convict in the prison. The porters are, as one of them says here, "their legs." The porters are the men upon whom the Death Row inmates most depend. Lawyers and family and prison doctors and judges are all distant folks, they all have other business, they may or may not want to or be able to respond to a request for aid. The porters are always there. Every day of every week, they are there.

Some inmates hate them. Sometimes the hate results from an incident that really happened. Just as often, it results from the mere fact that the porters have, from the point of view of the Death Row inmate, an enormous freedom. The porters work eight-hour shifts, they can go to school, they can go to the gym, they can go out into the hallway and let their eyes focus hundreds of feet away.

Some inmates focus their paranoia upon the porters. One inmate told us they read all his mail. Another said they deliberately held up his toilet paper. Whether these accusations are true is less important than what they signify: the porters are the condemneds' primary human contact with the world. That world extends no farther than the Row itself, but that limit does not minimize its significance. On the Row, trivial things are enormously important because the parameters of life are so incredibly small.

I'm the porter here. I start about five in the morning, start feeding at five-thirty. Start feeding one side, finish up over there usually by six. And then head over here to feed, make the trays up, pass them out on the run, pick the trays back up, clean up on the run. Set the showers up for them. Leave here, go back over there, come back. It's 10:30 and we start feeding dinner. Make the trays, put them out, pick them back up. Feed fifty-eight on this side and fifty-six on the other side. Take the trays back, chow cart back to the kitchen. I turn on the TVs, clean between the bars, clean the windows. Finish up with the showers, pick the dirty clothes up, clean the messes that's in there, put the TVs on the channels that they're watching.

Soap operas during the daytime. About 3:30, they watch "The Brady Bunch" and then *Gunsmoke*. After *Gunsmoke*, I put on the 5:30 news on channel 2.

In between, we have to clean up the dayroom for recreation. The biggest hassle is in the evening when we have to feed the last meal.

There's fifty-eight men on this tank and all of them want to watch something different. A lot of them have different preference. The officer, he has got to come up with the decision of which program they're going to watch, which movies they're going to watch, which specials they're going to watch. You got Chicanos, you have whites, and then you have your blacks out here. If it's a black program on, there's always a controversy if you watch it or if you don't.

I put them on whatever program they're gonna watch and naturally I catch all the heat. If I put it on the black program, the whites say I'm discriminating, putting it on something I want to see. Put it on the white program and the blacks are hollering. Movies—some of them like science fiction and some of them don't. A lot of the time, they'll holler and they'll scream. They all want to argue.

The hardest part of the job is dealing with the TV sets in the evening. During the daytime, the feeding is the most physical part of it.

What about the mental part?

Just dealing with the inmates here and trying to be fair with all of them that you deal with. When they're all locked up a lot, they get paranoid and a lot, naturally, have frustrations. A lot of them have never been in prison before. They aren't aware of the prison ways.

In other wings, they have more freedom to come and go. You have more access. If one of them has a problem, he can go to the lieutenant's desk. He can stop and talk with the lieutenant. Or stop and talk with the captain up there. He can go into the kitchen. He's around other inmates where he can get the latest news, the latest gossip. He's around his friends. He's in a much better mood because he can pick his associates, who he associates with, whereas in here, he's limited. He's in his cell a great deal of the day, all the weekend, all day Wednesdays. When they do recreate, it's an hour and a half a day and they do it with the neighbors that's next to them. They don't have any choice or say-so on who their neighbors are gonna be, so if it's somebody they can't talk with or can't relate to, then he's left trying to occupy his time.

A lot of them read. Some of them started drawing. Others just set there, be in another world.

When they have a problem, they have to write a request, and there's some 2,300 men on the farm. The warden or the captain, one of them, comes in at least once a week. And the major—he's in here at least once a week. They just have to wait until those times till they come through here to visit with them.

Besides being a porter and having to clean up, you feel you've got to try and understand them if you intend to try and deal with them. Each guy is different, has his own problems that he brought down here with him. We don't know him, really, but we have to try and figure them out with communication with him in order to deal with it. Sometimes that's the heaviest situation, the heaviest problem—you don't know who's off or who's who or just what the situation is with a lot of them.

Physical work, the cleanup, that's just part of prison life. Everybody has to work. The difference on this job is not just the work, but you have to be a social worker or a psychologist. Just a good listener at times. You come down the run with a mop, they'll stop you just for any little thing. An article in the newspaper, ask you questions just to stop you to have somebody to talk to.

The guys in their cells, they're all alone.

The luckier ones' people stick by them. Those ones are usually in the better frame of mind. They get letters often, hear from the outside world, are able to communicate. But the others of them—don't have families, some other reason their families aren't with them—they get depressed. The officer passes the mail out in the evenings and the ones that do get letters from home, they're apprehensive, they're waiting on the mail. This is the big time of day for them, when the mail comes. They looking for letters from their mothers, their sisters, their girlfriends, or their wives, and they're usually in the more healthier attitude.

And the ones that don't, when the mailman passes their cell, it's a disappointment. I imagine it's pretty hard on them. The guys in the cells next to him constantly gets mail. Well, he begins to feel envious, jealous. Naturally, after a while it's going to cause friction.

Or he'll sit there, he'll try to write whoever he can, whatever he can, and it has an effect on his mental attitude, his overall situation in here. Others it don't seem to bother.

From the outside, I don't know what I would write somebody on Death Row. Imagine it would be hard to say . . . you don't want to mention too much. What do you say to a man you're writing on Death Row? So I figure that's why a lot of them won't get mail.

After a while, they'll get paranoid, they'll think the officer's taking their mail.

I don't mind the physical aspects of this job, that makes the time pass a little faster. The only thing I resent about the job is it takes so much time. Seven days a week and sometimes eight, nine, ten hours a day.

I have the morning shift—4:30 till 12:20 at noon. Then we come back and feed at supper and clean up. That's about four to six. There's three shifts there.

The job is mainly janitorial. We serve the meals and keep the place clean. There is an officer in there twenty-four hours a day, except when he's out in the picket showering. We're there to assist him in what he tells us to do. Anything he asks us to do, we're responsible for that.

I watch out for who's mad at me or who's mad at another guy or who's cussing who out, just to know in advance, if I can, what may happen.

Do they get mad at you?

Oh yeah.

Why? Are you the Man?

No, not really. I don't think any of them think I'm the Man, they know my personality better than that. I've explained to them that I wasn't there to harm any of them or hurt them in any way. I've been over there a year and I've never hit one yet, and I don't intend to unless it's in self-protection. I've pulled a few apart, the officer usually helps. He pulls one and I pull the other, we'll whisper in their ear and try to keep them from hitting again. That doesn't happen very often. Once every two or three months tempers will flare over the television or whatever.

You're locked up in a cell with a sentence like they have—it's a small world. Teeny things tend to become big things. Like, "I don't like potatoes. How come you're giving me potatoes?" Or, "There's a bean on my potato!" Their world is real small right now and it's a small place for them to live, and they do get angry over little things that I wouldn't get angry over. But when they do get angry, they are impatient. Part of their impatience stems from what is probably the root of most of our problems at present, this lack of self-discipline. They seem to have it to a greater degree than most of the other population.

I think the main reason for that is their situation, what they're in. They don't know a lot about the law. They are locked up in a cell. They don't feel like their lawyer's doing what he should do. They don't feel that their parents on the street are doing what they should do to help them, or their girlfriends. They're feeling real neglected is what it is, and a lot of them don't know what to do about it. I can see the frustration they would be facing, especially with a sentence like they have.

One of the main mistakes I think a Death Row inmate can make—or any inmate—is that he comes to prison and listens to everybody else's advice. "Lawyers are not any good. All them girlfriends—they don't last but six months." Things like this. And they get to feeling real down about it.

Do you think they are, in fact, different from most of the population in terms of their personalities or their crimes?

In the situation they're in now, yes. I think they are different from most. They seem to be a little more impatient, like I said. They want things to happen faster, there's not much empathy or understanding. You can stand there and explain and sometimes they don't seem to like the explanation or they won't listen to the explanation. Their self is the center of what they want, what they say, what they understand. It's hard to change their mind or get them to see something another way.

Part of the reason is, the rest of the population can be out, up and down, and they can see what's happening. Like medical treatment. That's one of the major complaints on the Row. There is only three or four medical assistants or nurses that handle the hospital; there is one doctor each day who sees as many as he can. There is a full-time dentist. The Death Row inmates are prisoners of the county. The dentist doesn't do restorative work for them unless the county pays for it. To get eyeglasses, they have to get on a list and wait to be taken over to Huntsville to have their eyes examined. This going to take longer, normally, than it would for someone in regular population.

They keep aspirin on the wing. Aspirin makes some of their stomachs sick and they want something else. The man comes around once a day around noon and then again that afternoon. They deliver the prescription medicine three times a day and once a day he comes around for a general sick call. They'll have a complaint and he has a little container of medicine and he'll give them some.

They might not like it, and then that evening they'll be sick again and they'll call for him to come down. Well, he's down the hall with a knifing or something like that. There's an emergency that happens here about once an hour. Somebody's old and has a stroke or heart attack. Somebody's hurt in one of the shops or somebody is having respiratory problems, asthmatic attacks. There are 2,300 people here. And when they're not having emergencies, they are running the general sick call, the pill call for the general population. It's a busy and full day for them.

And these people here on the Row, they can't understand why when they call it's an hour or an hour and a half.

They get irritating, but you got to remember, they live in a real small world and you are their legs. Sometimes I forget. I'm sure when I do, they get mad because of it, and that's probably a good reason for getting mad.

There's other things. When I'm over there at night to shower, they'll ask, "Change the television."

I'll say, "The television is operated by the officer and he says what channel to put it on and that's where it's going to stay until he changes it or tells me to change it."

"You've influenced him."

"Have you ever seen me watch that television?"

"No."

"Then why do you think I've influenced him?"

I can't take it easy. I'm going to school in the daytime and working at night and trying to keep up with all of it.

When I get the clothes from the laundry, they're not put together. So they bring me a big buggy full of shorts for 120 men. And they bring me the pants and the shirts. They are put together by the number. They're in the big cart. Then they'll bring me 120 towels. Towels aren't numbered. And 120 pair of socks. And I sit down and I put all the socks together. And I fold all the towels.

Couldn't you get one of the men on the Row to help you?

No. They're off duty. See, only one Death Row porter works at a time.

I mean one of the inmates.

There's nobody there but Death Row porters.

I mean couldn't you get one of the men who's on Death Row to help you?

He's in his cell. You can't let him out to help. It's locked down.

I used to have a little retarded kid down there to help me fold socks, but they moved him. He kept going and breaking windowpanes out with his fist and they moved him where he couldn't.

When I walk in Death Row at night, I can tell the mood as soon as I walk in the door. I'll make one round.

The first thing I do every night is pass everything that they want passed. A lot of the guys send their newspapers to their hometown buddies and things of this manner. They'll pass their *Penthouse* books. This is every day.

And I see the mood right away. I know every one of those guys—what they think, what they do, and how they make their time.

When they get their bottle of honey-almond lotion out—that's the stuff they sell in the commissary to rub on their arms, but they put it on their penis when they masturbate—when I go in and smell all that, I know everything is going to be all right. There'll be about twenty-five of them masturbating and watching the TV.

A lot of the guys will keep it hid.

A lot of guys completely live in a sexual fantasy on Death Row. It's forced on them, really, because of the way they have the TVs over there. They watch too much TV.

Comes on in the morning at nine and they shut it off at eleven, twelve, one every night. And sometime in that period you're going to have two or three programs that's got pretty girls or sex in it, or violence. They get off on this violence. And they clap every time a police gets killed. Or every time a little old commercial got a little girl in shorts. You wouldn't believe it.

Every one of them are instant replays. They holler the same thing over and over. "Did you see that bitch? I saw her panties."

I came on the Row in 1970, under the old death penalty law. There's quite a bit of difference now.

I lived on the Row. I was in there by myself. There was no guard in there with me. I had it all myself. I lived on the Row twenty-four hours a day. Now the attendants work three shifts and they have a guard in there all the time.

The administration then didn't allow any glass, any tin, anything in there that you could harm yourself with. No electricity in the cells at all of any kind. Only plastic was allowed in the cells.

The food and stuff they bought at the commissary, I kept that in boxes out in front of their cells and I would keep that for them and give it to them as they wanted it, any time of day or night.

I had sixty-some-odd on Death Row whenever the death penalty was kicked out by the Supreme Court, ruled unconstitutional. I believe that was in 1972 or 1973.

I lived in there all the time. My job was to take care of it.

I think we had one suicide attempt. That's a strange thing on Death Row. Even though those people have the death penalty given to them by a jury and they are sentenced to death and they are down there on the Row, none of them give up hope. You couldn't find a man down there this morning that thinks he's gonna die. They just don't do that.

As a whole, they're very pleasant people to be around. I found it to be so. I found many friends there. Friends that I still have. Some of them are even on the outside now. They beat me out. People that I waited on down there.

We had a pretty well behaved bunch of people. They were all mature. Most of them had been in prison before. They knew what prison was like. You got a different breed of cat down there now. You got all those youngsters.

The reason for this is on account of the new 1974 law, when the death penalty came back in. It's a certain type crime now that you get the death penalty for.

Under the old law, it was up to the district attorney whether or not you got the death penalty filed on you. Now you have to commit murder and another crime in order to get the death penalty. And there are different degrees of punishment now.

Back then, I could go over and rob a store in Dallas County and kill someone and get twenty years or five years or five years' probation, and you go over in Tarrant County and kill someone robbing a store and you would get the death penalty for it. Or I'd be driving the car and you'd go in and rob someone and kill him and I'd never get out of the car and I'd get the death penalty driving the car. You pulled the trigger and you'd get twenty-five years.

Most generally, if you got the death penalty under the old law, you was an ex-convict, you done a lot of time, they felt like that you couldn't be rehabilitated and that you needed to die.

Under this law here, it's the degree of crime that you commit. So you get a younger inmate now. Most of the old inmates that I had on Death Row that I waited on and attended to were people that had did time before. They knew what a prison was. They had become used to prison. They knew what the rules were. So they were more adjusted when they came on the Row.

They had inmates down there that had been on the Row ten, twelve years. Joe Smith had been on the Row, I believe, almost ten, twelve years when I went down there. So they guide and direct those people in their actions.

It was altogether different. There wasn't any loud talking. You respected the man in the cell next to you. You held your voice down and there wasn't all that hooting and hollering and carrying on that you have now. They were just more mature. You got young inmates down there now.

The biggest percentage of them have never been in trouble before. Maybe arrested for being drunk. We have maybe twenty that's been in prison previously. Most of them are just youngsters.

One youngster out of Fort Worth, he was just seventeen when he got in. I was talking with him one night. I just noticed he was in a bad mood and I stopped and started talking with him. We were holding a regular conversation and he just come out with, "Man, I ain't never spent all night with a woman and here I am with the death sentence."

This is the kind of thing that's going through their mind.

You have others that go off into their fantasy world and never have any problems. They just lay there and that's it. They drift off into their world, shower, and come back in and eat and go right back to their pillow, and they are in paradise. They just completely ignore the whole experience here. The death sentence, capital punishment, is something in another world that doesn't exist to them. It's not real. And that's where they exist, that's where they live, that's where they escape—to that world.

I let them take their problems out on me. I let them cuss me out if they want to. I'll tell them, "You can cuss me out a couple times a night if you want to. Make you feel better."

"Oh, I'm mad at that other guy."

"Well, he's not over it. Cuss me."

"No, I can take it. I'm tough."

And I'll calm a guy down easy. See, I was a nurse in the Treatment Center four years and I learned it. I've got so many pacification programs going down there you wouldn't believe it.

Do they resent you?

No, they like me. I'm probably the best-liked Death Row porter down there. All the Death Row porters play games with them. They hustle them out of their money. They get them to buy them things on commissary day. I don't run no hustle.

If I need a shot of coffee, I'll go to Barefoot. He drinks coffee. Or if I ain't got no cigarettes, I'll go get a few from Corley. Or two or three men. I don't ever hit the same guy. I don't really have no money. I don't draw money myself. Charles, he draws thirty every time. He gets me anything I need. I was hoping they would start paying something.

When I first come here, you could draw one dollar a week. It went up to three dollars, and then to six dollars, and then to ten dollars, and then to fourteen dollars, twenty dollars, and now it's thirty dollars. Prison board keeps letting them draw more and more. That's because the price of everything has gone up.

Some of the work that the guys do here, they need to be paid. There's no doubt about that. And I guess in my lifetime they'll bring it in before it's over with. That's one of the things they need to do. If a man's got a little money, he doesn't cause problems.

Except for compulsive gamblers. We've got guys here that draw thirty dollars every time and they lose every penny of it. They ain't got a match.

Some got all kinds of businesses going. They sell sex books. They keep the racy stuff out of here all they can. But it's starting. You can get any kind of sex book in here now as long as it don't show two male homosexuals. Anything else goes. They're trading them now. They're going for pretty high prices right now until the place gets flooded with them, then the price will come down on them.

What turns these guys on more than anything else is girls sucking guys off. That's the top pictures right now. Especially black and white.

There's more goes on in the county jails than down here on Death Row because you don't have very much of a chance for any homosexuality to be going on down here on Death Row. You're in a cell by yourself all the time, or you're in the dayroom, which is about the size of your living room, and everybody's there looking at you. If somebody's going to be doing something, I don't see how they would.

Some of them up there play with theirself, masturbation. One dude plays with himself with a bottle. He's got that bottle and he's got some plastic around it and he puts lotion in it and he plays with himself like that. You got a bunch of things like that goes on.

Sex is gonna be there and if it ain't there, you're watching it on TV. Sex is the essence, the root of the whole dad-blame thing that hurts everything. That's the worst evil.

I say there ain't none of them down here that ain't in here on sex. Not all the way on sex, but it's pretty close to it. It's number three if it ain't number one or two. It'll be more of number one for sex than it is number two for sex. For some kind of reason or another. To buy this woman a new car or because this dude was doing it for his wife or because he was jealous of his girlfriend. Something that has something to do with sex down the line. To buy something for some sex or to do something for some sex. It's tied in. Everybody that I have ever talked to so far yet, bar none, it all ties in.

Including you?

Including me.

Everybody I've talked to, if they didn't kill directly for a woman or directly about a woman or didn't kill a woman, it had something to do with the woman itself. Everybody that I've ever talked to. And it's usually number one or number two.

You ask, "What was you killing for?" And it's money to buy something for her or she was going out or because he was fooling with my old lady.

I like a lot of the people over there.

It's hard, too, because you see somebody and you wonder how in the world they got into this. I try and stay divorced from their case. I don't usually discuss their cases with many of them.

But they'll offer to tell you about it, you know, their side. You try to stay divorced from listening to their case because that's not your problem—their guilt or innocence.

I've found that when people confide in you they are going to lie to you anyway. Most people. This is a personal observation and I don't mean just these people up there.

If you confide in people, I've found that it's going to be put back on you somewhat, in some form that you won't like. That's a human trait.

Like if that man set up there and told me all his weaknesses, what drove him to do whatever he did, even if I was sworn to secrecy that I would never tell a soul, it would be put back on him in some way—probably by me. Or I would tell somebody else and then somebody else would use it against him. This is human—to find out another person's weakness and wear it down like a boxer would. If he gets a guy's eye bleeding, he keeps hitting him in the eye. That's a human trait. If you tell somebody, "Now, if I tell you this, you promise you won't tell anybody else?" "Yeah, yeah."

Nobody keeps a secret.

I've found there's usually two kinds of people that will listen to your problems. This may sound skeptical. One of them is glad you've got them, and the others, they want to take advantage of them.

You look around and you see people with big problems and your problem isn't so big, so why would you want to tell about it in the first place? To go around and complain all the time. I was in the service and that was one of the big things people did—gripe a lot. I was an only child and I griped a lot. But now that I'm older, I think it's a bad thing and I don't like to listen to a lot of frivolous things from people. I guess there's a lack of patience there on me.

But they want to talk about them and I'll listen to them. I can't advise them because I don't know the law very well and they get frustrated because of that. They say, "You don't tell me because you don't want to tell me." That's what they are thinking a lot of times. That's one of the reasons I don't like to listen to the legal things—because I can't help them.

A lot of those that I would want to help, I still can't help them because I don't have the money to hire them an attorney.

I don't really want to get involved.

But there are some of them there that I just don't think they could have done that. Some of them. One or two I think I'm probably right on.

One of them had me convinced for a long time that he wasn't guilty. He's a young man and I would come by—when he got here he was nineteen or twenty and he was here for a rape-murder—and the first thing he told me was, "I don't know if you want to talk to me or not, but I'm not guilty."

I said, "That doesn't matter. I don't even know what you are here for. I don't really pay any attention to that." And I said, "If you need anything, let me know, or if I can help you."

That's a generalized speech. Really don't mean it half the time. It just comes out. I just try to get out of the way, get the rest of my work done so I can go home. I go to college too here and I study some. I don't study like I should, but I do study some. Right now, I'm taking the last part of biology and English literature. I graduate this May.

So he told me this and it went on for about two months and he said, "You don't stop and talk to me very often and it must be because of what they accused me of doing."

I told him, "No, I don't. I just don't have a lot of time. Is there something wrong?" I could tell that he's just lonesome, that's what it was.

He lived all the way in the back cell there on the row and there's not that much traffic up there.

So I got worried, and in the mornings I'd come over there and sit down and talk to him fifteen or twenty minutes before I had to go and get the chow cart. And I'd bring him some hot water. And he run his case down to me pretty thoroughly.

I talked it over with another man there one time. I told him, "I just don't believe that boy is guilty."

He says, "Well, I think he is."

I said, "He just doesn't seem that way." His lawyers, he told me, had lied to him several times, and his mother was not helping. In fact, she almost disinherited or disowned him. They are supposed to own something somewhere and supposed to be well off, but he didn't have much money to spend at the commissary. I found out later he had been down before for a car theft. He talked to me about his narcotic problem on the street. I can understand that 'cause I've had a few of those myself.

He said, "That was a cause of a lot of my problems. But I've never done anything sexually to hurt anybody."

And I told him, I said, "Well, if you're innocent, I'm sure that they'll . . ."

Words of hope. You don't mean them, but you try to give them something to look forward to. To keep them from getting so depressed. You do mean them, but you don't know if they are going to come true or not when you tell a guy that.

It went on that way for a month or two and I noticed he was having some problems with some of the other inmates on Death Row. They would get mad at him or he would get mad at them. One day he said, "Most of the guys whistle at me when I come out to the shower. Why do they do that? And what can I do about it?"

I said, "Don't pay any attention to them. Or tell them in a nice way, 'I can appreciate you think I'm nice looking but don't whistle at me because if you do it and I don't do anything others will do it and it will get out of hand.' Explain it to them that way. And if you still have your problems, the administration will try to help you with them too, if you want to tell them about it. That will be your decision." And he said okay and so it went on, and they moved him down to another cell and then they moved him to another one.

One of the others stopped me one day and asked me to take a note up to that boy. I said no.

He said, "Why?"

I said, "He don't want to get notes from anybody. Told me he didn't want any notes from anybody. He's not that way and he doesn't want to come on with you that way."

"Oh, yes, he does."

"No, he doesn't."

And he says, "I'll prove it." He gets his little mail packet and digs out this letter. He said, "Here is a letter I got from him." Now I know the boy prints and I knew what kind of stationery he writes on and everything.

I read it. It's one of the sickest things I ever read in my life. He's running down that he hates his penis and he really wants a vagina and this, that and the other; that at night he puts his penis between his legs and rubs in there and it looks just like a woman's parts. He's hated this extension of himself ever since he's been born and he really wanted to have sex in this other part of his anatomy.

I read about half of it and I handed it back and I said, "Well, that's his business and that's your business."

I got to thinking about that thing he done out there, and I haven't ever said anything to him about this, but it kind of destroys your faith. I was so convinced before. I'm not really convinced now that he's guilty, but I sure wouldn't want to make a statement one way or another. If I had been a juror, I would have voted for not guilty at first, and then to see something like this—it's hard. It's a hard decision for society. It really is.

He's up there, he's still up there and he still has the same problem. It's not getting any better. And it probably won't as long as he's on Death Row. It will probably get worse.

There's one there that will talk to himself all the time. I mean constantly. And he'll play with himself out in broad daylight.

You can say, "You know, there's only supposed to be one in that cell. If the boss finds there's two of you, he's going to get mad."

He'll say, "Oh yeah?" And he'll listen. You can talk and anything that's funny, he'll laugh. And then he'll be quiet. Or he'll stand in the back and he'll talk into the little vent holes in the back of his cell.

I said, "Have you met those people out there?"

He said, "Yeah."

I said, "I met them one time. George is an invalid. There's two of them out there. You know that, don't you?"

"Yeah. George. George—and who's the other one?"

He'll sing loud along with his radio and wake everybody else up, I told him. "Emily. Emily told me, man, that she wanted you to sing low and soft, that she liked that better than she did your yelling through there." He'll quiet down.

My first reaction was, if they'd get upset, I'd get upset. They'd holler at me and I'd holler back. That would never solve anything. It never has come to any violence, but it could, so now I tell them nicely, "Look, if you want me to do something, ask me in a nice way and I'll go ahead and do it. If you get angry with me, my reaction will probably be that I won't do it." I won't get angry back, but I'll do it when I get around to doing it. I'll explain to them, "I know you're in there and the door is closed and I'm your legs. I'll try to do what you ask, but I'm only one person."

One of them up on three-row wants the toilet brush, and one downstairs on one-row wants some tobacco, and another one upstairs will want you to take something to someone else, and the one that you take something to wants to answer back the one you got something from, and it gets to be a hassle when you also have to sweep and clean and mop and dust and the rest of the stuff. And about that time the chow cart is coming again and you don't have a lot of time for personal attention.

John Hayter, who goes on at night, the first thing he does is see that they got their toilet paper and the newspaper that they want from someone else. He tries to take care of their personal needs. I know he does because I've been there and I've watched him. And then I hear some of them say that John won't do nothing—but I know John Hayter better than that. He will and he does. He'll get all of that out of the way before he starts on the clothes.

There's one from the Row who's at the hospital right now. The hospital or the Treatment Center. One morning he cut himself. In jail, he set himself on fire and another morning he cut himself, and then they wouldn't move him and he sat on the floor and beat his head on the bunk and they came and had to take him to the hospital. He had told me before, "I don't want to die, but I sure don't want to stay here the rest of my life either. I got three or four more cases, and I'm just tired." He said he never was going to get out of prison and so he didn't want to stay here the rest of his life and he thought death would be a more humane alternative than staying here for the rest of his life. That's what he said.

It's always like there is a plot. That one over there, for example, he'll look at you and he'll be about half smiling, like, "I know you're going to get me one way or the other."

A lot of them act that way. You tell them something and if it's not exactly what they want to hear, they think it's a lie or you are lying to them or there's a conspiracy just to put him down. It's not a conspiracy, it's an uncaring thing.

That's probably colder than a conspiracy.

Prison is a jungle; only the strong survives. Dog eat dog. A man knows what he get into, so if you dance to the music, you have to pay the piper. It's that simple. They out there and they struggle; once you get there and get a position, then you got to worry about staying there and worry about being crossed or knocked out.

It's the same way on Death Row. A guy there wants to watch his favorite program. They know what officers come on and if they can be used, if they can be manipulated. They can give you a pretty good rundown on the type of individual each is. And if they can use them to their advantage, they will. We've been having a lot of young officers work down there.

Most of them are fairly decent. The young officers coming in now are more college-oriented, most of them go to Sam Houston State college, and you'll find that they are pretty liberal and decent in regards to their dealings with the inmates, more fair. Some of the inmates don't like them that way, but they still respect them because they know that they are fair. One dude in particular, Summerville, he's a fair man. But he's been down there long enough to know the inmates and they can't use him and manipulate him the way they could another officer. They don't all like him for that. He's hard, but he's fair. That's the way he has to be—a little stern with them. Let them know that they're going to have to pull their end of the responsibility too, it's not going to be all give.

They'll do what they can to help each other out in their cases. There's a unity there. You don't do the same thing in population. In population, a guy may buddy up with someone because he's got a little money and when he goes to the store he can maybe talk him out of a pack of cigarettes, a bag of coffee every now and then, and he'll be his buddy for that purpose. But it's not like that on the Row.

One man may be up there in 3 cell on three-row and hit one on 20 cell in one-row. He may holler through the pipe chase and ask somebody, "Man, I'm out of tobacco." He may hear about it up here and he'll buy two or three packs of cigarettes and send it to him and say to me, "So and so up there don't have no cigarettes." It's common courtesy, it's considerate. And it's without any kind of repayment at all. He knows the fella don't have money, he'll never get it back. He's not out to boost his ego in no kind of way, he's not done anything to charge it, to make the other guy feel obligated. He's just another fellow comrade in the same position. The man is out of cigarettes, he needs them, send them to him.

You find this quite regularly on the Row.

Like I say, when a new man comes in, they all want to know where he's from, what he needs. Does he smoke? Does he need some stamps?

You don't find this nowhere else in the prison. Usually, if a person does you a favor, you owe him and you're not going to get something for nothing. But it's not so down here, not in most cases. Some people down here don't have anything, except the death penalty.

A man has to be responsible for his own actions, whether he accepts it or not. Regardless what he's been through, what he has to deal with, he's still his own man, he still should be in charge of making his own decisions. We've all had our bad times and our hard times and we can't just say, "Well, the whole world is against me." It's not so. You got to stand up and be your own man. You got to be responsible for your own actions and until a man can accept that and do that, or try it anyway, then he'll forever be in tough situations.

Do the guys on Death Row have to wrestle with that?

Yes, it's the same thing.

They're in those cells. A lot of them won't spend their time constructively. One individual in particular, he's real paranoid. He'll sit there and he'll put himself on the rib. He's writing these people from churches and sometimes he won't get a letter. Says the officers are throwing his mail away, won't give him his mail. He's just putting himself on.

One day I come by that and see him, he had been kind of quiet all morning, and I said, "Hey, how you doing, man?"

"I'm doing all right, but you better tell this dude in the cell next to me, don't throw no more glass over here on me."

I said, "Throwing glass?"

The fella in the cell next to him is pretty quiet, he's not bothering nobody, always talking, switching books back and forth, trading ideas. I said, "Why would he throw glass on you?"

"I don't know, but he done it. See these pieces of glass?"

There were a couple of pieces of glass in front of his mattress. Well, that morning the fella upstairs had dropped his jar at the bars. It was put up there when we was passing by with the tea and the milk. And some of the glass came down and landed on his blanket.

I asked the fella next door what's wrong and he said, "I ain't throwing nothing over there. You can look and see, 'cause if I had there'd be a whole lot more glass. And you would have heard it 'cause it would have hit the wall."

When something like that happens, naturally we're going to be concerned about it. But it wasn't the case. I could see that it hadn't happened and I said, "What's wrong, man? The dude ain't throwing no glass at you."

"How'd it get here then?"

I said, "There's only a couple of pieces. A dude dropped his jar upstairs."

"Well, I'm not going to recreate today. You'd better tell him not to do this no more."

He's just paranoid. He puts himself on a trip. He's a real schizophrenic. And I said, "Well, man, the dude ain't throwing no glass on you. You guys were talking friends the other day. He ain't done nothing like that to you. You ain't had no argument. Get off your trip, man. Don't bother him." So I went home and when I came back that evening, he stopped me and apologized.

There's been others like that.

——, he's out of Houston. He was arrested for killing an old lady that let him stay in her house and kidnaping his common-law wife's daughter. He's basically insecure, he's afraid of his own shadow.

In the jail there, they kind of misused him. They raped him and made him shave his legs and misused him pretty bad. Well, he comes down here and he has had some bad experiences he brought with him. He goes out to recreate and he comes back in and stops the officer or stops one of us and says, "So and so came by here winking at me."

They talk pretty rough to each other. Just what they call "shooting the jive," passing time. He'd be playing dominoes and one might say "Man, come on out to the barnyard." And it's all just jive. Nobody's really mad at nobody, but they're talking pretty bad about each other. This is called woofing. And he can't take it. He says, "So and so threatened me."

I'll say, "All right, man, I'll talk to him, but I don't think he'd make no harm."

I talked to the guy and he said, "Man, I'm just doing it."

—— said, "This dude come on with me. I got raped up there, but I ain't no punk."

I said, "The dude didn't mean no harm. He was just speakin'." But he lays there and he rehashes it in his mind and he rehashes it. And he's basically scared and I imagine he's punishing himself and hating himself for being like that. And it's just getting the better of him because half the fellas he says were bothering him really wouldn't mean him no harm. A lot of them are concerned. They say, "Man, come out of your cell." He just lays there.

And he's stingy. I read his case in *True Detective* magazine. When him and his girlfriend were living together, he'd lock up his candy bars. And he almost took the top off the house because the girl got in the closet and ate one.

In jail they misused him, done everything else to him, but he never did holler until they got to taking his money. And then he hollered and that's when they found out what all was going on.

Why didn't he holler before? Afraid they'd kill him?

I guess it really didn't bother him until they tried to take his money.

He told me, "Man, I told them to do what they want to do to me, but just don't bother my money."

Either he was feeling guilty about the woman he had killed or felt that he deserved that kind of treatment, and he just never said nothing about it. In his own bizarre way of thinking, this is what he had coming. But when they tried to take his money, he blowed the whistle on the whole deal.

One guy just stopped eating and after three or four days he was real nervous, walking back and forth, pacing. Just before then, his fall partner had got a reversal on his case and he hadn't gotten one yet. His people wasn't really working with him or helping him, hadn't visited him in a while. I thought that was more or less on his mind.

So I talked to him, and then one day we were sitting there and he stuck his jar of hot water out of the cell and threw it on the fella in the cell next door to him.

The dude didn't know what was going on. He said, "Man, what did you throw the hot water on me for?"

And he said, "You know why, you know why."

I talked with the other fella and he said, "I don't know why he done it."

So I talked to him and he said, "The dude, I showed him a picture of my brother the other day and my brother had long hair. They wear long hair out there, and the dude made a funny comment about 'Who was that girl?' I said, 'That wasn't no girl, that was my brother.' The dude's disrespecting me, man."

So I asked the dude about it and he said, "It actually looked like a girl and I just misunderstood. It wasn't intended against him. He told me it was his brother and I apologized for it."

"Yeah, man," the other guy said, "the dude apologized, but he still disrespected me. Talk about my family like that. I just laid here and I got mad and throwed it on him."

The dude apologized again for making the comment and he apologized for throwing the water. Everything was all right. Four hours later, he jumped up and told the dude to come out swinging in the morning. He said, "You come out fighting in the morning, man, you just come out fighting."

"Hey, man, I don't want no trouble with you. Just forget about that."

The guy starting all the trouble, he had had a fight before with another inmate and he pushed him and it didn't go like he thought it should, so he's kind of mad about that. Feeling bad about that.

So at recreation, the guy didn't bother him, but he approached the dude and told him he wanted to fight him again and the dude told him he didn't want to fight. I noticed this and I asked him, "What's the matter?"

He was pacing back and forth again.

He said, "Well, man, they took me off my medication." And he had a clamp in his stomach where he had been shot, a metal clamp on the inside, but it came to the surface and was sticking out. They came and they fixed that for him.

I got off and I went back to my cell on the other side. The officer called me and told me the guy wanted to talk to me, it was real important, couldn't wait. So I come back over to J-23 and he explained.

He said, "Well, man, what do you think about moving me? I just want to get away from here. The pressure—I just can't handle it. I'm going to hurt myself or do something. I can't stand it."

So I told the officer and he talked to the major and the major said he'd be down there the first thing in the morning and he'd move him.

If one man moves, then somebody else has to be moved. How would the other man feel about that?

If he's in a place where he likes to be, it will inconvenience him. A lot of them keep their cells clean; some of them don't. He might have to move out of his cell where he might have been a year or two or more. He's got to move and get adjusted to other neighbors. Some of them are pretty well mature and can get by with a decent neighbor, somebody that they have something in common with or can relate to, or they've been there so long they know each other's feelings. When one usually takes his nap the other will wait till later on to type, or when one's up, they like to talk and can relate back and forth. If one gets moved to another cell and another man comes in there, he's got to get readjusted all over again. So it's not just the two men moving that's affected, but the four men on either side of them.

Well, that guy wanted to move because of the pressure and I told him, "The man said he'd get you the first thing in the morning."

He started talking about the people upstairs talking about him and I was wondering because I know the dudes all like him, they all have respect for him. "They calling me, they think I'm a punk," he said.

I said, "Man, they don't think that. I know that." None of the guys felt that way about him. They all liked him.

I said, "Nobody's talking about you."

"Yeah, yeah. They think I don't know it."

So I said, "Well, man, I think you should settle down a little bit. You're misconstruing things." A little while later on, I noticed he was hollering, cussing people out. He told me they're talking about him but all they were doing was talking about something on the TV. I go by his cell and say, "Well, man, well, what's wrong?"

"I heard them up there talking about me."

"Man, those people aren't talking about you. This is a nice night."

He said, "Man, get me out of here." As I leave he tells me, "You got to get me out of here tonight."

I said, "The Man's doing notary work. He'll get to you first thing in the morning and I know you can wait till then."

"I'm going to cut myself. I'm going to hurt myself."

So about nine that night he cut himself. They brought him out and took him to the hospital and sewed it back up.

Cut his wrists?

No, he cut down his vein. It looked pretty serious.

What did he cut himself with?

A piece of mirror. He just slashed it right down his vein. They moved him up to the other cell and they sent the psychiatrist or the sociologist to come and talk with him. He came down there and the guy said he didn't want to talk. He didn't want to see the man.

They took him off his medication. He said, "I don't want to see him. I don't want to say nothing." The man left.

I tried to talk with him and he wouldn't say anything.

He set his mattress on fire that evening.

His brother-in-law up the hall heard about it and so did one other individual that was on Death Row then but is back in population now doing a life sentence. They wanted to come down and talk with him, they'd like to settle him down. The warden was going to arrange it so the brother-in-law could come down and talk with him. Before he could, he set his mattress on fire.

They went in and put that out and they took the mattress out of his cell. He was just in the cell by hisself. He don't have nothing now.

The next morning we come in to feed breakfast and we hear this loud banging noise. We think he's beating on the bunk. We pass by there and he got his head, he's beating his head on the metal bunk. And it's a pretty sharp edge there. He's just sitting there, beating his head on it.

They called the medical captain and he come down, they brought the man out and patched it all up. They put him back in there. He was pretty dazed.

I talked to him for a while and eventually found out that when his fall partner got that reversal, his people had been behind him, but they weren't helping this guy. He hadn't been receiving no mail and he hadn't had no money in quite a while and he was just depressed. He told me, "I just don't care whether I live or die."

He's at the Treatment Center now and he's getting medication. His brother-in-law told me that the other day his people started coming down for a visit. He said they're going to start coming kind of regular, seeing him quite often, sending a little money, try and get together and work on his case, help him on his case.

Basically, what you have is a man, you take him off the streets, he had his friends out there, his circle he's associated in, he has his family, and you bring him down here, lock him in one of these cells. You're taking his identity away. He doesn't have his friends around. He's just a nobody, just somebody anonymous. He's in a situation where he has to start all over, start in a new world with a whole different environment and situation. A lot of them adjust to it pretty well and others don't adjust.

They come from jails. The weaker ones, they might have been messed around in jail, raped, taken advantage of in jail. He comes down here and he brings those problems and those complexes with him. So when he gets here, in working here, you have to be able to deal with him.

It's not just a matter of coming in, working eight hours, cleaning up and going back in. You have to come in, you wake up with them on your mind. If you're gonna deal with them, you have to have it on your mind. You have to try and be aware of their problems. You have to be sensitive as to what's going on and try and figure out what's the matter with them or just what it is going on in their head.

One fella in particular, he was raped in jail and messed over pretty bad, and he come down here, a person look at him wrong and he takes that as an aggressive act toward him. He won't come out to recreate or he won't talk to people. He's scared. He's paranoid. You have to try and deal with him and still try and be fair with him and treat him like an individual.

This is the biggest thing in trying to work over here, with these people whom I'm with all day, sleep with them on the same wings at night. It's just necessary that you have to do it.

One will stop you and you just listen at him. He'll bring his problem out and you have to try, as a human being one to another, to keep his morale up.

A lot of them have suicidal tendencies. Some of them will stop you a lot. You talk with them.

One, his people won't write him no more. He goes out to the visiting room, his girlfriend tells him they're through. He's coming back, he's depressed. You give him a tray and he might kick the tray all out on the run. Food is everywhere. Well, I'm the one who has to clean it up. I can just get mad and blow my cool. In situations like that, you can't afford to.

It's not an act against me, it's not something he's intending, something I've caused. But he goes out there, he's frustrated, he's mad, and I'm just the closest thing next to him to take it out on.

And I have to stand there sometime and it's hard to hold the anger back. You talk with him awhile and he'll blow off his steam. And then he'll settle back down awhile after he's had a chance to blow it off and then he'll tell you what the real problem is. His girlfriend left, somebody's not writing him anymore, somebody's messing with his wife on the street, and there's nothing you can do about it. You have to try and console him in whichever way you can for him to live here and get along with his neighbors, exist here as a whole.

Do many of them go crazy?

No. Just every now and then they'll get depressed, and it's their way of dealing with the trauma. There's one who is part white and part Spanish and he's caught a lot of hassle about having a Spanish father. It's been throughout his whole life and he brought the problem here with him. Right now he won't recreate, he's very quiet.

He's a acid user, he used LSD on the street. He was in Vietnam, he come back here and he was pretty well shell-shocked. At times he's intelligent, he's got good sense, he can sit and hold whole conversations with you. He was raised in California and he did a whole lot of surfing. He's spent some time out there. He likes to surf and we'll sit there and we'll talk about the good old times on the beach. And he'll sit there and hold a decent conversation.

Other times, you'll pass by and he's sitting on his bunk lecturing the wall. I mean really *lecturing* the wall. You'll come by there and he'll be sitting there swimming or just floating or just plain sitting there staring. He'll jump up and say, "I was on my submarine," and I'll say, "Well, you better come back here," and he'll say, "I'm all right."

He likes tea and Dr Pepper. We pass out tea. We'll come by there and he'll raise all kinds of hell if he don't get some tea. When he goes to the commissary, he'll order a case of Dr Pepper—twenty-four to a case. And that night, he might have three Dr Peppers left. He'll do without it for a week or so, then he'll get the case and bust it just like a man busting down a case of beer. It's nerve-racking for him, it's the ultimate high. He'll say, "Ahhhh. This is beautiful." Then three hours later, all the cans will be stacked up at his door, empty.

Sometimes we'll rib him. We'll come by and say, "They don't have no soda water this week."

"Man, you kidding me?"

"No. No soda water."

"Oh, no!" And he'll get pretty disturbed.

There's one man out of Waco. He's in for killing an officer, and he was shot with a .357 magnum. He claims somebody jumped on him up there in the jail and he's supposed to have a plate in his head.

He was normal when he first got here. He was recreating, real talkative. He was living in Houston the time the killing happened, going to Texas Southern and working as a car salesman. From what I understand, he was pretty popular in little social circles. He was recreating for about two weeks and getting along fine.

I brought his breakfast by one morning and when I came back, he hadn't touched it. He said, "Say, man, don't bring me no tray. They bit off my biscuit." They cook the biscuits a pan at a time and you have to break them apart, so a piece was missing off of his. He said, "Man, don't bite off my biscuit no more."

I said, "Nobody bit off the biscuit. What's the problem?"

"Oh, man, you know."

The day before I had asked him if he was having problems or was anybody bothering him because he had stopped recreating for a week. "No, man, it ain't nothing." He would not say nothing.

I said, "Well, man, I didn't bite off your biscuits. Those aren't teeth marks. It's just where we tore the biscuits apart. There ain't nothing wrong with the tray. What's the matter anyway, man? You quit recreating. Is somebody bothering you, been threatening you or what?"

"No, man. You know what it is."

I said, "I don't know what it is. Have I bothered you?"

"I put it this way—if you're not a part of it, you know about it."

I said, "A part of what?"

"There was a cooka bug in my food the other day."

I said, "A what?"

He said, "A cooka bug."

I said, "I don't see how it could get in there."

"Yeah, man. There was a fly in the time before that."

I said, "How come you didn't bring it to somebody's attention, man? You have an officer here. If there is something wrong with your tray, stop him and show it to him, because we're not going to misuse your plate in any way. Man, I wouldn't want it to happen to me and I know how you feel about it. We're here to do what we can."

"No, man, you know about it. You know what's going on. They followed me all the way from the county up here."

All the time I'm talking with him, I'm wondering, "Is he going through an act? Is the pressure really getting to him? What's the deal?"

I stood it for about forty-five minutes of talking to him, then I snapped: the pressure's getting to him.

He goes up to his vent. There's a pipe chase in the back and he's talking to somebody out there in the vent. "There's girls out there in the vent and I'm talking."

You pass by there and he's up to the vent and he's really talking, he's holding a conversation. It was so real, the officer left and went to the pipe chase to see if there was somebody back there. There wasn't.

He waked up in the middle of the night talking to little green men dancing on the shitter—on the commode, we call them a shitter here. He said, "I'm talking to the little green men dancing, man."

He had a plate in his head and he said they put some kind of bug in there, and this dude supposedly followed him here from Waco. "He's always bothering me, man," he said.

That went on for about a week and they started giving him Thorazine. He calmed down for a while, then he started back up again. Then he got tired of being in his cell, so he asked the sergeant could he come out and recreate. "When you get through playing crazy, quit seeing little green men, then you can come out."

He straightened up. He comes out to recreate, but now he's reverted back to the same things again. He talks to himself. He'll stand up there and talk to the radio. Tell you there's another guy in the cell with him.

I go by there and tell him he'll just have to hold it down and he'll get pretty loud and I'll say, "Man, you got to hold it down because if they find two of you are in there, one of you all got to go."

And he says, "All right, man." He's harmless.

You can't help nobody if you don't know them.

If you come in there and work with me tonight on Death Row, you'd see some pretty nice people. They would fool you. Some of them would. Some of them you would say, "Well, I'd better stay away from that guy." And you'd have different thoughts about another guy.

You'd feel sorry for that little kid, little eighteen-year-old kid we got down there. Everybody whistles at him when he goes to take a bath. If I don't give him the right pair of shorts, it makes him look too feminine. I have to take special care of two or three of them on their looks. I have to tell them how to act grown-up. They're that young. And some of them are retarded. And they don't know how to take care of theirself down there, never being in prison before.

They're scared as hell when they walk in. I don't know them when they first come in, but I learn them right quick. I have to. To live with it.

When they come out of that shower and people whistle at them, I stop the whistle. That's the first thing. Then I ask the guy to go from eighteen to thirty-five overnight. It's hard to do.

That's a cold-hearted, lonely place down there. There's no women there. The only women is on the TV, or one of them books that's wore out. They pass them down the row.

Inmates abuse everything here. That's what's wrong with prison. Inmates abuse other inmates. There's nothing wrong with the way they're running the penitentiary.

None of the ex-convicts on Death Row are hard to get along with but J——. He's an agitator. He comes from the old school. I knowed him for thirty years. He was down here in the fifties with me.

Him and three other guys killed a guy in a robbery and they tortured him and tried to make him open a safe and he wouldn't do it. So they just blew him away. He's a cold-hearted person.

He's what Death Row is about. He was made for Death Row. He doesn't deserve to breathe the same air you and me breathe. He's the kind the death penalty needs to be taken for, he needs to be out of society, he can't live in this society.

That's the kind of people that needs the death penalty—people that can't live in society out there or in here.

Death sentences are supposed to be for the sociopathic person, the ones just bent on violence. This is the way the legislation was drawn up and intended to be. But in my opinion, those aren't the persons that are getting it. I can go down the twenty men on each of the six rows, and on each of them you'll have only three people that's been in there before. Just not that many that are vicious. Most of them are just youngsters, just out of high school.

The prisoner on Death Row, he really doesn't have access to another prisoner on Death Row. He's being watched all the time. Nobody ever forgets what those people are down there for. You don't go around persecuting a guy because he done this or that. You got one guy who's killed sixteen people, one's killed seven people. We got six down there that's killed five people. But you can't go around being mad at a guy for what he done before he came down here. You just can't do it and stay in there and work. It's too hard.

I've been in prison for thirty years and Death Row is the hardest job I've ever been on. I've been on many jobs, being in prison as long as I have. I've been working on Death Row about two years.

I was doing a life sentence, and I got out of prison in '74 after twenty-five years and I only lasted eighteen days. I got off into some trouble again and I got another life sentence.

I'm not a bitter person. I try to maintain my sanity. I know I done wrong. I'm guilty. You hear a lot of them say they're not; they claim the criminal justice machinery done them wrong. But the courts don't make that many mistakes.

Some say they'd rather go by the injection, sleep it away, and others would rather be electrocuted. Others, well, you know: dying is dying.

Some think it's never going to happen. One, since he's been here, he's been talking about how he's going home. Even now, he still says that he's going home. His case is in the fifth circuit. They're going to rule on it. They should be hearing it now and in the next couple of months they should hand down a decision. [The case was reversed in the district court, then reaffirmed in the fifth circuit, so he is still on Death Row.] But he keeps his articles packed up and every time you go by there he says, "I'm going home pretty soon, man, I'm going home."

I've seen somebody who was executed in the electric chair.

When I was just a young kid down here. I had a horrible experience when I first come here. I come down here for two years for stealing a car when I run off from Gatesville. And they gave me two years and I was stationed at The Walls unit. After I was there a week, there was an execution coming up at night. I was in my cell. It was 1951. Nobody there could see the execution, but they told us whenever they executed one of them all the lights went dim.

I waited up all night. I'm waiting for the lights to blink. This guy hadn't got a stay or nothing. Sure enough, at about 12:15, the lights start flicking off and on and dimming. And they say, "Well, they took another guy down." I thought about it.

I was on a working detail at the tag [license plate] plant at the time. The next day, we took a bunch of tags that they had made and put in boxes over to the prison store to store them all away. And they had this guy that they had executed in a little icebox. It was a three-tier deal. I guess you've seen them. Like a morgue. And they had this guy they had executed in this box.

I didn't know he was in there. They put all new, young guys on this detail job. We could walk outside of the walls and didn't have a gun on us. I was doing two years, I wasn't going to run off. There was a bunch of other kids like me. Seventeen-, eighteen-year-old kids. They kind of took care of us back in them days because of sex, you know, guys getting raped and everything. That's when the raping was bad. There ain't none of that stuff going on now.

Well, this boss asked some of the guys in this group, "You all see that dead mother over there that they killed last night?"

I was the first one. "Yeah, yeah, I see him. I want to see what he looks like."

This guy opened this deal. I don't know if they've got them nowadays, but you can pull this deal out. And he pulled this guy halfway out and his feet came out first. He had on white clothes, just like I've got on now. He had a pair of slippers on.

Only he didn't have one on his left foot. But they had a tag, just like you see in the movies, around his toe. It was a black guy that they killed. His skin was real gray and all the hairs was off of one of his legs. It was the leg that they put the deader on.

I never will forget it as long as I live. His name was Thomas Black. He's from Dallas. Tried to do some research on him later on, what he done and everything. He killed a guy in a service station robbery.

But it's always in my mind, seeing him in there.

I couldn't adjust when I got out of here. I couldn't adjust to that free world. I had been down here so long. I went out and women wasn't hardly wearing anything. They had dresses on plumb up to their you-know-what. It was too much for me. I was going around with an erection on all the time. Biggest thing you ever seen. Just a potential rapist.

I've never been around any women in my life. I'm surprised that I'm talking to you as easy as I am. I've just been here all my life.

I was in Gates reformatory fourteen years before I came here. And then I was raised in Waco State Home.

I keep an open mind about everything and I like to play a lot. I'm really still young at heart. I played ball down there fifteen years. I don't play no more. They kicked me off the team. I ain't good enough.

I stayed in prison too long.

When I walked out, I had my head up and I went to a family that loved me. My sister and my brother-in-law love me. They wrote me all the time I was here. Twenty-five years. I done twenty-one years on a life sentence, but I done four years before that and I never did get out. I killed a guy here in prison by killing him with a pitchfork. I got into a fight on Ramsey One with the guy and they gave me a life sentence. From the time I was seventeen until I was forty-four, I wasn't out. And when I got out, I just walked into a world that I had never been in.

The biggest thrill that I got when I was out was I went to Shakey's Pizza a couple of times with my sister.

One thing I couldn't face was the women. I didn't know how to talk with women. All I did was sit there and look at their tits.

I had several places lined up I wanted to see. I wanted to see the Indianapolis 500, Niagara Falls, I wanted to see the Kentucky Derby, and I wanted to see a Rose Bowl game. It was several things that I wanted to see. And I wanted to see the Dallas Cowboys play.

Did you do that?

None of it. I didn't do nothing but just work and go home every day. I went twice to Shakey's Pizza. And we went to a restaurant.

I had never lived under air-conditioning. My sister keeps the air-conditioning on all the time. She had an air-conditioner in her home, and it just about froze me to death. Man, I got there and got on a coughing jag and I had to go outside it was so cold in there. Have you ever been in places where it's cold?

Now I see why them women wear them fur coats in the summertime.

I really became interested in my job, but it's so hard. It's taken its toll on me. I'm almost fifty years old and it's beginning to tell on me. I'm beginning to get bald-headed, my teeth are beginning to come out. In this job, I'm on sixteen hours a day, seven days a week. I don't ever have a day off. It's just eating me alive. Three years ago I had tuberculosis. I just got over that. That was pretty rough. I'm in fourth-class medical, but I still work.

They don't allow me to feed chow. My TB is inactive now, but a former TB patient or an arrested case, they're not allowed to handle food. So I'm the only Death Row porter down there that's not allowed to handle food. But I'll take care of just about everything else down there.

Most of them express their boredom by overeating. Some eat all they can eat at mealtime and through commissary purchases. If you put people in a small place and feed them three times a day plus what they buy at the commissary, they're going to get pretty heavy if they don't have the facilities to work it off.

I've never seen many of them go into these vegetative states where they just sleep all the time. There's one or two like that on J-23 that's not on medication. One is a very religious person on two-row, and he sleeps the majority of the time. There's another one that's asleep nearly all the time, but when he wakes up he's happy and he's smiling. I would think a person that slept that much would have to be depressed, speaking from my limited medical knowledge. I think he'd have to be depressed. His mind would be so unstimulated and slowed down that it would be vegetative.

The majority of them don't sleep that much. There's always noise. It's either the television or the chow cart or somebody on three-row hollering and talking to somebody down on one-row. It's very noisy in there during the day. That's probably another cause for the frustration or agitation—the noise pollution that they go through.

From eleven or twelve at night during the week to about five in the morning it stays fairly quiet. On the weekends, Friday and Saturday night, it's quiet from about one-thirty or two till about four or five. I know what bothers me and I know it's bound to bother other people.

I live on the other side, on J-21, on the Death Row down at the front, and it took me a long time to get adjusted to the noise. When I get off at twelve-thirty, I usually go take an hour-and-a-half or two-hour nap when I don't go to school. Then I get up and feed supper. It is impossible to rest in there because of the television, the conversation, and the people recreating and talking in the dayroom. I don't see how they can sleep during the day, unless they are exhausted, just wore out, and stay up all the time. It'll put people in a bad mood.

It's not a very good place. But it's not a very bad place. There's nobody there that is intentionally maltreated or mistreated. Some get a little more than others now and then, but I don't know how you're going to get around that. People form friendships, and jealousy is part of human nature. You can control a lot of it, but some of it you can't.

We just got two new porters down there and they're scared to death.

You have to go through an orientation program with a guy working on there.

Because you got to treat those people right on Death Row. You can't say the wrong thing. If you say the wrong thing to one guy, it affects two or three people. You don't ever hurt a guy's feelings on Death Row. That's where a lot of these Death Row porters make trouble. And they have trouble with them. But I don't ever say nothing wrong to them.

You got to talk sixty different languages in J-23.

Feeling Sick and Going Crazy Too

No one on the Row had anything good to say about the medical service. Inmates feel it is too slow, too careless, and inadequate. They say it takes a long time to see the doctor, he doesn't pay much attention when he does come, and doesn't do much before he leaves. They complain about optical and dental treatment: population inmates can get eyeglasses made fairly quickly, and they can get complicated bridge work done by convict technicians. But Death Row inmates don't get dental prosthetics, and they have to wait years for optometrist appointments. A measure of hypochondria enters here. There is little to do and some of the men become obsessive about the deterioration of their bodies resulting from the lack of activity and starchy food. Some men overeat the starchy food on their trays and order similar food from commissary, thereby complicating the problem. Nonetheless, the complaints have merit. The Death Row inmates do not have the kind of medical access all other prisoners have, let alone the kind they might have in the free world. Part of the anger about medical matters reflects something more basic: it is another area in which one has no control over critical things in one's life. If the doctor doesn't feel like responding or won't take a complaint seriously, one cannot call another doctor, one cannot elect any alternatives.

Death Row inmates are in a medical limbo. They are technically the property of the county governments, so the Department of Corrections has no budget for nonemergency medical services for them; since they are in physical custody of the Department of Corrections, the county governments avoid involvement in their care. When they need something like false teeth, the agency with the custody says it has neither the responsibility nor the budget, and the agency with the responsibility and the budget says nothing.

Some people go crazy on the Row, and there is even less help for that. Perhaps it is reasonable to go crazy, living under such confined conditions for so many years. In August 1979, forty-two men on the Row had been there more than three years. Further, some people were pretty much crazy when they got there. Everyone on the Row thought the man who beat his skull against the steel bunk was seriously disturbed. The Row was divided about the man who talked and screamed all night: some felt he was quite mad, others felt he was putting on a bothersome performance. It's a tough audience on the Row, and if one is faking, one had best be very good at it.

The first statement in the following section is by the medical assistant, the man who goes around with the pills; the second is by one of the porters. All the other statements are by Death Row inmates.

I'm the medical assistant on the Ellis Unit. I assist the medical officer in taking care of the inmates on the unit here. Each morning we have a sick call on the unit. I screen each individual myself. I have the health record on each inmate on the farm. I screen them myself. If I can examine and prescribe medication for the inmates, I do so. And if I can't, then I refer them to our medical officer and he, in turn, will examine the patient. If he can take care of them here, why, we do the medical work on the unit here, and if we can't, then we send them to a different hospital, where they have more facilities to take care of the inmates.

A minimum of once every day, I go through Death Row, and I take with me proper medication to take care of the inmates up there—if they have headaches and bad colds, et cetera—and I also take along with me prescription items which a doctor has prescribed for these inmates.

I take with me medication and I take different kinds of salves for sores and skin rashes. And if there's an inmate that I can't take care of myself, why, then I take his name and number and I come back and I put him on a referral list. Then I refer him to our unit doctor, and then he, in turn, will either have these inmates come down to the dispensary or else he will go up and examine an inmate on the unit. And then he will prescribe proper medication, and he'll come back and we'll make out a prescription, and, beginning the following day, or that day, this patient will start receiving the medication that's been prescribed by the doctor.

The inmates here on Death Row, they don't differ really that much from the ones that are out in the population. Sometimes these inmates are a little bit more tense, naturally, they've got more problems—medical problems and other problems. They're a little more nervous sometimes, but that isn't on a day-to-day basis. I mean it varies from different times. But as far as an inmate on Death Row, as far as being any different from the ones out in population, they really aren't that much different in the type of patient up there.

In here, they don't consider it a major catastrophe if you have the sniffles or a headache or a cold. They can't issue penicillin to everybody. In order to issue it, they have to stop and search your records. If you're outside, you can go to the doctor and get penicillin if you want it, but here they wait till it's called for.

I don't really agree with all that, but I don't see there's anything else they can do. To run down and give everybody individual penicillin shots, they'd need twenty, thirty people on duty all the time. And that seems to be what most of them want. "I want a penicillin shot." And some of them want an X-ray.

I say, "What could an X-ray do for you?"

And he'll say, "When I was outside, the doctor gave me an X-ray and I got well."

It probably speeds up the process of meiosis, kills a lot of cells and they have to divide again. It takes a lot of energy away from the other necessary body operations. They don't want to hear that. They know the X-ray cured them the last time.

We have one psychologist that comes by once a month. He says, "You want to talk to me?"

They don't care nothing about rehabilitation on Death Row because the whole goal is to kill us. I think they're really mad because they have to feed us. "Why don't we just let them all starve?"

The psychologist says he's fascinated to come by and talk to me because I'll talk real fast and I'll run a bunch of things down to him. I said to him, "You know why I'm talking so fast?"

He'll say, "No, why are you talking so fast?"

"'Cause I know any minute you're going to have to walk off and I want to give you as much from my mind as I can."

I have a lot that I can share or give and I don't mind giving it, but I have to have somebody to do it to. I can't do it to myself. I can't sit and talk to somebody on the wall. If I can give something or do something, I want to do it, to express myself. I have very little chance here for that.

Sometimes I get very bitter and I lay down and I get very depressed. Then I say, "Snap out of it, you idiot." And I snap out of it. I talk to myself sometimes but it's, you know, inside.

As soon as they hear a cold front coming in, they open up all the windows. They try to make you uncomfortable. That place is not a good place to live. It's not an insulated place. Oh, I could feel my bones hurting for the cold in it, you don't never be warm. You don't never be cool when it's hot.

You in a cell about nine foot long and three or four foot wide. A man sit down in that, he could lose his sanity. I'm looking at a guy now, he losing his mind more and more each day. Bruce has been seeing him in there every day, he know. He really losing his mind. They should put him in a mental hospital. The guy ain't got enough sense to eat his food sometime. If they don't ask him, if they don't tell him it's there, he say, "Oh, I never knowed it was there." He plain crazy.

I believe they kicked him in the head and messed up his head more. Doctors come there and give him some pills. I don't take none of them pills from the doctors.

I done had some bad headaches. But I just refuse to take them pills from the doctor. One guy next to me told me, "Never take no pills from them because you take some pills from them and you snap." I knowed a guy in the county jail. They got him right next to me now. He takes them pills from the doctor, the doctor brings him pills all the time, and he nutty as a fruitcake. Them pills do something to you.

I guess they old tranquilizers. Same thing on the street. I know what they do to you on the street because when I would take them, sometime the aftereffect make you ignorant. And it get you in trouble.

I'm going blind in there because I can't see good. That's why I'm telling my uncle to get me a Bible that's got bigger letters.

You should get glasses.

I wouldn't even ask them people. Look here at my teeth. They don't feel nothing. See, this one here is knocked completely off and this one over here is rotten plumb all in. And here's another one rotting right here.

They'll pull them, but I haven't heard of them filling none of them down here yet. I got a filling here that needs to be done, but if you're put on a list it would be a month or two or three before it would be done.

You should get on the list.

I've been thinking about it.

This eye is real bad, and then I got no hearing in this ear. It's about 65 percent deaf in this ear. I can blow smoke out of this ear when the humidity gets up. It will pop in there and it's got a hole in the eardrum. It doesn't hurt, but it's hard to hear people.

But about getting my teeth fixed: I don't like dentists no way. All he wants to do is pull them. I had one right here and they pulled that one out and he didn't hurt me none because I've stood all kinds of pain. I've been cut, stabbed, shot, and everything else. That wasn't hurting me. But the bones has stayed inside there. I picked them out of there for about four weeks, almost a month. It was pieces of bones. It busted in two and I kept picking them out. That hurt for a long time. It just now got well.

He's supposed to be a pretty good dentist, but they don't take a whole great lot of time with Death Row prisoners as they do with the other prisoners.

I made me a set of teeth about six months ago. I made them out of a piece of plastic. My lip had been falling inwards and it had begun to look bad and it bothered me, so what I did was, I made me a set of teeth. You can't eat with them, at least I can't, but they are a support to keep my upper lip from falling inwards. At night, just before I go to sleep, I put them in. They're made out of a piece of plastic out of a plastic cigarette pack. The teeth, you can't talk with them because they're not set in your mouth. But they do help with keeping my lip from falling in.

Now something as simple as a pair of teeth, I don't see why that TDC would deny any inmate some teeth to eat with. The reason why I want them is to eat with and wear when I speak so I can be understood without this hissing sound that you get from teeth being missing. And to keep my upper lip from falling inwards.

But TDC has constantly refused to give me a simple set of teeth. I have offered to pay for the teeth myself out of my own money, to have my own doctor come down here. TDC has refused my doctor to come down and also has refused for me to pay for the teeth.

They say, "Well, you don't need no teeth. You gonna die anyway."

He don't know this for a fact—unless he knows in advance what's going to happen, how the courts are going to rule.

They'd rather spend thousands of dollars in keeping me from getting a pair of teeth than to let me pay or even they pay a hundred dollars or two hundred dollars for a pair of teeth. I don't see why the TDC policies are the way they are. Inmates in population get dentals put in just about every day. But just because we're on Death Row we can't have them. I don't think that's right.

I'm trying to change that now. I've got a lawsuit filed in court.

So far, I've done a lot of legal research and I haven't found any law that supports the TDC position that would cause them to legally deny me teeth.

The way I do my legal research is, I usually take *Texas Digest* and I look up under "medical treatment for prisoners" and stuff like this. Once I find the law that supports my position, then I look it up in the law book. And once I find it, then I try to find some law that supports TDC's position. But so far, I haven't found any law—case law, statutes, anything anywhere—that would support TDC's position in denying me teeth.

It's a policy that TDC has always had. They have always did little stuff like this right here, for what reason I don't know. The main problem is, TDC don't have to answer to anyone, really, unless you take them to court.

I've been trying to stop the doctor for about two weeks now because I've been heavily constipated. This is probably due to a lack of exercise, lack of moving around. I haven't used the bathroom in almost three weeks now, and I stopped the little orderly. The doctor only comes up here once a week, and not really once a week. I haven't seen him in about a month. But these orderlies come down here and they are not allowed to give out nothing but aspirin and they tell you, "Don't ask for stuff to sleep." If you're having problems with your nerves to sleep, they'll say, "Look, man, you'll have to consult the doctor about this. We're not allowed to give out anything."

This is all fine, but then you try to get the doctor down here. You write a request and nothing happens. And finally when he does come down here, he gives you such a long story. He doesn't speak English too good, he's hard to understand. You really need an interpreter, an inmate who's been working down there with him so long he can understand him.

As I was saying, I stopped the orderly several times. I've told them about my constipation and I've been given a couple of pills and they've said, "This ought to do it."

But it didn't do it, so the next day I said, "Look, man. This is getting serious. My stomach is hurting real bad."

And he said, "Well, take these." And he gave me some more and that was it.

And I never really used the bathroom until I just finally got down and got the doctor up here, which took a lot to do. He finally come up here and I told him, "I haven't used the bathroom, it's hurting, and I'm scared I'm gonna lose my life. I'm gonna bust."

He gave me something called Metamucil, and I had a bowel movement then.

I've been trying to get medication for the last seven months. It's for my nerves. I'm nervous.

When I first come down here, I was not nervous. When I was on the streets, I wasn't on medication, so I didn't think I need them so I didn't ask for it. And about seven months ago, every doctor, every attendant doctor come down here to the wing, I ask him for medication. They won't do nothing.

I ask him again to get one of the psychiatrists or psychologists to come down to see me in my cell. I explained to him my problem. He went and told the doctor for them not to give me nothing.

The doctor [he means here the medical assistant] come and see me the next day. He come to pass out medicine and I ask him about it. He said, "That doctor said he didn't think you needed anything."

I told the doctor, "I don't think he is qualified to come and look at me and tell you that I don't need no medication. I asked you all to give me medication for my nerves or take me to have an examination to see what kind of medicine I need." I told the warden about it and he come over here to the wing. Four or five days ago, I talked to him again, and he says, like everybody else, "I'll see what I can do."

I talked to the doctor today. That Filipino doctor or Vietnamese doctor. And I talked to him about a week ago, and I tried to explain to him what was wrong, and he kept saying over and over, "What's wrong with you? What's wrong with you?"

I don't know what is the definition of the word *nerves*. I can't sleep at night. I don't need nothing to put me to sleep. It's just a kind of nerves. My hands start sweating. They sweat. And I'm nervous.

I think that when anybody asks for medication, they should examine him and see what kind of medication he needs.

One of the doctors, he looked at my hands and he said, "This sweating you have, that comes because of the nerves." He himself told me that.

And to this point it's been seven months. And what do you do, when you have asked for medication, when you have talked to them—I'm not saying for one week or two weeks, I'm saying for months. What are you supposed to do?

What do you do?

Deal with the fact that they ain't gonna give you nothing. Not unless there is somebody in society that knows your problem. But here on Death Row, there's no way that you're going to get medication. You can't say, "I'm going to get on the phone and try to see if I can talk to somebody and see if they can do something about it." You can't say, "I'll go to this doctor here and he can help, he can give me a medical examination and see what's wrong with me. And he'll give me something." You can't do that. You just deal with the fact that they ain't gonna give you nothing and that's it. "You got nerves. It's tough. That's your business." That's what they tell you.

You are forced to deal with your own problems, which I don't think you should deal with. They should have better conditions here on Death Row. They got you here on Death Row ready to die. "Well, you gonna die." Okay.

I got used to the idea knowing that I'll be here today and tomorrow. But I haven't got used to the idea of being here. I face the fact that I'll be here today and tomorrow, but I don't like being locked up, you know.

If you get one of those people that think this is not bad, lock him up in one cell for five years.

You have to go through a lot. It takes a lot to be on Death Row. It's hard. But you deal with it day by day and you learn to get along. And if you don't, that's your problem.

What happens to those who don't?

I had this old friend of mine who come down here on Death Row. They moved him a few times because he was asking for his medication. They finally put him back on this side again. And he said, "I want my medication." He talked to doctors, he talked to guards. They wouldn't do nothing about it. He cut himself. And they took him to the clinic, put some stitches in him, brought him back.

The next day, they put him in another cell, and, on the edge of the bunk, he hit himself on the forehead. And it cracked the skull. For one hour, he hit his head on the bunk, on the edge of the bunk. After one hour, the doctor finally come down here while the young boss that they had, he stand in front of his cell and just look at him and laugh. Laugh at him.

Did you see this?

That's right. And finally, about an hour later, came the doctor, took him out of the cell and took him to the hospital.

And we learned later that he had lost some fluid from his head. He lost a lot of blood.

That was his way of telling them that he needed medication.

I don't know what happened to him. The last thing we heard was he was all right. But his head had grown about twice what his head was on account of the beating that head took.

You saw this boss laughing at him?

That's right. It makes me so mad that I wanted to come out of my cell and go in his cell and stop him. I know him from the streets. And it just made me so mad that nobody would do nothing about it.

Do people here ever just snap?

That's what V— did. He's the one that beat his brains out on the bunk. He had cut his wrists. A person cuts his wrists, not just for the hell of it, to see what's going to happen. I know what's going to happen.

Okay. He cut his wrists. They take him out and then they bring him back. He bites all this stuff off. The dude's nuts. There's something wrong with him. They take everything. He lit his bed on fire. They take everything out of the cell. He beats his brains on the edge of the steel bunk till his brains come out. This is literal, this is not a figure of speech. Brain matter was running out of his head. They take him down and bandage it up and they bring him back. He starts beating again. And they stand there and laugh at him. You're not supposed to laugh at him.

Did they think he was playing?

He wasn't playing. He proved he wasn't playing. When a man is determined enough to beat his head that long, he's not playing a bit, especially after he's cut his wrists and tried to burn himself alive. This is obvious: there's something wrong with him.

We have somebody flip out here or get so mad or frustrated that something happens every week, just about every day. Somebody will get mad and yell. Somebody will get mad and just go screaming about the television. We have men here that sleep under blankets continuously, summer and winter, and they sweat all the time and they scream for the windows to be opened and the windows might be opened.

We have men that wake up in the middle of the night and start singing and some men have something drawn on their wall, an outline of a man, and they start talking to it, scolding it, cussing it, beating it, beating their legs, beating their bunk, just to get some motion, something in their life other than just sitting here. They're dangerous to themselves in a sense—they can't function. They have no reason for going on living.

We've had men sit here on the floor and beat their head against the bunk until they were bloody. We've had men try and cut themselves. We've had men that just couldn't tolerate it anymore. Nothing was actually happening to them, but that was just the thing—the waiting.

They scalded one dude here just a little while back for making noise.

This man, I don't know about him. I knew him before he got down on one-row. He was up on three-row. I'd go by and give him cigarettes, give him coffee, buy him ice cream. He seemed like he was all right. But then a little over five months ago, he started hollering and yelling and screaming.

This dude never did that before. I was up there for a year and a half and he never did that. He never made no noise. And now, he'll just all of a sudden start screaming. It don't matter night or day; he does it all the time. He don't never go to sleep. There's something wrong with him.

He needs help, but all they do is throw hot water on him or whip him. Put him in the cross and have two or three people whip him.

I don't think that man is crazy.

He tried that game in the county jail for the psychiatrists and the jailers. You can watch somebody and see if they're crazy. I think he's just running a game.

When he got here on Death Row, they had two building tenders. They didn't have a boss in the wing then, the building tenders ran it. And the building tender said to him, "If you start playing that goddamn shit here, I'm going to stomp the hell out of you." The man believed him. The man lived right above me for a year and I never heard his voice. And he's got one of them voices you'll always remember.

Then one of the building tenders died. He was meaner than hell. He died and the other one went to Santa Fe, New Mexico, to do some time. And he seen that the new building tenders weren't going to do nothing, that a boss was in the wing to protect him, and then he started playing his game again.

I heard he was beaten. Someone said the building tenders got an inmate to do it.

Two or three weeks ago he was beat up, but it wasn't nothing to do with no building tenders. His next-door neighbor whupped his ass. It was because he couldn't sleep at night, he couldn't sleep in the daytime. If you're just about asleep and somebody starts cussing out loud, after that happens so often, you got to do something.

Did that stop him?

For about three days. That day it happened, you couldn't even tell he was there. If he'd a been crazy, that would have just made him worse. 'Cause I seen that happen to crazy people before. In the county jail, something like that just aggravated them worse, made them crazier.

This one, he shuts up when it's dangerous. The psychiatrist comes through our wing, you never hear him say a word. He never tries to stop him. He's one of the only ones who don't. I don't speak to the psychiatrist myself, but he don't got nothing I need. Lots of people try to stop him and talk to him, but this guy, he don't want nothing to do with him. I don't think he's crazy.

He's dumb. Because even if he was crazy, these people don't give a damn.

"Dancer is at Rusk [the state mental hospital] now.

"A few nights ago, he just got worse and worse and was breaking glass and shaking the door at 2 in the morning and then on into the day. The guards were scared of him. They tried to give him a shot and he fought them off, then they tried to drug his food and tea. He refused to eat. He was winning, but only to a point. They had five guards and a warden get him, and three men from Rusk chained him and took him on.

"I have talked to Dancer in the recreation group when I was on the other side and we were out together. He talked some sense, but he was so screwed up body wise and hurting that he used his actions as a release."

That one is out of Houston. He's the one they had to take out of the courtroom during his trial 'cause he kept calling the judge "Jezebel."

Jezebel?

Yes. He's highly intelligent.

He called him "lying Jezebel, racist, pig, the devil, the beast." He's basing it on Islamic philosophy—Elijah Mohammed. He's highly intelligent. He was in the Masonic organization and he's real knowledgeable.

He spent his whole time going through the trial telling the judge what he thought and sticking it to him and eventually they had to carry him out of the courtroom and carry on the trial without him.

When he first come down, he wouldn't eat. He said Moto was coming down. Moto was his savior and was going to help him. He was delirious because he hadn't eaten for a while. They had to literally force food down his throat. He was just completely out of it. A sun worshiper or something he was supposed to be.

That went on for about three weeks, and one weekend his brother and his sister came to visit him. They had a nice little visit. They had to come down there in the dayroom and visit with him. He kind of straightened up, and then he just regressed again, so they sent him to the Treatment Center. When he came back he was on Thorazine.

He just walked around like a mummy on Thorazine. He'd sleep, eat, sleep, and when he wake up he'd run it down to you about Moto, the man of the Congo. "This is the man that's going to make it all right."

He had his case reversed, then he went back to trial again. He was trying to plead insanity. He still got the death sentence when he came back this time.

He was completely different. He got his sense together, all his motor senses are intact. And he's working on his case. His people are 100 percent behind him.

No more Moto. No more sun worshiping. He still claims Islam is his faith and religion. He prays every day. Sometimes you'll come by there and he's facing to the east saying his prayers.

He's highly intelligent.

There's some people here that's insane. There's one guy up here who told me of seventeen he raped and killed. They've only convicted him for two or three, but he told me of seventeen of them, and several of them they don't even know about him. To know him, I know the man is for real telling me the truth. He ain't lying. This is the type of man that's crazy in his mind. He has no business being in here. He needs to have somebody be talking to him or doing something for him.

People don't really try to commit suicide. You can give them knives or whatever, a gun. They wouldn't do nothing like that. They take all the razor blades away, they put the light outside the cell where we can't reach the electricity. That's not a security thing, that's a cruel thing. They are just trying to punish us as much as possible. Just like somebody, before you kill him, torture him before you kill him.

Do you really think that?

I know this. To commit suicide, it would be easy to take a piece of the sheet or a pillowcase or a bandana or your shirt sleeve and wet it and tear a strip and wrap it around your neck and tie it about four or five times. By holding your breath you're automatically going to pass out. And if there is no one there to untie it, you ain't gonna wake up and you ain't gonna feel nothing.

That's all make believe by the institution. All that not letting you have belts and all that, that's something they're trying to sell the public. If a man really wants to die, you don't have to go through them changes. Anybody can die. You can do it with Scotch tape. Anybody knows that with Scotch tape, if you just make a few laps around your neck real quick, it's gonna hold and it's gonna stick. Anything to cut your wind off. It don't take much.

They worry about cutting your arms to bleed to death. I've put eight hundred stitches in them arms plumb to the bone and it didn't do nothing but bleed the veins out and that's it.

Were you trying to kill yourself?

No. It's just the prison here. I went against them for approximately thirteen years. I didn't draw no good time. I wasn't going to work. They had to beat on me. They'd do different things trying to get me to work. And I wouldn't work for them. I'd cut my heel strings. I might go out there a day or two and see a lot of work out there and I'd tell them, "I ain't getting nothing for it." I just make them bring me back in the building. We'd go through some changes. They'd put me in straitjackets and I'd break out of the straitjackets and go to cutting.

You can't hurt yourself cutting your arms open. You got to cut a main artery. And the main arteries, everybody knows where they're at. They're in the bottom of your feet, they're in the thighs, they're under your arms and on both sides of your throat. If a man is serious, he knows where to cut. He don't have to be chopping on them arms 'cause you're not going to get nowhere.

The thing is, you're putting them under such pressure when you have to do this to get help. I could make them fire up the ambulance right now and carry me in, but it's only what you do when a person is pushed into the corner to where he needs help.

If I ever get out of this, I have got to have myself checked into a mental institution where I can talk to doctors and talk this thing—what hate and frustration is in my system now—talk these things out.

I've got to be brought back gradually. Right now, I would probably have a nervous breakdown. Maybe not literally, but it would unnerve me tremendously if the situation was suddenly switched and I could walk out that front gate and away from this.

I would want help to recover. I know myself and I know I'm not mean or cruel or dangerous. But what if there is something hidden that I cannot see that somebody else might see? That maybe a doctor would know and could bring out, someone who has been trained to observe these things and bring it out?

I might get out of here and nothing is bothering me, but I suddenly get trapped in a closed elevator and it brings it back. You know that fear? And then I want to strike out to stop it. Or what if I get into a room and the doors are locked and I can't get out?

See, those things are happening to me now, but I'm accepting them. What if I am suddenly free and exposed to those same things and I have no control against that feeling of total helplessness?

I might only need to be in there a couple of days and I might need a month. I might need to be there for a while. I just don't know. But I'm definitely checking myself in.

I would get used to being able to walk a long distance. I would reassociate and reacquaint myself with things. Control and being able to do something myself, like turning on the TV.

Finding God

Act crazy or announce you've talked with God and folks will say in neutral voices, "Sure, pal, sure." There is a curious tolerance here. If they think you're sincere, almost anything goes, almost anything is acceptable. But these men are not quick to assume sincerity. They've spent too much time in a world of mendacity, posing, ambition, and manipulation.

It isn't surprising that some men on the Row should get into a religious fervor. They are facing death and they come out of the heart of the Bible Belt. Some cynics say that most get into religion only in the hope that they'll get a good recommendation from the preacher or some of their free-world correspondents when their case gets down to the wire—when the governor or the Board of Pardons and Paroles makes the last-minute decision about whether to grant clemency. And some are even more cynical than that: to them the religious passion means only that the hated television sets are turned on earlier one day a week, stealing a few precious hours of relative silence.

I don't want to give these people no trouble. As long as they give me what I know I got coming, I'll go along with them. And any time they don't give me what I think I got coming, even if it's a kick in the butt, I want it. It belongs to me and I'm asking for it and I want it.

It's like this case right here. Even though I'm not guilty of this case right here, I got other things I have done that have slowed me down. I ain't in here for killing nobody. I'm in here because I disobeyed God, that's what I'm in here for. And whenever I pay that, well, His law overrides Texas'. Texas ain't nothing but a grain of sand on the sea. When I get what God wants me to learn of this down here, I'll be gone. These people can't hold me. They have to turn me loose. That's true. Can you believe that?

It kind of sounds like Jesus taught in the paradoxes: he that seeks his life will lose his life. Well, he damn sure will. Because his flesh life is not what all that counts.

For thirty-four years I tried it and I tried to do it and I fought a hell of a fight. But I couldn't win. I could not win. And I tell you, if anybody could have beat it, I would have beat it.

What is "it"?

The evil.

If anybody could have beat it, I would have beaten it. Because I done everything from pimping whores to selling dope to running whiskey to—you name it and I've done it. I didn't want to do it. But it was just a game that I had to do.

I had the things in the wrong order, I should have said, "God, I want you first." That's what I should have said. "And then come back and get my family and live for you the rest of my life. That's the three things I want." But I said, "I want out first. And then I want to get my feathers back and live the rest of my life." He changed my mind. He told me, "Here's how it is. You got me now and then you're getting your family back." He's showing me. I'm getting it back. The end has got to be just like He's told me it's gonna be. I asked Him for it. He's going to give it to me. He's got to.

I've been here pretty close to a year now. I read a whole lot of books on wisdom and knowledge or the Bible. I don't get off into TV like some guys. They just lust on some woman that come on TV. It hurt me to look at TV since I turned my life over to God because it look like every commercial is a lady has got to show herself in the six ways. Boy, what the world going to become. People base their life on TV. And they ain't going to have no room in the penitentiary in twenty more years. No way in the world. Right now, you can see all the laws that's done wrong. In Houston, they busting police officers like they busting common criminals.

You see God doing His work. A while back, they could never understand a whole bunch of birds dying all around the police station. Nowhere else, but just all around the police station. That was a message for them. They find nothing but a whole mess of them little tweety birds dead just around the police station. There was thousands. Each one of them going to become one of them tweety birds if they don't watch theirself.

I know, because as soon as them tweety birds died, that's when all these police started getting busted. You see, God sends signs to people.

The police is not bad people. They're supposed to be here for the good, but they not for the good. They here for the bad. They here for the take, the money. The take.

When I first got put in jail, when I would look at one of them lawyers, it would turn my stomach. I knowed they disliked me, but I liked them. I liked to joke with them and talk to them about Jesus and try to get them to turn their life over to Jesus.

As soon as you start talking to one of the officers here about Jesus, he cut away from you in a hurry. He don't want to hear that. Sometime I'd be tripping on myself and say, "They are the devil's servants." They hate to hear the word "God." Everyone I met, they don't want to talk to you about God. Even the preacher here, he don't want to talk to you about God.

He'd rather joke and clown around. I don't see him. He come in and be in the dayroom with us, and he won't talk. He'll talk to the religious guys, but if it get too far down into the religious, he'll ease off. He'll light his pipe and he's off.

What does he want to talk about?

Bullshit. You know, just regular old ignorant stuff. Laughing and talking. Playing dominoes. That's what he's off into. So I just don't bother him that much. A whole lot of things I didn't understand in the Bible, I would try to ask him, but he didn't want to talk about that. Now I get a Christian paper from an evangelist group and they really preach the Bible. They tell the truth of the Bible.

The chaplain doesn't know nothing.

You remember old Schultz from *Hogan's Heroes*? "I see nothing. I hear nothing." That's him.

I ask him something and he says, "I don't know."

He comes to the door, he comes in the recreation room when I used to go out there and play dominoes. That was such a waste of time I quit it completely. I even bought my own set of dominoes because I didn't like them to cheat out there with marked dominoes. If they had guns, they'd probably shoot each other. He comes down there, and if he can't give you spiritual help, he'll play you a game of dominoes.

Some of the men told me he isn't interested in spiritual help, that he doesn't want to talk spiritual things.

If the person is very sincere and pursues it, he will talk to them. But 90 percent of the time, he'll bring you a little pamphlet on how to get a certificate saying you've read so much Bible. A lot of guys have done that, the ones that get on the God trip. He'll talk to them. He'll bring down a little religious newspaper and he'll say what it's like and sometimes somebody asks him, "If they take me over to the death house, will you go with me?" And he says, "Yes, I'll go with you. I'll be there." This kind of thing.

I asked him that one day. I knew he was coming. I says, "Chaplain, if they ever take me to the death house, will you go with me?" And he says, "Yeah." I says, "And you'll be there with me?" And he says, "Yeah." I says, "Will you go with me when they take me to the stretcher?" And he says, "Yeah." I says, "Will you go in my place?"

I had him going, and I threw that monkey wrench in there.

We're supposed to be punished and rehabilitated. Shit. You can't rehabilitate a man in a place like this where all he does is get madder every day. There's no program to rehabilitate them. On Death Row, you can't go to school, you can't go to the gym, you can't go to the movie, you can't go to church. These other people, they go to the gym, they go to movies and church.

The chaplain, he's about the sorriest bastard on the farm.

There's a man on Death Row who was raised in a church where he was the preacher, was raised in the church with that man. And he gets to Death Row and it's "Well, how do you do. Good to see you." Then the man's dad had TB or something like that and they had to amputate his leg. The dude was going crazy worrying about him. He ain't going to get a letter from his mother 'cause she's too nervous to write. His brother, I don't know why, wouldn't write him. He didn't have no way of knowing what was happening with his dad. For a week or two he said to the chaplain, "You know my mother, you've known her for ten or fifteen years. Would you call her and see what's happening with my dad?"

He said, "I can't do it."

Now how could that hurt any TDC rule?

Every time you talk to him, he talks to the major. It's true. You can't tell him anything.

They have a priest here, but I've only seen him twice. I believe he might be a nice man.

Here on Death Row, there's a lot of youngsters. They're not used to this kind of life. They should have a chaplain who should come. A lot of them need help, mentally and physically. If you don't have a well-trained person that can come to you and try to help you deal with your problems, ain't nobody else going to deal with your problems here on Death Row. Everybody, they trying to take care of their own business.

I haven't seen hardly any other people down here except us and the guards all week.

That's it. Guards, they work eight hours a day. They have a chaplain and he comes once a week for a few minutes. When he comes, he just talks to two or three and then he leaves.

I asked him quite a few times, "Say, chaplain, there's a lot of people here that need help and they need to talk to you. Maybe you can help them deal with their problems."

He said, "I got population that I gotta take care of. I got thirteen hundred people over there that I gotta see."

I guess I can understand his position, but I don't think it's right.

Doesn't the priest come out here?

No. They don't have no priest that comes on here. We don't go to church.

I had been worrying about my four kids, what they was doing. That was my loneliest time of the year, and I was in here where I couldn't get no drugs, no dope, no nothing to ease my mind. I said, "I'm just going to go completely off of it."

And I said, "Why don't you just kill me?" I was talking to the Lord. I told Him, "Why don't You kill me? I can't take it no more. You know my heart. You know I love You. You know I want to love You. You know I'm trying to get out of here. Lord, why don't You do something? Why don't You just kill me? You can't do it, that's why."

I cussed Him. I done everything in the world. I really did. And then in the second breath I'd tell Him, "Lord, you know I didn't mean that, but I just can't understand. What do you want me to do? I'm around here all the time and I can't figure it out."

I'd been off drugs then for about three months. I'd smoked a little grass in the county jail, but other than that I hadn't had any hard drugs. When they first brought me in, I had an abscess on my arm right here where I'd been shooting it. And this vein here was cut. I've had my arm swell up about that big.

You're lucky you didn't lose it.

I've never had hepatitis. Never have. And I've shot with every kind of rig that's ever been. When I was in the federal joint, we used to shoot with one of them twenty-one-gauge needles, about as big as one of them that you take blood with. You put it down an eyedropper and you pump it to get the stuff in there. When you pull the needle out, that blood just spurts everywhere. Lord, let me tell you, I have been there.

Anyhow, it was Christmas on Death Row. That's when my heart was hurting real bad. I got to thinking about my mom and them.

My mom wrote me letters that she was having turkey and wishing that I'd be there with them. I said, "Boy, ain't that a bitch. They're telling me they wish I'm over for Thanksgiving dinner and they know damn well I'm here on Death Row. Ain't this something else."

I was going nuts. I wanted to do something to myself. I wanted to die. I didn't know what I could do. I would get on people's cases. I was real moody. They'd come by there and if they gave me any trouble at all, I'd jump right in the middle of them. I'd tell them, "Hey, get away from here," or way worse.

What was your worst?

I wouldn't even want to say. It was real bad. I'd cuss them out. Call them what I thought about them. I said, "You sonofabitches, you're done already. Got me down here on Death Row. What the hell do you think you could do to me any more than this. Shit!" What could they do? They couldn't do nothing.

Christmas was a special time down here for these people. It can't really be special because your loved ones is not with you, but they had a real big dinner. They brought us off into the dayroom and let us get our turkey or ham.

I got back to my cell and I looked at all that and it was good-looking stuff. And I couldn't eat it. I got sick. I got to crying. And I hurt so bad because I knew my family was out there and I knew they was probably on welfare. I didn't know if they was going to have anything. And what could I do? I'm in here. I just got disgusted and I wished I had enough nerve that I could kill myself. "Lord, if You could just give me enough nerve." And I couldn't get it.

I wrung my head and I asked Him, I said, "I want this damn shit. I want it!" I was wanting to eat, but my heart was hurting and I knew that I had done this to get in here, but I couldn't have no way to ease my mind. Not for what I'm in here for, but for the people that I'm making suffer while I'm in here. We went to the dayroom the next recreating time after Christmas. Everybody had *beaucoup* money. Usually, you can only draw thirty dollars twice a month, but on holidays you can have more money and you can buy different things. So everybody was trading this and buying that and I was mad. I didn't want nothing and nothing I had didn't please me. I told them, "Shit, I don't want nothing what you got over here." They was trying to sell me different things.

It wasn't nothing, Diane, but that I was mad I was in here and I couldn't be out there with my people. I got to thinking about my mom.

This guy was there and we was playing dominoes. I was beating him and I wasn't doing nothing. I was just throwing rocks around and beating him bad. I didn't even have it in my mind to try. He was getting mad too. He acted like he wanted to get up and I said, "I hope you do. You'd just give me a pleasure if you would get up." And he wouldn't say nothing. I won't call his name now, but he's about six foot one or so and he outweighs me by a hundred pounds. I'd a beat him plumb to his knees and he knew it. He wouldn't say nothing. So then I said, "I don't want to play no more dominoes anyhow."

I went over in the corner and I started thinking about it and I said, "Well, I ought to go over and whip that sonofabitch anyhow. He didn't have enough nuts to get up. I ought to just go whip him my own self."

I wasn't thinking about the time. Just about then, the guy came in there and said it was time for us to go rack up. Saved by the bell. "Saved by the bell"—I said it out loud.

Everybody said, "That sonofagun is crazy."

"Saved by the bell, saved by the bell." I kept saying it out loud. That guy knew exactly what I was saying to him.

I got to thinking about that later and I thought, "Boy, ain't this one a fool." I heard him talking about me down the row, saying this was just like me. I wrote him a note.

I said, "Hey, Mr. Sonofabitch. Don't use my name in none of your conversations no more. Forget that I ever lived. I wish that you'd die." I just wrote it on there and signed it.

Then I hollered for Shorty Walker, the floor boy. I said, "Hey, Shorty Walker, I want you to carry this down there to that guy." I handed it to him. He looked at me and went down there and carried it to him. I put my mirror out there to where I could see if he's gonna give it to him. I wanted to be sure that he got it. He got it.

It got way underquiet. He had been running his mouth about nine hundred miles an hour before that, and then he got real quiet about it and he didn't say nothing.

The next day, we was at recreation again and he said, "You know, you misspelled a word." I had called him a "supercilious sonofabitch," or something like that, and I think that's what I misspelled. And he said, "You misspelled it and I believe you used it wrong, too."

I said, "Did you understand what it mean?"

"Yeah, I understand."

So I went out and I was mad at that cat for two or three days.

But it wasn't him that I was mad at, not really. But that got them all off my back.

Were they afraid of you?

Yeah. Because I went crazy on him.

I got mad at my mother because she was telling me that she's wanting me home. Well, damn, I thought, don't tell me that, mom. I'm hurting enough as it is. I wrote her a letter and I said, "Goddamn it. You're killing me. Live your own life. Ain't I done enough to you already? Why do you even write me? I wish you won't even write me. You're driving me out of my goddamned mind. I can't stand it."

Then she wrote me another letter back and another letter, and I kept getting letters every day, every day, every day, every day. And I was getting where I didn't even want to read them. I'd just throw them away.

I said, "Lord, I can't take much more of this."

It was around the fifteenth of January at that time. I had made my mind up that I was going to either do one thing or another. They was either going to turn me loose—and I knew they wasn't going to do that—or I was going to make them kill me. I said, "I'll make you kill me then."

I had that in my mind. It wasn't that I didn't have enough nerve to do it, but that I couldn't make it come about.

That was January fifteenth and I had a plan.

I am a very, very careful planner about doing anything that I do. I don't care how big or what it is. If I get ready for something to happen like this, it's going to happen just like I want it.

But I couldn't do nothing with it. I said, "I'm going to make them kill me," and I couldn't do it. I could not do it. It would just seem like I was going to light a cigarette and I had it in my mind, but it just wouldn't light. My hand, it wouldn't work for me. My hands wouldn't work. I couldn't make nothing do nothing.

I said, "Lord, there's something wrong here. Why don't You just show me what it is that You're wanting me to do?"

And I cried. I cried and I cried and I cried. So much so that in my head, right there, it was hurting. Have you ever cried till your head hurt?

It was hurting me so bad that I just bumped my head on the cement and it felt a lot better because it wasn't hurting as bad.

I said, "Man, I just got to know what's going on." And I said, "I'm crazy. That's what wrong with me. I'm nuts and it ain't going to make no difference. Shit, I'm just nuts."

I kept thinking. I said, "Well, it can't be that I'm nuts. If I'm nuts, how in the hell am I going to know I'm nuts? Crazy people don't know if they're nuts. I know I got problems. I got a bunch of problems. But what can I do? I can't do nothing about them. I know this."

I'm thinking about 990 miles an hour in my mind and I'm wanting to get something. I was going to break a glass. I said, "I just can't do that. I can't take my life. That would be about like blasphemy if I take my own life. I sure can't."

See, I'd been reading my Bible all along this time and superficially I knew what it was saying to me. I'd heard about the Spirit and I thought all those people was liars.

I had been up now for these two days and two nights, the fifteenth and the sixteenth, and it was the seventeenth coming around. I had been reading the Psalms, the thirty-fourth psalm, the sixth verse is what I was reading there. It said, "The poor man, he cried out and God heard him. And He saved him from all of his troubles."

Well, boy, when I heard that, I got to thinking in my mind. I said, "Well, by God, don't You see me as a poor man? Look where my heart's at. Look where I'm at right now, Lord. Don't You know where I'm at? You don't care about nobody. You ain't even real."

I got mad and I was throwing shit in here and I was mad, I was wanting to do something. I was wanting to kill something or anything. I was crazy, I was an insane man. Boy, it was old Satan. I was jarring him loose is what it was. I didn't know it then, but I was jarring him loose.

I got to reading and I think it was in Romans, I can't remember exactly where it was. I got it marked in there. It said, "If you read this here and listen to my word, hark not so hard to the provocation."

Well, what in hell is he talking about? "My heart ain't hard. Here's my heart. Listen to what I'm saying to you." And I was crying bad then. When people came around, it was time to eat and they were putting plates in for me and I don't want nothing and they was writing down in their book, "He don't want to eat," and I thought they'll probably carry me to the hole. Maybe I'll get a chance to knock one of them in the damn head here.

This was about six that morning and I done accepted the death. "Well, hell, I'm dead. That's it. Forget it. I'm ready." I done accepted it. I'm ready to die. I said, "By God, You're going to do something to me," and I couldn't get no peace and I'd cry and I'd beg and I'd plead. "Can't You see where I'm at? You know I love You, Lord."'

And you know what? I was truthful to Him. And He knew. He knew. He could tell that my heart was true. But I said, "Well, it can't even be true. There ain't no Holy Spirit," and I cried, and I went over there and I sat down on my shitter and I just had my head down and I said, "I just don't understand none of this. It don't make no sense. My folks' hurting and I'm the only one that's done it. I'm the only one. Why do I have to be the one? Them people is crazy. I've got me, they don't have to worry about me."

And you know what? I wasn't even caring about me. And I think that's what done the trick. I don't really know, I'm not sure. But that's what I think.

I said, "Mom, I just wished you wouldn't worry about me like that. I'm giving you one more chance."

I picked that Bible up and I opened it one more time and I come to James in there and got to talking about how you live like this and if you do like this, that you got to act like that. I'm reading James and I didn't know what I was reading. I had no idea. I was reading it all, word for word, but I couldn't figure and I got to keep thinking, so I turned back to Psalm 34. Something was striking in my mind about it. I got down towards the last where it says, "The righteous will not be distant. He's not going to leave you. That He'll always be with you." And I said, "Well, I guess He's always been with me, but I'll just read it again." I turned it over and I read it, but I was reading and I didn't know what I was reading. When I got down again to that sixth verse and it said, "And the poor man cried out and God heard him and He saved him out of all his troubles," well, I felt light-headed.

I felt light-headed. It was like nothing I'd ever done. The most best dope that I'd ever done in my whole life. I was just light. My feets is like on fire and I was just—I don't know how it was. It was just, I said, "That's it, that's it. I know now."

I couldn't say nothing. I didn't know how my mind was. I was thinking, "This is the Holy Spirit. This is how it's supposed to be. Yeah. I know now."

And I was in limbo. I was in a daze. I was cussing every other breath and anyone on Death Row will tell you that. You won't believe it. I was cussing every other breath, every other word that come out of my mouth was MF, SB, GD. For three days and for three nights, I never said one more cuss word. And one day, it was Shorty Walker, he said, "I don't understand. You ain't said no cuss words."

And it dawned in my mind and I said, "Well, I'll be dad-blamed. I haven't even said a cuss word." I had not known that I didn't say no cuss words. It was more of a habit to me then, more so than me breathing. Ask anybody on Death Row here.

I've gotten back now to where I will cuss every once in a while. Nothing like it was. But for three days and for three nights, I didn't utter a word whatsoever. I had no thought in my mind that I was even thinking about anything that was bad.

God was telling me then, "Hey, this is how it is and it can be like that if you want it to be like that. Do you want to live like that?" And He just let me have that for three days.

From after that, I have never wrote another letter out of here that I didn't write about the Lord. I said, "I'll never do no more wrong. When I get out of here, I'll do the work for you and that's all I'm going to put my life in forevermore. If you don't let me out, that's good. If you keep me in here, that's good. I don't care none. I'm just satisfied to be just what you want me to be. And just let me know anytime what you want and I'll be right there to do it."

From then on to this day, I don't have no troubles. I don't have no problems. I don't have anything. I know my family is there. My daughter is pregnant and I wrote her and I wrote my mom and I said, "Mom, see if you can figure this out right here," and it can't worry me because God's taking care of it. He's going to. I just look on the other side of everything now. I see the ashtray and that's God. Everything to me is right. It's right. I look on the other side, I don't care how dark it is. It don't make me no difference. I look all the way through. "Well, yeah, that sure is pretty." It ain't raining outside, this is picnic time. Don't resist it, because God's way is easy. "Just take my yoke, it's easy." You know what? When you yoke up with Him, He'll pull right there. Sometimes, I'll get too far with Him, I'll try to drag Him. I'll drag Him because I want to hurry up. And He has to slow me down.

What did everybody say to you?

They thought I was nuts.

They actually thought I was nuts because it was a more miraculous change than ever I've known. You know, I have shot heroin to the point where I was beamed so far out of my head I'd nod. And before I could get the rig out, I was knocked plumb out. When I'd come to myself, the rig would still be in my arm.

I was more higher when the Spirit come on me than I have ever been on any kind of drug.

I've tried to do that again. I went over the same things to try to be high again and I can't. I'm happy, but I don't have that flash like I had. I don't know if you ever get that high again or not. Or maybe that's how heaven is going to be, because it was close to heaven. It was real close. It really was.

But maybe you don't get that no more.

It's sparkling, like. It's more. It's everything and nothing ain't nothing. Everything is just everything. It's no thoughts. It's everything and nothing don't mean nothing. Everything you say, you don't care.

Heroin ain't like that. You got bad thoughts and you got good thoughts that's all mixed up. I have shot cocaine when I was overseas till my eyes cried blood teardrops out of my eyes. I would be so hard, I have seen my heart just pump, pump, pump out of my shirt whenever I'd hit it. I'd go into convulsions. And I'd set there and fix me another shot. I've been that high on the uppers and I've been that high on the downers to where I just fell out.

I went over it again and again, and it won't work.

Trying to get it again.

It won't do it, it won't work. And really, I've tried hard. I think it's because, they say it's faith, and I haven't gotten this far into it yet.

But from what I'm knowing, I'll never be like that again until I drink the blood, until He drinks that blood with me.

Searching that Bible out, that's all I do from sunup to sundown. I do it as long as I can see. That lighting, you can't see in there very well. I write letters. I got a knot right here on my finger from writing letters. I write anywhere from fifteen to twenty Christian letters out of here a week. I never write one letter out of here to nobody without me telling them about Jesus Christ. If they want to get a letter from me, they're gonna know something about Jesus Christ in my letter because I ain't gonna write it otherwise. I write everybody like that. Some people write back. I get letters and they tell me, "Oh, that really blessed me, made me feel good. Boy, that gives me power."

You'd be surprised at the people that does write me over here. I got an uncle that I haven't written yet. He's an evangelist, a doctor, I don't know what-all in. He made the highest grade that's ever been made at the Baptist seminary in New Orleans. He's a professor or some kind of something. I haven't seen him in eight or ten years. I'm writing him a letter now. The president of the Jesus Christ Lift-Up Organization, which administers to thirty-some countries, the president, she writes me all the time. There's one old lady, Boo Strange, she's out of Dallas, she's eighty years old and she writes me letters. Boy, you talk about being spirit-filled—this woman is really something.

That's how I spend my time, writing those different people.

I'll pick out somebody's name. This guy, he got busted for something and it says where they're sending him, so I write him a letter. Sometimes they'll write back, sometimes they won't write back. After I put it out and say how it is, then I've done what I've supposed to be done and the next of it is up to him.

My dad won't write me. I've wrote him many letters, but he don't write me. I write him every week anyway. I don't care whether he writes or not. Let him write when he wants to. I write him. What I'm doing is I hold my end up, that's the only end I got to be responsible for.

He'll have to come around. I'm hoping that all this right here is going to bring my people close together. Bring them into unity to theirself, where mother is not against daughter-in-law and father against son. I hope God will use me in this way. I'll be glad to die right now. I tell Him, "Bring me the needle right here. I'm ready for it." I've been dead for years. And right now, I'm as happy as I have ever been in my whole, complete, internal life. Ever.

I've learned me a bunch of words too. I got me a dictionary. You would be surprised how much I've learned. I know I might sound kind of lower down to you, but when I first came in here, I was dumber than a day-old deer. I didn't know nothing about anything. Spelled everything wrong. Shit. But I've been looking them up, I check them words out. I got time and I just do it. It makes it count. It's like if you have to be inside 'cause it's raining outside and you can't play, do something to figure out something where it's gonna do something good for you.

I had been trying to get my life figured out, what I was gonna do. The Friday before I got picked up, I told this girl, "Well, honey, it's about time for me to go back to the penitentiary again." I didn't have no idea they were gonna have me here for Death Row. I just knew in my mind that it was about time for me to withdraw back into my little safety, where nobody wouldn't get me and do something. I mean, I was seeking something within prison that I thought it was a safety, a love or something. To be sure that I was secure.

In prison, they would feed me. Hell, I was sleeping under bridges sometimes and I didn't know what to do.

As far as working, I'm as good a worker as you ever think about in the whole world. But each time I got out of prison—and it's been four times, this was the fourth one—I find myself getting right to the same rut again. Them deep ruts, they just going right back to the same place again.

I figured it all out now how it is. And I will get out of here. I know that. God told me so this morning.

He did?

Yeah. He's telling me that this morning. To cope with this down here, you just can't resist it. If you resist it, it will get on your nerves.

They feed fairly well down here. I'd say pretty darn good. Now if anybody would hear me say that, if it was a whole group of them overhearing and I said that they fed good, they would grumble and carry on. It wouldn't make a darn to me anyway because I tell them, "Yeah, they feed me pretty good."

I'm not gaining any weight or anything like that. I've lost a little weight since I've been here. But it's not because of the food. I've thrown away food every day. It ain't real good, but you get plenty of it.

The worstest place is the county jail. When they put you in the county jail, that's the worstest place. That's way worse than Death Row. The county jail is way more terrible than Death Row ever was.

How?

Because you have riffraffs—that's what I call it. Riffraffs, in and out. They're going in and out. Whereas at Death Row, you have the same neighbors all the time. You know they're gonna be there and you know they ain't gonna do nothing, and if they borrow anything from you, they gonna pay you back. In the county jail you got somebody who's mad because he comes in and he's drunk and puking all over the floors and everything. It's pitiful in county jail.

But Death Row, Death Row ain't bad to me. Everybody, they see it how they see it within their mind.

I'm finding out more about Death Row every day.

Death Row has really just brightened me completely, because I've slowed down enough now that I realize that all of what is is really not there. It's only been an illusion of what I thought was.

I found the Lord when I come down here. I knew that it was always in me, that little thing that said, "Don't do this and don't do that." It makes me know now that He's always been with me all the time. I feel that He's got something He's really training me for, a special job. What it is, I don't know.

Before, Death Row was a bad and dark place. People think that on the street. My folks, for instance, they think, "Well, this is really a terrible place to be." That it's dark and dungy and gloomy and damp.

It's not anything like that at all. It's a state of mind, that's all it is to me anymore. If you resist it, then it's nothing gonna be happening but putting knots on your head and pain in your heart. That's all it's gonna be.

And if you accept it?

If you accept it and go right along with the current that's flowing, you come out victorious every time.

There's nobody that I have any hard words with since I've been down here on Death Row, none whatsoever.

I see them, they fight and carry on and stuff like that every so often. Not real often, but every once in a while the anger will rise in them. But I ain't never had a bad word with nobody. I talk to everybody. Everybody that come by, if they don't talk to me, they better get away from my cell because I'm going to talk to them. I tell anybody what I think. They never bother me.

It's like I be walking around in a little protective shield and nothing can't bother me.

It's not that way for most people.

No, indeed it ain't. It wasn't like that for me either for a long time.

When I first come down here, I was really worried about everything that was going on. You know: like how my folks is gonna be taking this. That was my main concern, always. As far as them killing me, I ain't never had a worry about that.

Really?

Never have. Truthfully, I have never worried about these people killing me one bit whatsoever. 'Cause I done been dead for thirty-four years anyway. It don't make no difference if they did it. They wouldn't be doing nothing but burying me, you know? I'm serious.

Now that you're alive, wouldn't you hate to have to see them do it?

Sure. Now that I'm alive, it don't make no difference because I'm just as happy right here as I would be if I would be in the Taj Mahal Hotel.

Of course, I'd like to be with my family, where I could help them to gain the peace of mind that I know, that I thought people was lying all these years when they said they had it.

Then I would lie and tell them, "Yeah. I've got it too."

But I was ashamed. I thought they was crazy, actually. But then I wanted to have that for myself and when I couldn't get it and I knew I was trying, I said, "These people are just lying and if I don't go along with their kick, they ain't gonna like me no more."

I was being rejected, rejected, rejected all my whole life. I just didn't have no other place where to go. Every place I'd come to, the state was looking for me for this, for that, for something they thought maybe I might did do.

If I would have done all the things that the people said I did do, Jesus Christ, the Savior, would have done took me. He would have.

I made this cross.

I got a piece of black walnut. We got some plastic spoons, and I took a pair of nail clippers and I hollowed the wood out. Then I melted that plastic and poured it down on the inside there and made those white blobs.

It looks like mother-of-pearl from over here.

After I done that, to smooth it off after this big old blob, I cut what I could with my clipper, and then I smoothed it down on the cement there. It's smooth like glass now. I bored little holes in there to fit the pieces together. You can see where it comes apart right there in the middle.

Some of them put up a front.

I've read quite a bit of the Bible. I haven't read all of it, but I've read a lot of it. I was a youth counselor for church. And I have studied it quite a bit. So whenever someone talks to me about the Bible, I know pretty well what it says in there, and they come up with some strange, off-the-wall stuff that I ain't never heard of. I'll say, "Where did that come from?" And they'll name something that ain't even in the Bible. I'll tell them, "You sure about that?"

"Oh, yeah, I read it."

"Well, show me."

And you hand them a Bible and they don't know if it's in the New Testament or the Old Testament.

They bust theirself.

Then they tell you, "I would never do this again, but if I ever catch that blah-blah, I'm going to pull his head plumb off."

So this is a case of a man that is putting up a front so people will feel sympathy for him. But in feeling sympathy for him, you got to know how much has he ever done, how many times has he ever been busted, what is his mode of speech, what is his philosophy? He is a religious man, but he wants to kill somebody.

I played dominoes with one individual who seems to be what you would call a born-again Christian. I say "seems to be" because I'm not an authority on it. I have my own religious beliefs, and I don't try to impose them on anyone else. But, by the same token, I am not opposed to a man seeking religious gratification if that satisfies his mind and eases his conscience or whatever. More power to him.

Some people think it's a game, a strategy.

I would have to agree with that. I'm sure there are some who are looking down that road to the parole board. To them it is a game. But I don't think that man is really fooling anybody but himself.

You don't resent it?

The only thing I resent is the fact that it has a tendency to get the TVs turned on an hour and a half earlier on Sunday. That bothers me a little. It's not the fact that it's religious services, it's just the fact that it's more noise to put up with.

The thing that is most demoralizing to me is the constant and incessant noise. That does more to irritate me than any other single factor.

These people that are on the God trips get the TV turned on at nine in the morning so they can sit there and watch those crying evangelists. That right there is the most nauseating thing. I would much rather watch soap operas run in reverse than to watch these hypocrites, these salesmen, these

Bible-thumpers getting up there and crying and screaming and wanting this and wanting that, and be saved, and hell, fire, and brimstone. I'm sitting there saying, "Garbage, garbage, garbage."

I got one on each side and they stand at the bars with their hands in a praying position watching it and when they say, "Let's read," I can see their hands disappear. They're getting their Bible. They thumb, thumb, thumb through their Bible.

I say, I hope this is helping them, 'cause it's making me sick.

It's those ones that are like that that don't like "Saturday Night Live" because of the sex and all this kind of stuff.

TV

Television is the Row's window on the world, and some men on the Row look out that window constantly. Almost all of them watch the news. Many watch the soaps. For some, the characters in the soaps are the only constants in their lives beyond the Row.

The choice of what program will be shown on each side's eight sets is made by the officer on duty. Sometimes he decides on the basis of a suggestion made by a porter, sometimes he puts on what he wants to watch, sometimes he listens to some of the inmates. Except for the soap opera and news times, there is never unanimous approval of the selections. People yell and scream, demanding another channel. One officer told us that the hardest part of his job was selecting TV shows. We asked about the physical work, the danger, the occasional flare-ups. "No," he said. "It's picking the TV programs."

Television is not an unmixed blessing. The Row is close to a behavioral sink: a great number of men live in a small space, and every intrusion is a further insult. The noise level, from early in the morning until late at night, is a continuous assault upon the senses. Some men are able to block it out, to concentrate on their reading, their Zen, their art; many have their nerves continuously rubbed raw—they lust for the few hours of silence in the deep dark of night.

The first two comments are by wing porters.

You don't watch too many black programs down on Death Row because most of the guys on Death Row are movie freaks. In other words, they like to watch movies. The only time, really, you can watch TV and enjoy it is when the soap operas come on in the evening—one, two, three, four o'clock. And the movies at eight, nine, ten, and eleven.

I'll just go through the 23 side and this will help you understand a little better. We got about fifteen people there that likes ball games. You got about the same fifteen people that like "Saturday Night Live" and "Midnight Special." The rest of them like movies. Anytime you put it on "Saturday Night Live" or one of those sports programs, you upset about thirty, thirty-five, forty people.

But I don't have too much trouble with them at night, because I've got them set in what they're gonna watch. I've had to open up a pacification program down there just to keep the racket down. During the daytime, they're bathing and feeding them all the time, and nobody has the time to walk around and calm them down. The officer that bathes them is off the Row out there opening their doors and he isn't in there physically with them to say, "Well, look man. Everybody else wants to watch the movie . . ." They try to pick up a sports program or two on the weekend; about every other week we'll catch "Saturday Night Live." But we don't try to even it out. We try to put the TV on the best program at that time slot.

Like last night they was all mad down there. They put on a program—there was a Burt Reynolds movie on. Anything that's got sex in the movie, they like. They got a lot of masturbation freaks in there. They're heavy. I mean heavy: five and six times a day.

These guys have formed these habits because they look at the TV and they see the sex on the TV. A lot of them have *Penthouse* magazine and stuff like that. But where you're living in your own world, in a single-man cell, and you got a TV right in front of your cell and not too much traffic, man, you just completely entertain your sexual thoughts all the time. That's about 45 percent of them, or more.

Some of these guys really get upset. Some of these guys that masturbate, they'll do this for about two hours before they do anything. They keep an erection that long and I don't know how they maintain it. But they're waiting for a good part to show—a kissing scene or something like that, and then they'll go in and have a climax. And if they're watching a movie where it just keeps hinting everything and they don't ever do nothing, they really get upset.

I kid with them a lot about it. I can't stop them from doing it and I can't just walk in there. I don't try to stop no individual from playing with himself or anything like that.

Mork and Mindy, that's popular. *Gunsmoke* is almost a prerequisite. There's 80 percent of them that want to watch sports and 20 percent of them that hate sports. There's never 100 percent agreement on any program that they can put on television. All the cells are located where they can see the TVs pretty good and hear them because they are all on the same channel at the same time.

They turn it on the best program. I don't know how they determine the best, but the officer makes the decision. To me, what TV program is on, it's not a very big deal, but to some of them it's the biggest deal in the world.

TV would be the last thing that I'd ever be interested in if I was in there with that penalty. If I wanted to stay around awhile and have some longevity, I'd have my nose against that book page or something.

It's hard for me to understand their line of reasoning sometimes.

Right now, it works on you mentally. They use the TVs, your mail, your medication. They're trying to get this prison now on a psychological basis where they work on a man's mental capabilities.

Just like one of these bosses here. We watch channel 9 all the time on TV where the movies is at certain nights. He'll come up there and maybe he'll let us watch part of the movie, then he'll change it. See what the men says. We get interested in that, he changes it again. Then, when somebody talks to him, he'll stand there—"I can't change it back." Agitate you.

I used to watch the tube a lot, but now I just like my soap operas. I like *The Doctors* and *Days of Our Lives*. Iris and Rachel. Boy, I tell you, she's really doing a job on old Mac now.

I used to say, "Mom, I can't understand how you watch that shit. It don't make sense."

She's in prison in home, see? A woman is in prison in home. I look at everybody's situation by how I'm in right here. And I realized that she's in prison in home. Well, she could go somewhere, but I mean that is her little domain. That's where she is at. And that's all she has. She has this place and she does her housework.

I said, "Mom, I wouldn't watch all that. That is plumb stupid." Well, I see right now, now I can appreciate that.

The only trouble I ever had was I got into an argument over the television.

We have a problem here with the television—and this is not necessarily a racial statement, but the situation is that the blacks believe they have a right to watch all black programs and all rock music programs. That is fine, I can understand that. But they hate western music. There was a three-hour western special coming on. Very seldom is any western music on anyway except *Hee Haw*. And me and this friend of mine had been looking forward to it for weeks and weeks and weeks.

It was about a year ago. It happened March 8, 1978, to be exact.

There was a rerun of one of these James Bond movies, we saw it four times before, and then there was this three-hour country-western special. The blacks started beating on the wall that they didn't want to hear no goddamn country-western music, so they flipped the TV over to that damned rerun movie.

And in the thirty-three months I had been here, that was the first time I lost my temper. When the floor boy come by there, I started cussing him. That damned television, if I had my way, I'd take them all and drop them all from the top floor. Because they're more trouble than they're worth.

I broke myself of watching television this last year while I was out on a bench warrant because I knew what it would be like here when I came back. The only thing that frustrated me about this prison system, about Death Row, other than the boredom, is there would be some educational television on—*60 Minutes*, say—and we'd watch reruns of Walt Disney.

There would be wildlife-type programs and they would want to watch these stupid cop shows. You'd think these people would have had enough of policemen and sirens. And you always know that the good guys are going to win. You know James Gamer is going to come back next week, and so is *Hawaii Five-0* and all that stuff. You watch television programs that are on a fourth- or fifth-grade level, and after a while it just gets so irritating. And it's always a matter of who makes the most noise.

I don't believe in beating on the bars, hollering and screaming and acting like a savage. And yet they give in to the people that do exactly that. We're just outnumbered as far as that goes. It would make me so mad, I just got so damn mad over the television, you know, and there wasn't a damn thing you could do about it.

The most frustrating thing is to lose out. They don't even vote. That wouldn't even work because if they voted, we never would watch anything on television because you're outnumbered by fools as far as I'm concerned. People just don't have any interest in reality is my opinion. They're not interested in world news. If the news didn't come on all three channels at five-thirty we never would watch it.

As it is now, say the football game on Sunday gets over with at six, and *60 Minutes* comes on immediately thereafter, then you might get to watch *60 Minutes* if somebody is too lazy to get up and go turn it.

That's the most frustrating thing: to lose out, to have to listen to that junk when you know that there's something that would be really interesting on another station, and you have to lay there and you can't get away from the sound.

I intended to bring some earplugs back with me this time, to have my brother bring me some earplugs at the jail. I knew I could get them in the jail and I was going to try to get them back in here, but he didn't get them to me in time. But I lucked out. The cell they put me in, when I lay back, I can't see that damned television at all. Before, I've always been right in front of them. I had to see them as well as listen to them.

That officer and me go round and round all the time. I ask him something and he says, "That's not my job."

Like last night, after the tornado in my home town, I was trying to find out about my wife and kids. I called him down there and I asked him to turn it to the news. He was watching *Gunsmoke*, He said, "Don't worry about it."

I said, "Look, there's three hundred people in the county hospital. There's two hundred people in the other hospital. They showed a short strip and I saw my wife and my father-in-law outside the hospital. They said they were waiting to hear from injured that are in the hospital. I got three kids. I don't know if they're dead or alive. And you tell me 'Don't worry about it.' "

"That's not my job."

The other day, we was trying to get a hold of him down there to tell him something, something he was supposed to do. We couldn't find him. You know where he was? He was up in the washroom shaving the floor boy's head. This was the day before yesterday.

He goes down in front and he talks with certain individuals. I'll set there and watch him with my mirror. He'll go over there and talk with them and pick up the *TV Guide* and close it and turn the TV to some old rotten stuff nobody wants to see. Call him over there and say, "Say, boss, how come we can't see so-and-so?"

"I just decided we'd watch this movie."

The movie comes on at eight and he goes home at eight-thirty.

The other day, I went down to take a shower. The floor boy was sitting on that bucket, just taking it easy. That boss was leaned up against the bars with his feet propped up. I got to thinking, "It sure would be funny if somebody came down and caught him setting like that." They're not supposed to do that.

I come out of the shower and was drying off. I started talking to him about this prosecutor's coordinating council that I contacted. I had their attention so they couldn't look down the hall to see if anybody was coming.

Well, here come the warden, the major and a few other people. They walked dead up behind them before they even knew they were there and the major says, "Is that all you got to do is set around like that?"

And that chair the boss was setting in and the metal bucket that the floor boy was setting on got hot real quick. Like to tore them up getting out of it.

Oh, it was funny. I started laughing. I was trying to put on my clothes and laughing at the same time. Wound up dragging my clothes down the hall. I couldn't stand it.

See, they hold watch. One of them gets back in there and sits down to watch TV. He's not supposed to watch TV. That's not his job. His job is to walk and make sure ain't nobody beating their brains out or cutting their wrist or doing whatever. But they get up there and set up in the middle, drink Cokes, and have a good old time.

On Death Row, you're locked up twenty-three hours and fifteen minutes out of every day, on the average. That's a lot of time spent in a five by nine. You get to know every grease spot and fly speck on your walls intimately. And when you're deprived of even the momentary privilege of recreation, it sometimes gets to be more than some people can take.

The major problem that I have here is the noise. I don't like noise. That's something you can't escape from.

At six-thirty every morning, the radio comes on. It's an intercom system. Even though technically they can be turned on and off in each individual cell, the noise itself is reverberated and carried quite well through the ventilation system so, in effect, you can't turn it off. You're subjected to what would be electronic white noise from six in the morning or six-thirty in the morning until approximately eleven at night.

And then there's the ever-present television set, which I, personally, have very little use for.

It's almost impossible to concentrate on anything, to give anything serious thought. It's hard to even read. You can't do serious reading. You can restrict yourself to light novels and fiction, but as far as being able to study anything that requires concerted effort, it's virtually impossible just because of the background noise. That's frustrating.

I tune the TV out. I don't use earplugs, I don't put nothing in my ears. I adapt myself. I set my mind to adapting. I get up in the morning and do my exercises. Sometimes people have to holler at me two or three times to get my attention. I concentrate on my work, and everything else going on around me I just don't pay no attention to, I don't let it distract me.

I told somebody the other night, I could adapt myself, if it came down to it, that if I had to sleep hanging by a nail, I'll adapt myself. That's the reason I'm able to function here and not let it drive me down.

Sometimes Hayter comes by and says, "Get your mind out of that cell." I say, "Why?" and he says, "There's things going on out there." And I said, "I've seen what's going on out there. That's the reason I'm in here."

Everything really makes you bitter. Watch soap operas all day and get depressed. Think, if people on soap operas are that stupid, that evil and stupid, I just had to quit watching them. I watched them for about a year. I just gave them up. Some people will give up a visit out here to watch that soap opera. I can't understand that. Some say about some girl that's in it, "That's my girl." All right, if you think so. One of my neighbors had a visit, the first visit he had, and he cut it forty-five minutes short to make it back to see that. That kid is crazy.

Little old speaker with three knobs on it. Call it a radio.

They got three radios down in the picket stacked on top of each other. They set one on the black station, one on the rock stations, one on the country station, and walk away. If they have a rain storm or any kind of atmospheric condition that butts in with them stations, then we got to listen to all that static in our house. And it happens all the time. If you notice when you go out, there's about six antennas around this building. There's always something wrong with the radio. Usually something wrong with the television. So I try not to watch any television and listen to the radio when I can. Walk around or play around in the cell.

Death Row is oppressive. There's a feeling of helplessness. You're locked up. You have no recourse. There's no appeal. You're there and there's nothing you can do about it. There are very few diversions. The diversions that are available are distasteful—I don't care for TV.

From eleven-thirty in the morning until three-thirty in the afternoon, there is nothing on the TV but soap operas, with the exception of the noon news. There are very few things that I consider to be quite as asinine as a soap opera.

There are a lot of soap opera fans there.

I would say that it's the lesser of two evils. They can either sit on their bunk and pick their nose or they can watch the soap operas. That's probably a poor parallel, but that's the way it is. I, personally, don't have any fingernails, so I read.

Filling Time

Summer is hot on the Row. Ellis is in east Texas, and summer in east Texas consists of long, humid days, and nights in which the temperature doesn't drop and the humidity doesn't go down. A wet towel might refuse to dry for days. Air moves in the cells of Death Row because the building's central exhaust fans pull it through the pipe chase and suck it up to the roof. Some inmates have small fans. Sitting in front of the fan can be almost cool if you don't move too much.

Summer is a time in which there is more light, a time in which there are more things to do.

One man had two coffee jars with spiders in them. Each jar held a different kind of spider. He had collected them during outside recreation; if they were discovered during a cell shakedown, they would be taken away. The man was on his knees, gently swatting flies with a loosely rolled newspaper. "They don't eat dead things," he said, "so I got to knock them flies out. Just stun them, put them in the jar. They come to, the spiders eat them." He had a name for the largest of the spiders. He pointed to the other jar: "But that one, that's the baddest." It was a small black widow.

On the other side, an inmate in one of the J-21 cells had two spider jars suspended from the underside of the upper bunk. J-23 has always been Death Row, so it has all one-man cells, but, until recently, J-21 was segregation, so it has two bunks in each cell. Having the upper bunk is considered a great luxury because it is a shelf to put things on. The man with the spiders there came in from recreation with some insects he had captured. He unscrewed the jar tops and dropped the insects inside, screwed the jars back together, then lay back on his pillow and watched the spiders for a long time.

Two men were growing tomato plants. They had taken the seeds from tomatoes a few months before. They had brought the dirt inside the building in small batches, hidden inside handkerchiefs or just dropped into a pocket. The planter was a piece of aluminum foil from something bought at commissary. "They're contraband," one said. "When the Man sees it, he'll take it away." We pointed out that his cell never got any direct sunlight; the plants couldn't fare very well anyway. "What difference does that make?" he asked.

On the Row, everything is used. A photographer threw away several small plastic 35 mm film cans. They are about two inches high and one inch wide. The containers were rescued from the garbage can and immediately became salt and pepper shakers for one man, watercolor paint mixing containers for another, instant coffee containers for another (for taking to the recreation room; it meant he didn't have to carry his large glass jar with him).

One man made a postage scale. The frame consisted of a ball-point pen sleeve; the spring came from the heating element of a burned-out stinger; the platform was a small piece of cardboard glued to a small metal rod; the lower tip of the rod was the indicator. The scale was calibrated on the outside with small black bands at half-ounce distances.

Cigarette and tobacco packages—particularly Marlboro, Camel, and Bugler—are folded in special ways and woven to make crosses, picture frames, photo album covers. A Marlboro pack can give four different designs. The packs are smoothed out, neatly slit (if one has a contraband edged instrument, like a razor blade, that is used; otherwise, a strip of wood from a matchbox works as a cutting edge), folded, wrapped with cellophane, folded some more, and then put into the weave. They teach one another how to do it. One man shines other men's shoes in exchange for their tobacco wrappers.

Perhaps the most bizarre aspect of life on the Row is how very rational it all seems to be. The clock is regular: recreation, showers, mail, meals, the soap operas, all occur at predictable times. The variations are themselves regular: one week J-21 gets its meals served first, the next week J-23 has its meals served first. The recreation groups rotate so each gets to go out at different times of day. On different days, the officer starts showering with differing groups—but always in order.

The only real business of the Row is maintenance of individuals who have been told they must die soon. They are almost all healthy; they are almost all young. Their job is to get through each day without going berserk. Most of them do that fairly well.

It is very different from the cancer ward. In the cancer ward, nearly everyone is under a sentence of death, but it is a sentence hated by all participants—not just the victims, but the attendants, the surgeons, the administrators. And the enterprise is dedicated to foiling the fates, to delaying them as long as possible. On Death Row, only the condemned fight the sentence, and not all of them do that. The workers on the Row are dedicated to order more than anything else. Their successes are not found in a man redeemed, a life saved, but rather in another day gotten through without incident, without trouble. This applies equally to the porters and the guards, to the chaplain and the medic. The job of the cancer ward is cooperation in an angry struggle; the job of Death Row is maintenance of a bizarre placidity.

One can spend only so much time making picture frames out of cigarette pack wrappers, only so much time going over once more the transcript or law book, only so much time reading the Bible, rolling cigarettes, watching soap operas and *Gunsmoke* and the news. There is a delicate and desperate management of spaces of time—all deeded to keeping the madness at bay.

We live in a world of ongoing processes; they live in a world of terrible pendency. They find little things that at once consume the time and hold time at a distance. Most men on the Row wear watches, but there are few calendars. Filling time is their woeful job, and the passage of time marks their miserable destiny.

Day after day is consumed filing writs, reading Bibles, watching soap operas, waiting for the mail, jerking off, manufacturing bibelots, sleeping, waiting.

For prisoners in population, each day consumed or transpired is a movement closer to freedom, and the days are counted. For men on the Row, each day is a movement closer to death, and all counting is retrospective: "I've been here since . . ." rather than "I have X years to go."

There is another difference between this place and the cancer ward: here the sentence is grotesquely rational. You can't rest in hatred of the random, the gratuitous, the inexplicable. The death sentence comes with all the considered logic and care the state can muster and accumulate. If you have a question, the state will answer your question. The precipitating event—the murder—is so far in the past that guilt becomes an abstraction. There is nothing to fix the anger upon, there is only irrelevant busyness, desperate searches for relevant facts and cases, long sleeps, noise, and days without meaning or end.

I had a spider. We call them wolf spiders. They're kind of furry and they've got green eyes. It's a little too early in the year for them to come out.

I caught one in my cell one day and then I put a cockroach in there and it was fun to watch. The patience they have. Funny thing about a spider, they look around and once they see they can't get out of the jar—I put them in a fruit jar—they start building a place to sleep. I don't know who they figure they was going to get their meal from, but they couldn't get anything unless I fed it to them. And then I'd catch another spider and I'd put it in there and it was always interesting to watch them fight.

They'll fight until one of them is dead, and then he'll get eaten by the other one. Then I got hold of a big one, a big black spider with a white spot on his tail. It had a little fang, it's a funny thing. Their fangs are sideways, a quarter-of-an-inch fang on each side. I called him Jaws because of that.

I've had as many as eight of them in a jar at one time, but not with this Jaws, because he didn't let anything stay in the cell, in the jar with him. I say "him," but it was a female because I saw her lay eggs.

I'd put spiders in there and watch her battle them and cockroaches, flies, whatever. It was just something to pass time. When I left, I gave my spider to my neighbor and he finally wrote me last year and said he had died. But we kept it almost a year.

It was just something to do. It was interesting to watch the patience they have. I let it out, I let it crawl in my hand, I'd be gentle with it. You could put a pencil down there and he'd rear back in the corner and bare his fangs and I imagine he could probably be pretty painful if he bit you.

I had a jar just like this one with air holes in it. I had it upside down on the top bunk. These spiders will build a little web at the top of this thing, never at the bottom.

She was there the night before. I know that, because I looked at her. I knew she was a she because she had laid some eggs, but she was frustrated because she had been in there nine months and hadn't had any companionship.

Maybe it was the eggs that drew the piss-ants. I don't usually leave anything open, so it wasn't something else they came for.

The next day, I reached for the jar to look at her and I looked around the neck and I couldn't see her. I thought, "Where the devil is she?" I opened it up and I opened the nest and she wasn't in it.

Then I got to looking real good and I found little tiny pieces of leg and what not. Then I noticed—my eyes, unless I wear my glasses, I can't see real close—but I put my glasses on and there was piss-ants all inside this thing.

The only conceivable thing that could have happened to her was the piss-ants just ate her and carried her off.

I make different things down here.

They got Dr Pepper cans and Coke cans, which is made out of all aluminum. They allow us to have glasses and everything in there, but they won't let us have no razor. You can take our mirrors, which I'd say are six or eight inches around, and you could take and break it if you wanted to kill anybody. I have been in the life of crime all my life and I would know how that you could harm somebody if you wanted to. Or the wire around the notebook papers. You can cut a man's neck completely off with it. But they won't let you have a little ole razor, which, if anybody came at me with a little ole razor, I'd laugh at him. It's crazy. It wouldn't even hurt nothing. But they won't let you have it because they got fools down here that will cut their arms up. Those people don't really want to hurt nothing, they ain't gonna hurt theirself. If they wanted to kill theirself, why hell! You tell me I couldn't kill myself if I really wanted to? Sure I could.

All they want to do, they want to have their little light shine. They want a little attention. And they don't care if they have to cut theirself or bang their head against the wall. They're going to get some attention. They're going to get it one way or the other.

Anyway, I take the cans. There's a sharp edge on the side of my bunk. It's a rough-like steel edge. I take that aluminum, it's a lot softer. I have cut my fingers a time or two doing it. I took the top of that can and I started scraping it on the bunk until the top of it separated. I knew that's how it's made. So I plucked that top off there. Then I took and put it on the cement floor and smoothed the rough edge off with the floor and rubbed it down with my nail clippers, and I made drinking glasses out of the cans.

I had been breaking glasses after glasses, so I said, "I'll fix that son of a gun." So I make these cups, I don't break glasses no more. They drop, but they won't break. It holds just as much as a mayonnaise jar or a jelly jar, which is what I used to drink out of. I put it up there on the bars. There's an accident every once in a while if I don't lean it against the bar when they're pouring from the outside. It will tip over because it's light. I use a holder I made for that. It'll last for a long time and it won't rust either.

I got different hooks too. I take that wire out of the back of this notebook and I twist it together and I got different hooks that I hang my toothbrush on, that I hang my stinger on and that I hang my roll of toilet paper on. And then I got a thing I made where I can hook my mirror on the bars when I can see when I shave. The light is so bad, there's no light in the cell.

It's kind of funny what a human being can acclimate himself to. It really is. I've seen the time that I didn't even want anyone talking to me, I didn't want anything, I just wanted to be left alone for my own processes.

I think you must subconsciously know it's not going to do you any good to want to be out or hope to get out.

Of course, we all have hopes, because anytime you talk to someone about the future it's always, "When I get out"—and they are sitting on Death Row. But they'll say that. I do it myself.

But as far as your living accommodations are concerned and where you are in this cell, it's a way of life that you either consciously or subconsciously learn to accept.

I'm sure this is what causes these depressions. Maybe it's a subconscious depression because you're fighting, thinking about being away from it and having some activity. I don't know.

I guess you could say that, under the circumstances, I've become content in my cell. That sounds strange, but you have to accept where you are.

It's kind of like when I got that eighteen-year sentence. I recall when it first started, I thought, "You're going to be here a long time so you may as well accept what it is and go on about your business. This sitting around moping and wanting to be outside and feeling sorry for yourself because you were stupid enough to get yourself into this position is not going to do anything but screw your mind up."

And I've seen the times, during that eighteen-year sentence and even here, to some degree, that I was perfectly content doing what I was doing.

I went into the penitentiary that time with $12 and left with $2,100 because of my leather work. I found something to occupy myself with. I've even got a little thing in here I do to make a dollar or two with.

I have never been able to draw anything in my life, but I got an art book up there and I started. Now I can draw a beautiful rose and, by golly, to prove it, I sold one for fifty cents for a card. I made a little card.

So that is some accomplishment as an artist. It's not very much, but the rose is good. I've made a couple for a friend of mine and I've drawn other things too, but what it is is just a matter of shading it around the right places. That's how I look at it.

But I don't enjoy it.

I've sent these roses that I've drawn to my mother and aunts and friends, and all of them compliment me on them. And I'm sure—well, I know—that it's a pretty good little rose. It's a single rose, but I don't enjoy doing it.

I've drawn other things, and when I get through, I look at a piece of artwork and I say, "What is that? What have you accomplished other than killing time?"

I do not have an appreciation for art, I guess. Some people can see a great deal in art. I can't. I can in a statue, but I have never seen a painting or drawing that did anything at all for me.

The most beautiful picture I have ever seen was a photograph of the earth from the moon. Now that turned me on. But that's not art—that's a piece of science.

I think it was because I thought, "That's where I am. That's where we are." You're looking at it from a distance and it is amazing. But it still is the most beautiful picture I've ever seen.

When I came in, I had a watch. It was an Accutron. I'm one of these sticklers for time. And it broke. I went crazy until I got another watch, and time means nothing in here, but it does.

I've noticed that people in here are really upset whenever the schedule changes.

Because you are so accustomed to something. You don't know what the hell is going on. If something changes, it's like a shock to you, and the slightest little thing can make this happen, and you'll hear them yelling and screaming and everything else.

Max in the next cell, he's got a little digital watch over there. He'll tell you the time to the second when you ask him, and he'll even make a point of doing it. Sometimes it even gets irritating—simply because I don't have a watch like his, I suppose.

Time really means nothing, but you are absolutely lost without a watch.

It's a funny thing. With that TV on, this radio going all the time and people laughing and talking, I can lay down at one in the evening and go to sleep just like that for maybe an hour, hour and a half. And wake up. And at night, sometimes, even with the TVs going, you'd be surprised how you just get to ignore that thing.

Some way or another, it just happens.

But now then, at eleven, when the TVs go off and the radios go off, I've lain there for several hours and not been able to go to sleep. And not particularly had anything on my mind. It's the depression.

It's not a depression like I've ever experienced in the free world. I think, really, when it gets down to it, maybe you're subconsciously thinking of the hopeless situation you're in. That's the only thing I can come up with.

Because when this mood hits me, even if I have letters to write, I can't do justice to a letter. I'll just put surface things in a letter and let it go.

Whereas if you're not in this state of depression, I'll sit down and write three or four pages and just write about anything.

I spend most of my time studying German and English. I left school when I was about fifteen years old. Most of the time I spend studying and keeping my mind occupied at almost anything. But still, you have depressing periods when you can't study.

It's nothing like a depressing period I've ever had in the free world. There is nothing in particular bothering you. It's just a feeling of "I don't want to do anything." You don't even want to think. It just gets so depressing sometimes it's miserable.

You get up and you try, say, "I'll clean house." And, of course, it doesn't take long to clean a five-by-nine cell. I mop my cell every morning and clean my toilet bowl. I let my lavatory go for a few days at a time, especially when I'm doing a lot of reading.

I get kind of particular about what I read anymore. So much of what we get in here are books that bookstores have torn the covers off, and apparently they are rejects that they can't sell. I understand that they send book covers back to the book publisher for credit. We get so much junk that I just can't read most of it. All this sex in books doesn't do anything for me. I don't give a doggone about reading about some other guy's experience anyway. But once in a while you run across good books.

The way I spend my time in here is reading law books, keeping up with the news every day, and discussing legal problems and stuff like this with other inmates. I don't take out too much time reading fiction, novels or stuff like that. I'm more or less into things that can help myself get out of here. I don't have too much time to watch TV and stuff like that—unless it's the news—because I'm trying to help myself get out of here.

I think this is one thing that's being overlooked by a lot of inmates on Death Row. They depend on their lawyers to do everything, which is okay, but a lot of people don't understand that capital punishment and being under a sentence of death is something that should be given a lot of attention to. And if you can educate yourself, try to help yourself, I think this is what a lot of inmates should do.

I sleep like a rock. I put this out of my mind. Not totally: I wake up and I know where I'm at; when I go to sleep I know where I'm at. I'm in full control of my faculties.

I could fall out on the floor and have a fit, but I won't.

I try and make a joke of it. Not really a joke about death and what this thing is, but so I can keep my own sanity without beating my head against the wall or running my hand through my mattress. Some men upstairs are constantly having a boxing match with their mattresses, propping it up against the bars, beating the stuffing literally out of their mattresses or tearing up their sheets or breaking glasses or doing something just to let out their frustration.

The way I'm able to keep my sanity, what I started to do when I first got here, was by picking up my pencil. I consider my pencil my best friend here. I started sketching, I started drawing. I started doing things that I used to do when I was much younger and out there in the free world. I used to love to draw and cartoon and come up with funny little things—jokes. I've always liked to find humor in things. I prefer being happy. I like to see people happy. I like to see people laugh. I like to make people laugh. To help them to laugh, not actually make them, but to help them.

And I got into more cartooning and drawing, and it developed into cartoons to the point that people would see it and like it, and I was here for six months before I found out that I could send out business mail. And then I started to mail it to these magazines, and I offered them to these magazines to say, "If you all like it and you want it, you can have it. It's free, just if you all like it."

I started getting checks back. And since that time, my family has not sent me any money. I support myself. I buy my own commissary, I take care of my own things. If I need anything I take care of it because I'm making a living—or I'm making money here to buy my own commissary.

Mainly, I draw horses, but I draw all types. I draw mainly horses because I have such a love for horses. They can be so loving and such. So many things happened to me when I was a horseshoer in the free world and a trainer that I could relate back to them. Remembering about something funny that happened. And I know horses have a personality. All animals have a personality.

And you always kind of wonder what goes on in their mind.

Since I've been locked up, I've come to realize what it's like. If I was a horse thinking, if I was locked in a stall, like horses are stalled all the time, what would I be thinking if I was looking out over that door. And I related to that.

I believe the psychologists would look at it and say, "Well, that's really you hanging over that stall door or cutting up or saying something or sticking your tongue out at somebody that walks by or the person that is keeping you locked up."

I have worked on that idea and I've developed horses being restrained or tied down or in a stall or having their feet worked on or somebody having to take care of them like they couldn't take care of themselves. But it's a known fact that horses for centuries took care of themselves.

And then suddenly they become owned by somebody. They end up being controlled and locked up and being told what to do and what they can't do and where they can go and where they can't go.

I have to kind of relate psychologically to these horses.

Plus, I have always been associated with horses and been working with them, so I've kind of developed up from that that everybody who gets a letter from me sees one of my envelopes has a horse head on it. And that's become my trademark, my logo. Editors see it now and they know it's mine without having to look at my name. They know my work, my style. I've been working on it over two years.

I've had one editor say, when he knew where I was, "Don't send me no more work." And then I sent him some more work, the first of this year, and he took two more pieces and said, "Fine, keep it up." Nobody minds. I've had maybe one or two letters that I've written since I've been here that weren't answered.

I like to hear from a lot of people. I like to help kids. There's a little boy in Ohio, I'm teaching him how to cartoon. He draws a picture and sends it to me, and I tell him what he can do to improve it. Then I draw my little cartoon and I say work on this here, but develop your own style, and I send it back to him. We've been doing this for months now.

I originally started drawing to give my work away, if they just published it or if somebody liked it. And from there it just mushroomed. I sent some work out once and got back ten dollars. My first money I ever got back. I said, "This is unusual. Why would they want to pay me for this?"

I do different breeds, different organizations. Not a breed of horse that I don't draw now. I got a little cookbook coming out. It's going to be called the "Cooking Cowboy Cookbook," and it's got a cartoon with a recipe. Say the recipe is for chicken fried steak. The chicken is sitting there frying the steak and the cowboy's got a bat in his hand saying, "Rider, you're next." And I'm putting out a little book on how to make your own horse-head soap, how you can put pictures out of magazines on a bar of soap. I got some Christmas cards coming out this year, and I've got a trail-riders handbook I'm doing with the University of Oklahoma Press.

I have the time. I hate to sit. I'm writing articles now. I just finished one up and sent it to the *Horse and Horseman* in California. I've been writing about bridle trails. I've written every state in the Union, and to Canada, and found out where all the bridle trails are, where the stables are. I've got boxes under my bed that are just full of information. And I'm going to put out a book called "The Horseman's International Travel Directory."

I'm doing all those things, and if they do kill me in the state of Texas, at least somebody can look back and say, "Well, he was worth something."

Do you think they will?

I can't say. I really don't know. They are so down on people that they say killed a police officer.

I'm supposed to have killed a DPS—Department of Public Safety—officer for no apparent reason. I still can't figure out why I'm supposed to have done it, but they say I did it. They were looking for a stolen credit card, an Alabama card, and they happened to see my car, and they stopped my car because it had Alabama plates. They never found no credit card, but they sure tried to kill me.

When they take me for my date, I'm trying to get the US marshals to come to take me because my girlfriend had a nightmare of me getting shot in the back. You know, you hear about the things that's happening in Houston with the cops lately.

My thing happened just outside of Houston. The dead officer was taken to Houston. It happened back in '76, when a lot of these things was happening.

Since I found the Lord, the worst vice that I have right now is cigarettes, but in a way it's used for my good also, because it takes a lot of my time to roll my cigarettes, which I roll on different days of the week. Wednesday I use to roll my cigarettes for the rest of the week, and that way I do my thinking and meditating on what I'm going to do and what the Lord wants me to do.

The first couple years I was here, I worked crossword puzzles almost every day. And I finally got burned out on them and had to find something else to do with my time. So one day I picked up a pencil and started to do a little sketching and it turned out to be nice. So I kind of felt that I possibly had a little talent and I started in drawing and I've been drawing for the last two years.

I make greeting cards and I've gotten off into doing portraits, larger painting of scenes of birds, trees, et cetera. Most of my work is with colored pencils and regular drawing pencils, and just recently I've gotten into watercolor, about three months ago. Having a few problems with the watercolors, but I'm sure it'll come around.

If there is anything good that's come out of receiving the death penalty, it's that I've discovered that I have a little talent in art so I can be thankful for that.

People don't realize what it's like here.

If they were just to go into their bathroom and just sit and be able to see a television but they couldn't turn the knobs, they couldn't control it. They have to sleep with their toilet, and they have to sleep with their sink and they have to just sit there day in and day out, not being able to say, "I want to go walking someplace for a little while," or "I want to do something else different."

It's continuously having the same walls, the same bars, the same papers, the same books. Nothing changes. Only the outside, the light. We have day and we have night, we have day and then we have night.

The programs on TV are almost always the same. The mail runs at different times and that makes things a little different. Meals run pretty much the same. One week it might come a little earlier, one week it comes a little later. But the food hardly ever changes.

The food is sickening to somebody that might be from the free world, but here we have to get used to it. Our stomachs, our systems get used to it. Men have to constantly get something to be able to digest it. Get medication from the captain or the male nurse that comes by here with some aspirin.

Men sit here, thinking about what they've lost and what they did wrong or what others said they've done wrong. Such men as myself that didn't even think they were going to get the death penalty, had no idea what the death penalty actually meant, and ended up coming here and almost freaking out. We've had kids come in here—we call them kids, anyone from seventeen to twenty-one, twenty-two—kids, really, because they just don't know unless they've been in and out of reform school. I came here when I was twenty-four. I just turned twenty-four and now I've seen my twenty-seventh birthday here.

And it doesn't change.

Only if you get moved to another cell is that a change. Or if they take you away from here for a visit or something. Then that's a change. You want some kind of change continuously—or at least once or twice a week. Recreation does not give us a change because it's the same pattern. They form a system. We leave here, we walk down to the same visiting room or the same recreation room, and play the same game of dominoes with the same dominoes. To see the same old faces.

Only if they move a man into another cell will you see somebody new.

We harp, we hash, and we talk about all the same cases. Always looking for something that might give us a clue to what we can do to get off of Death Row, to get away from here.

All three times I've gone back to Dallas for execution dates, I've caught myself running my head ninety miles an hour. Talk about anything, everything, ridiculous things, just anything to carry on a conversation with anybody.

I don't usually talk much to people up and down the tier or anyone else because I don't have the opportunity. Max and I talk, but after you've set and talked to a man so long, you know everything he thinks, or practically everything—if he's being honest with you you do. And pretty soon you bum out on him.

So I caught myself when I'd go back to jail around people and then get up in the tank that I'd just talk, talk, talk, talk. As a matter of fact, I couldn't sleep for two days once when I went up there. I'd just keep talking.

I would sit while I was talking and think, "You don't do this, what's wrong?" Trying to turn it over in my head. I knew it was because I'd been away from people so long and it was a spontaneous thing.

There's no doubt about this being a lonely place.

Although, I'm perfectly content never to talk to anyone hardly anyway. Most of them probably think I had some strange ideas anyway, but I don't sympathize with them. I've told more than one of them, "Well, if you did it, they need to kill your ass." And that's just to me simple. I'd say, "I'm not putting you down in particular or anyone else, but anyone that does something like that should be disposed of."

Some people may think the same thing about me, but I know what happened in my case and I know I had no intention of killing anyone. But I'm still not trying to put myself above them, either. Because I'm really in the same boat from the point of view of a person outside looking in. I'm just in the same boat they are. They probably make no distinction between my case and theirs. I'm on Death Row and I'm something to be shit on. And that's just about the way they look at it.

I'm a voracious reader. I read light fiction and I read textbooks, technical books, anything I can get a hold of I read. It frustrates me and it aggravates me and I feel contempt—even though it's unfounded—for the men that will lay here and vegetate.

Are there many?

A great percentage of them. A lot of the men in this particular unit are functionally illiterate. Even though they can read and write, they can't help themselves. They have no working knowledge of the English language. They can amuse themselves with simple texts, but if it were a life-and-death situation, they couldn't help themselves. They could not file even a simple writ themselves.

You don't have to be a lawyer to help yourself. You only have to be able to read and comprehend the written word. Everything in the Texas Penal Code, the Code of Criminal Procedures—all the laws are set down in books. If you can read and comprehend it, you can do things for yourself.

That's something that you need to do here. If you don't help yourself, nobody else will help you. In the general population of the prison, they have what are known as inmate attorneys. Some of these men were free-world lawyers, some of them are just like me—they read and they're aware of what's going on around them and they know how to file simple litigation in their own stead. The general population of the prison has access to these inmate lawyers and they can, in a lot of cases, help themselves. In Death Row, you don't have access to that.

There aren't any in Death Row?

You just don't have access. You can't sit down and talk with a man. Library privileges are very restricted. It's about like a multiple amputee trying to type: you have to get a pencil and hold it in your mouth.

To get library books, first you have to think back and say, "Well, I heard about a certain book. Maybe I'd like to read that. Now if I could just remember who the author was, I could order it from the library." They have an elusive will-o'-the-wisp here called a library list. On this library list there are compiled all the books in the library. I've been here a little over five months and I've not seen it yet.

How many books are in the library?

I have no idea. I have not seen a comprehensive list. And I have not seen the library, therefore I could not even make an estimate.

Legal texts are a lot easier to order, but, by the same token, it's hard to do anything with it when you get it. The text is brought up either late in the evening or early in the morning. If they're brought up late in the evening, you don't have time to work on it before rack time and lights out. If they're brought up in the morning, you're confronted with a noise problem and an inability to concentrate on what you want to work on. And you don't have sufficient time to spend in research. It's frustrating at best. If you don't know what you want, you can't find it.

I heard last night that a new list was being compiled.

As far as I've been able to ascertain, they have closed the library right now for an inventory to make a new and comprehensive library list, which will be pinned on the bulletin board in the dayroom of the recreation area. And I would venture to guess that it would probably stay on that bulletin board for about an hour and then it will be mysteriously whisked away to someone's cell, and we'll never see it again.

Everywhere you turn, you've got some kind of frustration. You have problems with the library. You have problems with medical attention. And what frustrates me more than anything is the fact that even though the state of Texas has an educational program for the inmates in general, Death Row inmates are not given access to this educational program. I don't know if the state goes on the assumption, "We're going to kill them, so why educate them?" or what the reason behind this is. I don't know.

They say it's a matter of security. The school situation is fairly open.

I fail to see why myself. I don't understand all the uproar that's made over security for Death Row. You have murderers on Death Row, granted, but you have murderers in population. You have rapists in population. You have multiple murderers in population. But because of a technicality in the wording of the law, they were not tried and convicted of capital murder. That is the only distinction. There could be no more heinous crimes committed by men on Death Row than the ones by the general prison population. So I fail to see why we're subjected to so much security.

It just seems to be the procedure. We are the ne'er-do-wells. I have not heard of any stabbings, any weapons, or anything else being used by an inmate on Death Row.

There was a stabbing there recently, wasn't there?

If so, it was before I came. It may well have happened. But I do know that in population it's a common occurrence. There are fights every day in population that just don't happen on Death Row. Now that's not to say that we're a bunch of could-do-no-evil, because there are plenty of people here that don't mind getting down. But it just doesn't happen that often.

You're locked up so much of the time.

That's true, but by the same token, the men that go out in the recreation area, there's an hour and forty-five minutes there to expend any energy that may have built up or any grudges that may have accumulated.

It's a hell of a boring place here.

I published an article in the *South Africa Citizen* newspaper and I got over a hundred letters from the people over there. And I picked out several and it's been going pretty well. I've got several people writing me from South Africa and that helps pass the time.

I support South Africa. I think that this country is really screwing them around, you know, asking those people to commit national suicide. The one man, one vote thing, that's a bunch of bull over there. And so I wrote a letter saying that I was ashamed the way this country was treating South Africa and Rhodesia and that I'd like to correspond with South African women. They put men and women in the article, but anyway it's been working out pretty well.

I read through the letters and I tried to pick out the ones that seems to write interesting letters. I'm writing to one married lady; she's fifty-five years old. And I'm writing to one lady I believe is about forty-five years old; she runs a hotel there. And I'm writing to another lady that's thirty-seven; she's a long-distance runner. She's an interesting person. She's a—I can't pronounce the term.

Afrikaner.

Afrikaner, yeah. She spells very v-e-r-r-y, so I know she's bound to have a fascinating accent. There's one lady that we've been getting on pretty good. She's a pretty good-looking girl. She's been writing me some real interesting letters.

It's easy to get by here. You just keep your mouth shut and mind your own business.

Before I left here, I kept a diary. I've been keeping a diary ever since the first year I was arrested. I kept this diary and it had incidents of violence that I witnessed. But I got paranoid. I was afraid they was going to spot the diary and beat my brains out. So I went back to the diary and I marked through the places where I'd wrote down who had been whipped and everything. I didn't mark out the date, but I marked out the things I remembered. I marked out the names where anybody couldn't read it.

Ten days before I left, I sent the diary to my mother by certified mail. The major took it out of the mail. They didn't tell me about it. And the day that I left here to go back to the bench warrant, my mother came, and that's the only thing that kept me from signing the little card you have to sign when you leave here saying that you got all your property. As I got ready to leave that afternoon, my mother went and checked with Warden Lightsy. She asked if the major had my diary. As I was getting all my stuff to leave, the major said, "I've got your diary. Take whatever legal action you want. You're not getting it back. I told you not to mail it." He told me I couldn't mail a manuscript. He told me he didn't like what was in the diary.

My mother fouled them up. If she hadn't come that morning, they would have had the diary. I would have went out and signed the cards saying I had all my property and they could have said, "We don't know anything about a diary. See: he signed." As it was, I caught them, so then they had to admit that they had the diary.

When I got back to the county jail, I filed a lawsuit against them for thirty thousand dollars. The attorney general made them give me my diary back. But I still have a suit pending charging them with fifteen thousand dollars punitive damages for taking it.

I haven't seen the major since I've been back. But I just got back yesterday. I'm not looking too much forward to seeing that sonofabitch.

Anyway, I had stayed out of all this stuff that was going on, this Ruiz case, minding my own business the whole time I was down there, and then all of a sudden as I fix to leave, they've decided they ain't going to let me alone.

So as soon as I got back to San Antonio and filed this lawsuit, I also sat and wrote an affidavit to the Justice Department, told everybody about all these beatings I had witnessed and everything else. I sent copies to the

NAACP, to everybody I could think of. I never did get any response from anybody.

I was never offered any time and I wouldn't take it now. I wouldn't take it then. Some of them say that you can come off of Death Row if you'll take life. Say to me, "You're crazy," because I wouldn't do that. My mother wants me off Death Row, they're so scared.

I tried to explain it to them that it would be more dangerous in population than it is where I'm at. I'm pretty well protected here. If I was in population, I'd be working in the fields, maybe getting jumped on, they wouldn't allow me to do my work that I do now. I'd have to go through a piddling shop or get special permission and that's just another headache I don't want to have to go through. I'd much rather stay where I'm at.

I've got a little nest. I sit in the middle of it and I work. I get up and walk around when I get tired. I even have a piece of Plexiglas.

I used to recreate, but it's such a waste of time. To play dominoes for two and a half years. If we went outside to play volleyball and get some sunshine, I'd go. But to go in the dayroom to sit there and rehash things we've rehashed for years and play the same game of dominoes got very boring and a waste of time. I could be drawing something or thinking about something else.

A lot of people, that's all they live for is recreation. "Open the door, let me out of here."

As far as I'm concerned, they can weld it shut, I don't care. I live in my nest. I have my connections. I'm not celled in, I can get out of there. I just set my own schedule, little things I can do to control my life. If I want to go to that dayroom, I will go to the dayroom. By them opening the door and say, "Hey, you can go now," and me not going, that's one of the choices I can make. I'll stay here. A little triumph. I have climbed Mount Everest, you know.

I can take a tray or not take a tray. I can shave or not shave. I can shower or not shower. It's these little things.

Some guys think they've got to do it, or some say, "Because you say I have to do it, I'm not going to do it."

About two and a half months ago, I decided I just didn't feel like wasting my time going out in that dayroom. It is, to me, a waste unless we can go outside. I want sunshine, whatever that is.

I tried to buy it in the commissary. "We're sorry," they said, "we're fresh out of sunshine."

So I drink orange juice, it's the closest I can get.

Dayroom holds nothing for me. It's just four walls with some windows in it just like this, it's no different. It's got three tables and a walking area. To me, it's just going from a small cell to a bigger cell with a bunch of other people in there. Same people I know, same people I've been seeing, same ugly faces. Oh, this is an ugly bunch.

I shower real late at night and I say, "I see all the bats and the bears in their caves." I walk by and you can't see nothing. I walk by Wolf and he's black as night, he is a black one. I say, "Smile, Wolf. I want to be able to see you in there."

He says, "Get out of here, George."

Your name's not George.

That's why he says it.

What caused me to get my paralegal degree and to study law was because after being here for a while, you need some help. It's kind of hard to fight ignorance with ignorance. Muscles against muscles and try to win when your muscles is not as big and strong as TDC. TDC wants you to fight them back with muscle because they can deal with you.

But inmates are more educated today than they was yesterday. Instead of trying to fight with muscles, they'll fight in the courthouse now. And some of them are winners. About fifty-fifty.

After you be here a while and if you are not the type of person that wants to stand and to be just stepped on and crushed like a common insect, you want to fight back. You know you can't fight with muscles and win. So you have to have an alternative. Try to fight back legal and win.

I didn't have anything else to do, so I started studying law. It cost me five hundred dollars to take the course and I had to buy all my law books. That was another thousand dollars. I had the money to do it.

What I do is I help and teach the inmates that want to learn what I know about the law. I let them read my law books and help them do their legal work. I have a typewriter and some of the newest law books that come out.

I'd say about 30 percent of the inmates on Death Row are really off into law, studying law. And I'd say about 50 to 60 percent of them are off into this religious thing. And there's a few, like say 10 percent, that just sit around and don't do anything.

I wish they'd come and give me a date and get it over with. I'm sitting here in limbo waiting for them to come.

Why?

It's moving one step forward. I'm sitting here and other guys would dread it, but I don't want to be gone one day to miss my mail. I've been sitting here two and a half years and I'm not leaving Death Row. When I get the date, I'm just going to be temporarily misplaced or displaced—I'll be right back. I don't want to leave in the first place if I can't stay gone. I don't want to leave and be gone for a while and then come back. It's just going to be like reentering hell all over again. 'Cause I'll get used to the quiet or something.

So I want to go and get it over with and not miss none of my papers or my files that I have. I have a lot of material, and that has taken me a long time to accumulate. I don't want to misplace it.

The most miserable in there are the people that don't do anything. You can hear them, their comments. They set up there and watch TV all day long. They have nothing to do. They don't read or work crossword puzzles or do anything constructive or anything to keep their mind active.

Because they don't have the discipline or the talent or what?

Probably don't have the discipline. I'm sure a lot of 'em's got some talent. They haven't found it. Haven't tried. I'm forty-three years old. It took me a long time to find mine. So it's hard to say. A lot of the guys in there are a lot younger, so maybe it will be years before they do. I think I've kind of reached a point in life that I'm just tired of that type of life that I've led and things have got to be better than what I've been doing.

I don't get off into other people's business very much, so I'm not really too good as far as saying what other people do. But I do hear guys asking for books. I know that there are a lot of them that are reading, but there's a few that live down there around me that don't read. And I know what they do because I hear them—soap operas. I try to blink that all out.

Since I've started on my art, I can do that. I can pick up a piece of paper and start drawing. I don't hear the radio. I don't hear the TV. And I don't hear all the talking and hollering.

Was it always so noisy?

No, it wasn't. When the other building tenders were there, it was a lot better as far as quietness and control. Most of them that were the type to make noise were probably scared to make noise. I've lived under both conditions even when I was in population. I lived on a unit that didn't have the head-strumming, and then I've lived on a unit that did have it. And the noise level is considerably different.

Is it worth it?

No, it isn't worth the head-strumming. I'd rather have the noise than the head-strumming.

I won't say that everybody got their head strummed didn't deserve it. Some do. But there was so many people that got their heads strummed that didn't deserve it. See, the penitentiary is so strange because one person can say, "Did you know this about so-and-so?" And it might not be true. Then they take it for a fact, and then this person is whupped behind it. This is kind of standard in the penitentiary.

This is the reason I keep to myself. I don't want anybody to know my business, and I don't want to know anybody else's business.

You get where you can block most of it out. There's constantly a low hum going on all the time, except for the occasional person that screams out. You can just block everything else out.

If you're reading something that's dull, it's totally different. The least little thing just pulls you back because you're not really interested anyway. But if you're reading something that's pretty interesting, you can just block it out, concentrate totally on what you're reading.

I read anything I can get a hold of. I read fiction, nonfiction, newspapers, whatever. I enjoy reading.

I am bored. I am bored of things that happen to all of us. I want to do something that is going to benefit me or profit me or benefit where I'm at. I'm going to try to help it if I can.

Everybody's bored because who wants to be just in a place where you can't run around? Just being locked up every day, it'll make you sick. Make you tired. I mean, some of us can't sleep at night, got so much to think about. Every day that goes by, you just think about it. Can't do nothing about it.

I wish I had the things that I had before. I might have put myself in this position, I don't question that. I just question why we are not treated equal, why we are not treated like human beings.

I think about my family, I think about my little girl, I think about my little boy. But I can't see them.

It's really hard for me to just think about it and can't really do nothing about it. But as time goes on, I have to be strong. I can't let my mind play games with me. Because it's me that I have to take care of. Nobody else going to do my time, nobody else going to tell me, "Well, I take your time for you." Nobody else going to do your time for you. You have to do it your own way, your own time.

Mostly, I just stay in my cell and read my Bible and try to make out with all the noise and stuff. Most of the things I think about is going to church sometime and trying to understand why the people don't want us to go to church over here anymore, and do some of the things we want to do. Other than that, there's nothing to do but stay in the cell and wait until your appeal come up. Wait mostly for them to hear your case in Austin, I guess. Nothing too much to do in here.

It's just not no good for your health or nothing. You don't get exercise or recreate enough. A man could lose track of his mind in here if he don't watch himself.

All of it is hard to me. It's just all hard. Just being away from life is hard. Seeing all that goes on over here, you just try to cope with it. It's just mostly a bunch of sick people run this place and they don't care nothing about you or want to care nothing about you. They just figure you're just a whole bunch of criminals and find you guilty of something you never really did. They just want to satisfy this society, I guess. That's about the only thing I know.

I've been here about eight months now. Same thing go on every day. Just try to keep out of trouble most of 'em, you know. Mouth could get you in a lot of trouble.

Just try to live with life, the way it come.

3. Dying and Killing

To Kill a Killer,
Is that not a Crime, like any other?
To take a man's life
To Avenge the Death of Another.
And what happens to the Family of a Man sent to Die?
Do they go on the same or do they just set and Cry?
Capital Punishment is Murder!
It's the taking of a Human Life
It's done without any Consideration for Mothers Children or Wives
Crucifixion Hanging Electrocution
Gassing and now Drug Injections
Ain't it funny our killers are the people you look to for Protection.

—Donnie Crawford, execution number 569, April 24, 1979

The Death Penalty

A fair number of the men we interviewed believed in the legitimacy of capital punishment. Most of those who endorsed it said it should be reserved for special circumstances, such as killing children or killing innocent bystanders. None of the men we interviewed who were in for killing children or bystanders said that.

It isn't surprising that some residents of the Row should believe in the death penalty. Most of those men are lower-class Texans, and, among free lower-class Texans, particularly whites, the death penalty is fondly supported. There is no reason they shouldn't continue to share the attitudes of their own communities.

They do argue the specifics—the applications, the fairness of trials, the adequacy of representation, the political ambitions of prosecutors, the greed or laziness of attorneys, the long years of waiting—that is, the unfairness of it all.

Some said it was perhaps unreasonable to ask anyone on Death Row what he thought of capital punishment. We asked why, and they said it was difficult for them to imagine that outsiders could consider their answers as being offered in anything but a state of acute self-interest. "Whatever I say about it," one man said, "you got to wonder if I'm telling the truth. If I say I'm against it, period, then you can say, 'Sure he's against it, look where he is.' If I say I'm for it, but just for certain kinds of freaks or something, then you can say, 'Sure he's for it for them, but he's making sure the definition doesn't include people like himself.' I can give you what I think is an objective opinion, what I think about it. I think about it a lot. But can you listen to what I'm saying objectively?"

Not everyone on Death Row claims innocence. Most, in fact, do not. We didn't meet anyone who thought he deserved to die by lethal injection, but we did meet many who thought they did deserve some measure of serious punishment for what they had done. Many of those who had never been in trouble before and those who insisted they had never done any criminal work before felt they had done something that seriously scarred the community, something that deserved some measure of social revenge.

We didn't meet anyone on Death Row who thought the administration of the capital sentence was fair or equitable. Most were aware that if they had a better lawyer or had copped out early on, they would have received a life sentence or a sentence of fixed years. Some could point to fall partners who were serving fixed sentences, who might even be out and on the streets before they were finished with their appeals and put to death.

A porter who had been in prison most of his life said, "I don't know how anybody can think it's fair. They've got some guys living right across the hall in population that's done worse things than a lot of people on Death Row. We've got several that's got off Death Row living down there across the hall. They got life sentences. You can line all of these people up and you couldn't tell the difference by talking to them or anything else."

The question isn't one of guilt; no one seriously denies that most men on the Row are guilty of the charges. But so are many other men in the penitentiary guilty of similar charges. The only difference between the two is that some are on Death Row, waiting to die, and some are out in population, serving their time.

I won't be popular for saying this, but I believe they should have something—if not the death penalty, something to stop people who can't be stopped any other way.

But I'm a first offender. They don't have any idea what I'm going to do tomorrow because I don't have no past record. I have a perfect military record. I got in trouble in high school, but I never got in any serious trouble.

They have some down here been in trouble and in the penitentiary all their lives. One said he had been in prison the last eighteen Christmases. He's been out in that time for a month or two at a time, but he's been in eighteen Christmases. He cops out to his killings. "I did it and I'll do it again." If what he's saying is true, there should be some place for him. Whether it's the death penalty or not, I don't know. I'm going to be against it because I'm on Death Row.

Were you not against it before?

For certain things. For certain things I wasn't. Killing kids. To me, little kids are what make the world go round, and anybody do anything to hurt a kid, somebody ought to do something to hurt him.

A lot of people feel that way.

There's a lot of kid killers around here.

Are there?

There's three or four cases where a kid was killed and they didn't try for the adult that was killed, they tried him for the kid 'cause a jury is going to get them. And they get them.

Anybody who can hurt a little kid who can't hurt them, or hurt a woman who can't hurt them, or anybody who can't hurt you, there's something wrong with you. Just to intentionally hurt somebody who can't hurt you back. To take a little kid's life before it even starts. If it was my kid, I'd kill him without even hesitating about it.

Wouldn't help the kid, though.

No. It wouldn't help me either.

Are men who are in for that disliked the most?

No.

Do people know?

Everybody knows. Everybody knows from the newspapers. Capital murder is a subject that comes up in the paper, everybody reads it except a few who don't read at all. Everybody knows about everybody's case or knows what the case involves: what kind of murder, whether it was a robbery, kidnapping, rape, or cops. They have one down here who's famous around the world because he's accused of putting potassium cyanide in a pixie stick and giving it to his kids on Halloween. He's famous. He's famous all over the world because of that. He's not disliked. He's friendly to everybody. I lived next door to him for about six weeks. The bosses are even friendly to him, which is unusual 'cause they're pretty hard on some people. Some of that ole Texas redneck sticks out.

What kind of people are they hard on?

Rapers, baby rapers, and stuff like that. Or people who've been in trouble down here. One inmate threw glass in the boss's face, so no boss will do anything for the man.

Some of these people have no right to live, in my opinion. They should be disposed of because they are a threat to other people.

If you sit here and listen to these people giggle, for instance when the reporter was executed in Nicaragua, they giggled like a bunch of children. I am dead serious. You see something on the TV news program. For instance, there was either a Cambodian or Vietnamese woman was holding her baby, a little two-year-old child, and crying, and a large number of these people here hollered, "I'll be good," and "He he he," and giggled, like it's funny. It's sick.

The reason I think some people should be put to death is because of what they done, because I can see their mentality. I know with a mentality like that they'll do it again. I feel sure they would.

If I said I don't believe in the death penalty, it would be self-serving, because here I sit and I'm practically at the front of the line. I would feel that my viewpoint is really prejudiced.

It sounds strange, but I believe in capital punishment. I do. If it's applied the way it's written, and if they are sure beyond a reasonable doubt, as the law states, that the man is guilty.

I think it should be applied for all crimes against children because that has been a pet peeve all my life. A child is defenseless. That's all you can say about it. And it just irks me.

I don't want to get gruesome, but I can think of some things that I would do to anyone that ever did anything to my kid. Because my kids are number one. That's all. And if somebody does something to them, they're in trouble. And, therefore, I can see why other people would be mad at the individual that was convicted of killing their kids.

Well, this is fine. But what if this individual didn't do it? And then what if they go and kill this individual and then find out he didn't do it?

Say that the person is guilty. Would you apply capital punishment for a child murder or anything else?

Any situation where a man does not have to kill. In a robbery, where the store owner grabs a gun—this, in my mind, changes it. See, the man knows when he reaches for the gun, he knows the other man's got a gun, and this changes it. I'm not saying that this man, once he kills the store owner, should go free. No. This is not right. But I am saying this should not be a capital offense where both people had a gun.

Now, when a man goes in and kills another man and then takes his money, yeah, that's capital punishment there. It should be imposed.

There's a number of guys here that feel there should be a death penalty for mass murderers. But I can't condone that. I feel like that you can't have half good or half evil. I don't feel like it works like that. I feel like there is no conceivable crime that would justify the state's taking a life. I just can't see it.

Don't get me wrong. I also feel that it's not right for anybody to take a life. Me. You. Anybody. It's not right.

I feel like no person should take anything that he can't give. Anything. It's believed that only God can give life. So I feel like only He is authorized to take life.

I simply cannot condone the death penalty for any crime whatsoever, regardless of how heinous it might be. I feel that regardless of what anybody has done, there is possibly some help for that person. As the saying goes, you can turn them into a productive citizen.

Now there are some people who would be called mentally deficient where, perhaps, they could not control their urges to be violent. But I don't feel you should take those people and kill them.

There are a lot of people here who don't know any other way to get but to take. You could take these same people and teach them some way to make a living. You could teach them a trade, give them an opportunity to go to school and learn a trade and they wouldn't get in any trouble.

There is also a number of people here that are just simply victims of circumstance. They just happened to be in the wrong place at the wrong time. We've got at least three who have not killed anybody. One wasn't even there when it happened, and there wasn't any plot to kill nobody.

A lot of the people here were people that had jobs, were working, and they lost their jobs. And they ended up crossed off in a robbery and somebody got killed. That's really most of the people in here.

We don't doubt that these people, they can do anything they want to do. We always expect the worst. They feel: these people got you down here to die. And if they have their chance, they will kill you.

The only thing that saves us right now is the appeals. They have to go by the law. But I would assume that if they didn't have no appeals, they would kill you. Just as good as they convict you. There's no doubt in my mind.

That's what they call frontier justice. You commit a crime and they kill you for it.

To me, it's not going to solve anything. Two wrongs is not going to make a right, either way you look at it.

Why is the death penalty wrong?

Maybe not the death penalty. I'm saying that killing another man is wrong. Death penalty is just a word: death penalty. But the people, they put you to die. You have a man that gonna sit you in the electric chair or however the crime gonna be, he gonna put you in the electric chair and then he gonna push that button. Now, he's committing murder. He's getting paid to kill you. You're not going to know him. Even if you do, what can you do? You gonna die. But he's getting paid to kill you.

It's not wrong for them to kill, but it is wrong for you to kill. Not them; only you.

If people, whenever they first made guns, I don't know if they realized if that weapon they were making, they were putting their own life in their hands. "This gun, I made it today and tomorrow I sell it."

And the next day?

And the next day, they might get killed with their own weapons.

All this, "Lay them down and shoot them with a poisonous drug," that doesn't deter nothing. If you were to hear the conversations about lethal drugs that goes on on Death Row.

What are they like?

Oh, it's funny.

What do they say?

One of them hollered, "If they'd use heroin, I'd go on down there." You know, it's a big joke. Another one said, "Well, kill me, kill me. If you don't kill me, I'm going to go ahead and fight them." And they wouldn't kill him. Same thing as with that Evans in Alabama. He told them, "Kill me." They wouldn't do it. Now they don't want to kill him. And there's always one that says, "Kill me, kill me," and they come and say, "Wait a minute, let's talk about it."

You don't think it should be by lethal injection.

No.

How should it be?

Well, I don't like the idea of burning a man's brains out with the electric chair. I like Utah: firing squad. This is the most humane way. Because once a person gets hit, his body is in shock and he don't know he's hit. By the time he figures it out, he's dead. This is the most humane way. Maybe a little more gruesome than this other—how would you call it? I call it childish ways of dealing with a man. Put a man on a stretcher, lay him down like a dog and poison him. This isn't right, this does nothing. It's not humane, not at all. Because you're going to kill the man. The man don't care whether you kill him that way or not.

You mean he's got to hate it?

Not necessarily hate it. See, this man put another man in great fear with a gun, and then he killed him with a gun. So why should it not be the same way as it states in the Bible? If he puts a man in fear, he should be killed the same way.

The majority of your crimes are committed with a gun. And a gun is the most humane way to end a human life, if the person that's firing the gun knows what he's doing. And whenever you get six men up there with rifles, there's just no chance it's going to miss.

And then again, let's take this man and take him down here and put him on this stretcher and fill him full of all these poisonous drugs. What if he don't die? They say he will, but they've never killed anybody with that drug. How do they know that drug is going to kill him? What happens if it puts a man into a coma? What are they going to do, beat on him a while?

This is not a sure way of death, they don't know the results of this. This could be the most inhumane way to do it. What if the man they start poisoning goes into convulsions and flops around for an hour or two before he dies?

This is my objection to it. Now cyanide—cyanide works. When they had this Guyana deal, it proved itself pretty well 100 percent effective. But they don't want to tell people, "We're going to shoot them up with cyanide." Cyanide is a terrible poison.

What are they going to use here?

Sodium pentothal.

Isn't that just to put them out? That's not the poison.

They said that a massive dose of it combined with some ultrashort-acting barbiturate would be used.

I've messed around with drugs. During my junior high and high school days, I took massive amounts of barbiturates. They never killed me. I've gone through surgery two or three times and they had a hard time knocking me out then, too.

So, I don't know. All this IV stuff with conventional medicines just may not work. If they're going to do it that way and they're going to poison somebody, use cyanide. Cyanide is poison without a doubt.

When you go out—at least me—to rob somebody, you don't realize that you could end up shooting him. I mean, you have no intention whatsoever in the first place of killing anybody. Most of the guys here, they had no intention. I've talked to many of them, and they had no intention whatsoever of shooting anybody. That's just the way it came down.

You want to know something? In my opinion, most of these guys along the Row, they're not what you call hardened killers, hardened criminals. They're not. Matter of fact, most of them are like me: they're first-timers. Like—have you talked to J——?

Yes.

That's ridiculous.

Holes in his brain.

Right. I cannot see how the state could rationalize taking his life. The man, he actually has no idea that he really did anything wrong. I mean, he has no idea. Something else: he has no idea that he is on Death Row.

Doesn't he understand it?

No, he doesn't realize this. He actually feels like he's doing time. He says, "As soon as I get out of here, I'm going to do this," you know.

He told me he was going to see his fiancée.

Yeah. Right. Oh, you talked to him. I cannot see how the state can rationalize that.

But then again, they tell you that the death penalty is to deter crime, which is a lie, you know. I mean, yeah, if they execute me, it's true. I will never commit another crime. However, executing me is not going to stop that fellow out there from going down to the neighborhood store and robbing him. Executing me is not going to stop some dude who's out there in the streets, got a wife and kids who are starving. That's not going to stop him from doing something to feed his wife and kids.

The human body has a strange habit; it likes to eat. When a man gets hungry, he's gonna eat regardless of what he has to do to eat. If it's any way at all possible, he's gonna eat. He's gonna do something so he can feed himself.

They say, "We kill you, maybe this man here won't do this."

The idea of the death penalty being a deterrent is so full of holes. How is it going to be a deterrent when you can go up and ask anybody up and down this Row, "You knew there was a death penalty. Did it stop you from getting caught?" "No, I had no plans on getting caught." How's it going to be a deterrent to a man who's doing his damnedest, his best not to get caught? It doesn't work like that.

All the death penalty is—and they should say that it is this—is a form of revenge.

It's nothing but for revenge, and, on top of that, it is premeditated murder. State-sanctioned, true enough. But it is premeditated murder. You gonna send a man down here, you gonna be planning on doing him in for anywhere from five, six, seven years, and when you go over there and you do it, like with the lethal injection, you gonna have everything all set up on a nice little clean silver table. Nice little sanitary setup, you know, with IV holders running through it and with three guys there to push it.

Clean.

Very clean. Now tell me that ain't premeditated.

They don't look at it like that. "Oh, no. No, no, no, no. This is the state performing justice."

Justice for who? Killing me is not going to help the victim. It's not going to help his family. It's gonna hurt my family. I mean, for all I know, they execute me and my daughter or my son, he could grow up with extreme hate in his heart and go out and do something totally ridiculous. Call himself getting even because they killed me. It's totally irrational, that's what it is.

I feel that things are gonna get better. I seriously feel that if within this state, well, within the United States, if they can hold off executions for three, four more years, I feel like the people will possibly realize that they serve no purpose and that there should not be any.

You know what the view of the country is right now.

It's running two-to-one in favor. I read the latest NBC polls. I can't understand that because no later than last year, it wasn't that high. I can't understand why it would increase like this considering that the latest FBI statistics say that crime has gone down.

Maybe part of it is a reaction to the sixties. More conservative. It's not just "kill the nigger" anymore.

No, no. It's everybody now.

White boys are going to get those tubes.

I can appreciate the equality side of it anyway.

I have never believed in the death penalty. Never. I grew up on the streets and I guess I have always known that it was there. And in this state, with the exception of the one-year moratorium that they had, there has always been a death penalty. Always. I came up the hard way: hustling here, hustling there. And from the time I was just a little kid, I've been on the streets and I have known people that come in and out of the penitentiary. I realize, and I have always realized, how fragile a man's freedom is and how fragile human life is.

It's very fragile. I've seen people get killed just because they happened to be sitting in the wrong place at that time. I saw a girl get blew completely in half with a shotgun because she happened to step into a door at the wrong moment.

People say it probably makes a person callous to grow up like this, but it's not true. It just puts a man in a position where he understands what reality is. A person that grows up down on the streets and knows what it's all about every day, his number-one thing is that he wants to get away from it. If he can't get away from it, he wants to be damned sure that his kids can get away from it. I have always had no intention that my children will grow up on that street corner. I'm sure that my parents didn't have that intention either.

I just happened to run across some of the fellas. "Well, let's go to the pool hall and shoot some pool." Drank a couple bottles of wine and from there it was, "Hey, we can make some money doing this."

But, strange as it may seem, I had never been arrested before this case. Not even a traffic ticket. No juvenile record, no nothing. According to the statistics, I was a saint. Of course, I'm not saying that I was an angel. I have did a lot of things, but not anything really serious. I never had really been much of a lawbreaker. Never did any burglary, never did any theft.

I guess I had a lot of opportunities that I never did take advantage of. I could have gone to college on an athletic scholarship, but I wasn't really interested in college at the time. So I went through the service. And then I came here.

There is no deterrent value in the death penalty as long as it's set up as it is right now, where you take somebody out at midnight in the presence of only a few select people and you kill him. Now if it's really for deterrent value, then why are the politicians and prison officials and all these other people that are pro–death penalty afraid to put it on national television at eight at night? I don't know that that would be a deterrent either, but if there is any deterrent value in killing someone, the person that you're trying to deter has to see the effects of what you're trying to deter him from. As long as you keep it hid, it's just an abstract concept rather than reality. But if you see somebody dying . . . however you kill him, whether you throw him off a bridge or whatever, maybe it would strike home. But as it is now, there's nothing to it. You read about it in the paper the next day. You go to bed at night and the next morning read that old so-and-so was executed last night. Big deal. None of the drama was involved. I think it's all a bunch of bullshit.

If they would use the death penalty for what it's really for—revenge. What they do makes me so mad. I can understand them saying, "Max, we're going to kill you for what we believe you did 'cause that was a sorry thing to do and you took that guy's life. We're going to take yours. Now kiss my ass."

I can understand that, because I got a mother and daughters out there, just like everybody else. If somebody hurts one of my daughters, I want that sonofabitch dead. If the state won't do it, I'll do it if I can get hold of him. It would be hypocritical of me to say I'm against the death penalty.

But what I am against is the fraud in the way it's carried out. And also I'm burned up that people with a million dollars or so can get off where the rest of us can't. There's no doubt in my mind that if I had $500,000 I'd walk out of here. I wouldn't be back here this time. That's justice. Money talks and bullshit walks. That's what it's all about.

Do you think money helped Cullen Davis?

Cullen Davis will never see a day in jail.

He'll see a day in jail. He's not going to see a day in prison.

And I can't think of anyone that deserves the death penalty anymore if he's guilty of that, if he killed that little girl. I can understand him killing that bitch and the old football player. He was just doing what come naturally.

But the kid . . .

That kid was innocent. A twelve-year-old kid. I'm a little suspicious about all this plotting to kill the judge. But the point is, if it had been me in that situation, I'd be right where I am today. The only reason he's not here is because he had the money not to be here. That makes a mockery of all the rest of us.

Somebody told me he spent two million dollars.

I imagine he paid that much to Racehorse Haynes. I wrote Racehorse Haynes a letter and I said, "Say, you've been making money off these people. How about giving a poor man a break?"

Didn't get any response.

There is nobody that should ever have the right to take nobody else's life. Nobody. The murders that I've committed, I didn't have no right. I wouldn't have any right whatsoever to have killed anybody. That doesn't exclude anybody. God has that right. God don't even kill nobody.

If a person has mental problems, he needs to be in a mental hospital. If a person is just an out-and-out vicious and dangerous person, don't let them back out into the free world. That's the way I feel about it.

If the person is a good person but committed a crime at the spur of the moment, what they call a crime of passion, then he shouldn't be here, because there's a 99 percent possibility he'll never do it again. It is known and documented that people that were bad, or was termed as bad, was able to live normal, good lives after their fit or whatever it was. That they were able to go back out into society.

I don't think any should be killed. I think I would put them under a category of criminally insane. I don't think there's no man should be killed. I think they should have a special island to put people on instead of letting people have to go through the trouble of killing them or be on their conscience. Put them on the island and put the stuff there for them to survive if they want to survive. If they don't, let them die off themselves.

I don't think mental deficiency excuses a person from these sorts of things. That's like saying that man up there is insane because he killed five women and screwed this two-year-old baby in the ass after it was dead. I don't think that justifies anything. There are people that need to be killed just because they were mean sonofabitches. It doesn't have anything to do with deterrence, or with morals or religions. It's the fact that the sonofabitch ought to know better.

Futures

Some men on the Row believe they will die in the execution chamber at The Walls. They are probably in the minority. When this book went to press, Texas hadn't executed anyone since 1964; when most of these interviews were done, Richard Spenkelink was still alive in Florida. The Gilmore case was special, according to men on the Row. He forced Utah to do it; he refused to pursue his appeals.

A lot of men are either working on their cases or have lawyers working on their cases. Talk is continually of reversals, new trials, commutations. Many men say they would rather be executed than have to serve a life sentence, even though a life sentence for many of them could be as little as twelve years. Some of them really might prefer dying to spending years living as a regular convict and working in the Texas prison fields or at one of the prison's industrial jobs, but the posture is, at this point, hypothetical: no one is being marched into the killing room. Someone who adamantly insists he prefers death to regular prison life might be somewhat less adamant if the choice were offered while he was on the gurney with the three tubes in place.

It is also difficult to weigh the judgment—held by Death Row inmates, porters, and guards—that the number of men who truly believe the state will kill them is very small. Refusal to accept that fate, rejection of despair, may be the only thing keeping some of those men sane. To accept the likelihood of death by execution means these spare days are only a torturous holding operation, dead time before the final death. We have known terminal cancer patients who continued smoking cigarettes that threw them into agonizing paroxysms of coughing and gasping for breath—proving to themselves, for a brief moment now and then, they were still alive; denying, for a brief moment, what their body told them was a hard fact of life.

Richard Spenkelink's death in Florida's electric chair on May 25, 1979, made the death penalty real for some men on the Row. Spenkelink was no Gilmore: he fought it all the way; reports a few days after the execution said he had physically struggled when they came to take him out of his cell. They dragged him to the death chamber and clamped his jaw shut so he couldn't even make a final statement to the press and the witnesses.

But Spenkelink's death didn't matter to everyone on the Row. Some had been sure all along that the Texas capital punishment law would be upheld and that the state would kill them. Spenkelink's death, for them, only proved that the Supreme Court had no principled objection to killing by the state. And there were others who distanced that reality: that was Florida, nearly another country.

Men on the Row do many things to dull or busy their minds. All that activity is deeded to one goal: keeping at bay the kinds of thoughts expressed in this chapter. None is really successful.

I'm not scared of death. Feel like everybody gonna die sometime or another. I know that they're gonna die. Livin' in the world with a whole bunch of helter-skelter people, trippin' out on takin' people's life anyway, you really wanna leave it anyway, in a manner of speaking. Since I've accepted the Lord Jesus Christ, I look at things a whole lot much better.

I'm not scared of dying. I feel that dying, death come to everybody.

You look at it in a different way when you accept Christ as your Savior. Then you think back on people, like when you go to court and stuff, see how they all be there looking at you. Specially when you're bein' tried on the death penalty. All wonderin' if you're really scared.

What will really be on your mind, what's on my mind, how these people's all helter-skeltered out, freaked out, more or less.

The only thing I really like to talk about is Christ. Talk about death. It don't scare me or nothin' because it's like I say: everything die. I know I'm gonna die and everybody else gonna die. The whole purpose of life probably is death.

I don't think the executing is nothing to be afraid of. Now, after the first person is executed, I imagine some of these people will get kind of upset.

I won't go along with the theory that the NAACP and some of these other groups come out with that it's going to start a landslide of executions. They said that during Gilmore and it didn't take place. So that doesn't hold hot water. Every case is an individual case. Some people have got good points of law and some people don't have a chance in hell. Probably 75 percent of these people are going to be dead in another four or five years. The other 25 percent are going to get a new trial or get life sentences or get some help.

I keep up with politics. I get a lot of newsletters. John Birch Society and other things. I read liberal and conservative stuff, though. I even subscribed to *Playboy* for a long time.

Most conservatives are for the death penalty down here.

I'm not against the death penalty. I'm not judging any of these people here. But in my own case, I'm not fighting for my life, I'm fighting for my freedom. I'm not like old Evans or Gary Gilmore. I'm not going to give up trying to win a new trial, unless the courts reverse and dismiss my case. I'll have to either get a new trial or get my case reversed. I've already had one new trial and lost it. This is the second time for me.

I have been fighting this case five years and eight months. But I'm not fighting for a life sentence or twenty years or ten years. At the punishment phase of my trial, my attorneys begged me to let them make a closing argument to the jury after the jury had found me guilty. I said, "No, to hell with that jury." As far as I was concerned, it was over with. I wasn't going to take a chance that they might make some statement that would sink through to that jury so they would give me a life sentence instead of death.

I prefer a death sentence to a life sentence for several reasons. First, I've got more of the law behind me in the death penalty case. That's because any error can't be considered harmless because there's a life involved. Also, I killed a man in Dallas before this. I was dating his wife and they were separated. He had her by the hair, was beating her in the face and I walked out and shot him off of her. I pled guilty to murder with malice in return for a five-year sentence. And I've had four other felonies. I've already discharged that murder case, I discharged it here on Death Row. Behind this case in Dallas, I had some enemies, relatives of this guy, so when I was eventually arrested, I was caught carrying a sawed-off shotgun.

Anyway, I've got several prior convictions and I know that the parole board is not going to release me. I'm thirty-eight years old. I don't have time for a life sentence. And, from my point of view, it's not just a matter of time. With me, there has to be more to life than being allowed to have three meals a day and to work for nothing. Especially in this savage system, which is the most brutal I've run across. Well, I've never been in other prisons, so I can't base it on anything but what I've seen here.

I've instructed my attorneys to use our priority rights over all non-capital cases. I'm in a hurry. I'm not willing to sit back here like I did last time for thirty-three months and wait for them to make up their minds. The judge assured me that time they'll have my transcript ready within ninety days. The last time it took two years. And my attorneys have agreed to have my appeal filed by August 31, and we're going to file our priority motion along with it.

Your case gets priority because it's capital?

Right. Most people don't use that because they may be rushing their death. I may be doing it, too, but I don't think so. But I want to find out whether I'm going to go free or die. Hopefully, I'll go free, but if not, then what the hell difference does it make?

At least if I die within the next year, my daughter is going to get Social Security. I got a $10,000 insurance policy, and I think they can draw about $360 a month Social Security. One is sixteen, the other is twelve. I'm not any good to anybody down here.

Don't get me wrong. I'm not in here to die. I don't want to die. I feel like I've got my head together because of having this time to think.

These people haven't rehabilitated me at all. In fact, they've made things a lot worse. But by sitting down and writing everything down about my life and laying back here and thinking about it, I realize how stupid I was in the past. I'm not referring to this particular case. I pled guilty to this case ever since it started.

Two brothers implicated me in this case. One of them got ten years and the other one went free. He spent nine days in jail. They are both free right now. I was in Dallas in jail on another case when I was charged with this. So when I say I'm thinking about my past, I'm not referring to this case, but all the other stupid things I've done.

I know if I'm ever ready to go home, I'm ready to go home now. I'm not getting any younger. If I'm going to die, what the hell. I don't want to live down here, let's just put it like that.

I would prefer death over life imprisonment. I would much rather be free of this. Either free in the sense of really free—out doing what I want to do, being with my family, with people I care for and love, being able to do what I want to do—or free by being dead.

I have told my family many times that they should be prepared to understand and accept my decisions pertaining to this here. If I am ever given the choice of a new trial or being commuted to life, if I have a say-so in the matter, if I have any choice, I'll take the new trial, even though that means I might get sentenced to death all over again.

If it comes down to the bare choice of life imprisonment with no parole or death, I'm afraid I would choose death.

That's only if they came to me with the possibility of life with no parole, which the state of Texas does not have—unless they've got it hidden away someplace.

If they were to come out with that, that would be more of a deterrent to crime than killing somebody. I don't think anything that they've come up with so far is a deterrent to crime because if somebody is going to commit a crime, if somebody is going to rob, if somebody has a drug habit to support and they need the money, they are going to do the crime whether they think about it or not.

I think 75 percent of the people here did spur-of-the-moment things. Crimes of passion.

I hear of cases of people out in population that have life sentences, maybe two or three life sentences, and they are suffering because they are going to be here for years. Years and years. Maybe die here.

Their suffering is worse than having the death penalty on you, because once you're dead, you're dead. You're no longer suffering.

It all depends on what your religious background is, whether you're going to go to heaven or hell or whatever the case may be. I, myself, consider death a conclusion. You're dead. You're no longer suffering. I don't believe in this hell, fire and brimstone, and I don't believe in heaven.

The dead—they're no longer suffering. They're just no longer enjoying this life either. This beautiful country to see and all the wonderful things there are to do and see and to have. I'm not talking about material things. I'm talking about mental capabilities—knowledge and such: things to learn, things to see. Things to remember.

I'll never cop to a life sentence. They'd have to give it to me, I won't cop to it. I'm not suicidal or anything, but I'd rather stay on Death Row here and wait till they execute me than go out there and do a life sentence. I couldn't do a life sentence. I don't know why, I just couldn't do it.

But a life sentence for you would really only be twelve years.

I could pull that, I think. But it would be going back out in the free world after being locked up twelve years. . . . I had a hard time the last time I was down there and that was two and a half years. I had a hard time getting situated when I got out.

I think now that they have the injection instead of the electric chair, I think I could face it. I think that's a lot more humane than the electric chair. I'd cop to a life sentence if they still had the electric chair. I couldn't face walking up to the chair and just waiting. . . . I've been electrocuted before. I stepped on a bare wire and was knocked out for a few minutes. I know what it's like to be shocked, electrocuted, and I just couldn't stand being strapped down in a chair waiting to be jolted.

But I know what injection is like because I shot dope all my life, and from what I hear, it's something like sodium pentothal they use, some cousin to sodium pentothal, and I've been put to sleep with that. During an operation when I broke my arm once. You just go to sleep.

I'm not scared of death. Death don't mean nothing. If it's gonna come, it's gonna come. Because you leave here and bam! Get in a wreck and get killed. It's something not to think about. Because if you dwell on this—

—Yes, everybody is going to die. But to have to think that somebody is going to do it to you . . .

You think about that, but then you think about how they are hurting theirself. They not hurting you.

They are hurting you, too, though.

They are probably hurting my people, but they are not hurting me. They hurting theirself.

You know, they are hurting me over here waiting on death. That's the hurting part. Waiting on death.

The real cruel and mean things what they done in here is keep you locked up waiting on death. Waiting on death. Every day go around, it come in your mind: "When all of this going to be over with?" That's how they really punish you. They know how they punishing you, they know how they hurting you.

But just by putting that needle in or putting you in the electric chair or whatever, they not hurting you that way. If they do come, I'll probably be glad they fixing me up because I won't have to suffer days in that cell.

I was kind of more prepared for it when they killed Spenkelink down in Florida on May 25 than many of the younger—or I could say less-time—guys that are here now.

I was here when they killed Gary Gilmore up in Utah in '77, I remember that quite well. We all didn't think that was going to happen. We figured somebody would step in at the last minute and stop that, but they didn't.

I had heard of Spenkelink off and on ever since I've been here. Nothing in any great depth or detail, I just had heard his name pop up here and there, that he had an execution date set and that he had gotten a stay and that his case had a lot to do with what was going on in the Supreme Court.

Now it seems to me that just about two or two and a half weeks before his death on May 25 that his name was popping up more and more. Before him, it was Evans in Alabama that was pulling all that crazy stuff of asking to be killed just like Gilmore.

Spenkelink's name came up around the first or middle part of May and we were all discussing it and everybody was wondering whether they would carry it out or what would go on. Talk was just about like it would be in the free world, except it was more of an event, something that had more of an effect on our lives than on anybody that was in the free world.

We all knew that all the appeals had been exhausted, if you go by what the newspapers and TV tell you. And we heard nothing much else about it, except when he did get the stay the first time in May. We were feeling pretty good about that, as we would feel good about anyone getting a stay.

The next thing we know, we hear that his stay has been cancelled and that he's had another date set by that crazy governor that they have down there that seems to have blood in his eyes or wants blood on his hands. Something about a campaign promise that if he was elected governor he would carry out these executions for the betterment of the general population of his state, to do his bit for law and order.

The next thing we know, his lawyers have gotten Spenkelink and a black man down there another stay. It seems to me that his execution was coming up on May 23, we heard he got that stay, and then we heard it was reset because the federal judges had decided not to rule on it or review it or even listen to it. The next thing we know is he's got another date set because the warrant is still in effect that was signed by the governor.

On May 24, we heard just before the TV and the radio went off at eleven that some judge had granted him a stay. So we were relieved. Somebody had stepped in.

But waking up on May 25 quite early, as I normally get up, I heard something about him being said on the radio, and I thought it was that he had gotten a stay. And then it became evident to me that they were talking about this was to be his day to die, that the stay had not been granted.

I jumped up and started asking questions. My neighbor to the left was a little more up on it. I didn't have my radio turned on all the way, so I could just hear other people's radios. He said that the stay had been revoked and that he was to be executed at ten, nine Central time, our time.

We were all sitting around, hanging out at the bars and talking. You could hear people talking up and down the run wondering about who would grant him the stay. I had my hopes up that the stay was going to be granted.

A little bit before nine, they started running around turning the TVs on. I don't know if it was an order from up front or from down here. Normally they don't turn the TVs on till nine, but they turned them on just a little bit before 'cause we couldn't get everything from the radio and they knew that we wanted to hear.

I had just come out of the shower. They were showering from my end back. When I was in the shower I was thinking about him, hoping that the man was still alive. And he was because it wasn't ten yet, or a little bit after as we know now.

As I was turning to walk back to my cell from the shower, the officer in the picket handling the doors asked me what station we have the TV on. I went and looked and said it was channel 11, CBS for the Houston area. He relayed word to the other side.

As I walked back to my cell, they were starting to have flashes or news breaks to the prison in Florida where Spenkelink was at. And they were saying that they were waiting to hear whether Spenkelink was dead.

We were watching ABC. I know that because two people were talking and one of them was Marvin Zindler, the "doer-of-right" reporter. He goes out and finds something is wrong and tries to correct it or finds out who to write and such. He was on the TV, which means they had changed from channel 11 to channel 13, which is a station we normally do not watch. ABC cut into that program where Marvin Zindler and the talk-show host were talking, and they told us that Spenkelink had died a few minutes after ten.

The minute we heard that, you could hear cussing in the background from somebody here on Death Row. You didn't know who it was. You didn't recognize their voice. It was just saying, "Goddamn." You could hear, "Shit . . . goddamn." Little else was said.

I remember hearing somebody say, "Goddamn, they've gone and done it."

It was racing through everybody's mind. We had heard the DA and the attorney generals all saying that once they could get one, they could start getting everybody else. That's what they were in the business for—to get us.

The guards on duty that day were real edgy after that. Recreation still went on as normal, but the men seemed to have a blah feeling.

I felt for Spenkelink's mother and sister and all those people that were there. They showed us on television all the hundreds of people that were in front of that prison demonstrating and hollering at the police, trying to stop it. So we do know that people are out there trying to stop it, that people see the wrong in it.

I was just standing there, watching the TV with my arms through the bars, just propped up, looking at the TV and thinking.

My mother called the governor of Florida numerous times and kept talking to aides, trying to get hold of the governor to find out why he was doing this. She called many people. She was planning to go but, like us, she had heard on May 24 that the stay had come and that they weren't going to kill him. So they weren't there when they killed him. My mother told me they woke up just hours before Spenkelink was killed and they were totally shocked, as I was and everybody else here on Death Row.

He's no longer suffering, he's no longer locked up. He's no longer a prisoner. He's dead. He's no longer enjoying this wonderful life we have. He's free—although it was feet first.

I've tried to understand his case. The more I found out, the more I felt—as I've heard other people say and as I've felt all along—that he was just a victim. The state of Florida wanted somebody, and they got him.

He hadn't gone out and robbed someplace and killed three or four people. He hadn't raped a bunch of women and killed them. He hadn't killed a baby. He hadn't committed a robbery. His was a case of going in and killing another man that he had been with that was supposed to have attacked him in homosexual acts. Spenkelink was not the type of man or the type of case they should have used if they were trying to build up or promote the death penalty. He was just a small fish in the sea.

When that guy Gilmore was killed, I was out in the population. The day he was killed, it seemed like my time stopped. I never knew I was going to be here then, but it seemed like my time just stopped.

I said, "If they want to just kill somebody, why don't they just send them to Iran?"

I read the paper a lot. I like to collect articles out of it. I did it in the streets. There's one I want to show you. President Carter, he's way over in South Africa trying to get somebody clemency on a death case. They gonna execute a man and he's getting him clemency way over there.

What about the people here?

There was very little reaction when Spenkelink was killed. There wasn't too much comment on it. I felt maybe there would be.

I think there will be if one ever dies in Texas, because that's close to home. I sat here and thought to myself, "Boy, I want to be here when the first one goes." Because I want to see if some attitudes change.

Now, some of these people at times treat this thing like a big joke. I have heard them make the statement, "They'll never kill us. No." After Spenkelink, I said, "Well, do you still believe it?"

They said, "Well, that's Florida."

Still walking around in a daydream. It hasn't dawned on them yet that these people are serious about killing them.

The way it affected me, it just verifies what I thought and what I've been trying to tell them: these people are serious. You can walk around with your head in the air all you want to, but they are going to kill you.

I think if they ever get the legality in Texas straightened out, they'll start getting them two or three a week. Or at least one a week. They have to get two or three a week 'cause they'll have so many by then they'll never catch up if they don't.

I have no answers to the deterrence of crime. I can hear about it and I know what's going on. I hear how people say they do things and how they would do other things or commit a crime or kill somebody. It upsets me. It makes me sick. But I have to just put on a cold, sterile-type face, you know, pretend it doesn't bother me. Deep down it bothers me. I don't want to hear about killing. I don't like to hear about death. It's something we're all going to do, but I don't think any man has the right to help another man along, or a child, or a woman. Life is too precious to anyone and everyone.

So when they killed Spenkelink, it's kind of hard to put into words how I felt. I was shocked, depressed. It was just like a giant shadow had suddenly come over all of Death Row, and it stayed there for a couple of days.

I just had to go through an execution date myself. I was getting myself prepared for it. I had done as much as I could up to less than a week before my date was to be carried out. I was within five days before I got my stay and four days before I was able to sign the papers.

The sergeant happened to come down here and said, "Oh, by the way, you got a stay."

I said, "Well, thank you for telling me."

It turned out my mother had called down here with the message and the warden had taken it and was still waiting for it to be verified, so he sent somebody down to tell me that I had gotten a stay. That's all he could tell me, that they weren't sure on all the facts.

I had just gone through it and I had gotten my papers and personal property and belongings and ideas and thoughts together. I didn't think they were going to do it, but there again, I didn't think they were going to kill Spenkelink. I figured somebody would step in and stop it.

So many of us thought it would be stopped. We had actually thought it would be stopped till we woke up and there it was. We had all felt that Spenkelink had a fighting chance still, that there was still so much to be decided by the courts, that some judge would step up and say, "No, this isn't it. Let's don't do this. Let's review a bit more of the case."

My neighbor was really upset. He was very upset because he couldn't get his lawyers to correspond with him at all.

I don't know of a single lawyer that wrote his client when Spenkelink died, to reassure that man sitting on Death Row, in that cell, that everything possible was being done in his case.

When Spenkelink was murdered, several men went to praying for him immediately. I call them Bible-thumpers or religious freaks. They weren't religious on the outside, but as soon as they got in here, they jumped on the God-wagon bandwagon.

I felt a loss. The loss of another human being that was dead from this earth, no longer enjoying it, that was here just minutes before. It's like seeing somebody in a speeding car run headlong into a brick wall. Seconds before they were alive and you couldn't do nothing to stop it, but you knew that they were headed for certain death. And it was just like you were riding with them up to the point of impact, and that's what separates you because you're not there and they are and they're dead now.

Knowing that Spenkelink was dead, it affected so many men so many different ways. I know some men who didn't even get up to watch it, some men who didn't even acknowledge it. Some men are so deep into their little world of fantasy. There were others that, there on Death Row, just took it in stride and kept going. They wanted to get out and play their game of dominoes.

These are the ones that I believe are really the cold-hearted ones, the ones that didn't care. They wouldn't care if somebody off of Death Row here in Texas had been taken to be executed—it wouldn't have mattered. They would have wanted to get out and play their dominoes.

There's some here that would like to see all the blacks taken out and executed. I know some blacks here that would like to see a few of the whites or all of the whites taken out and executed. They'd like to do it themselves. There's that kind of hatred here. It's in the air.

I asked my neighbor what went through his mind the day Spenkelink died. He said, "When I saw what they did to him, I had goose bumps all over me . . . those pictures they have on TV about his eyes, the look of fear in his eyes knowing that he was about to die. If I was to sit in that chair, I'd probably have a heart attack."

He said that he would sit there and probably have a heart attack before the switch was even thrown because he knew that it was coming. He'd be sitting there waiting for it to come, waiting for it to hit him, 'cause he knew he was about to have the shit knocked out of him.

We talked a little bit about it. He felt nothing for Spenkelink. He was worried about himself, about the fact that he had this death penalty case on him and that they might kill him.

So many people have no feelings, no compassion, no understanding, they don't try to relate to another person's feelings. That's what really gets to me down here about the way these men talk about women, the way they talk about each other, the way they talk about so much. There is no compassion. Even down here.

Down here, if a man has a tear in his eye, he is weak, he's a sissy. Somebody that needs to be beat up, killed or done away with. It really makes me quite mad.

I felt very bad about Spenkelink. Not just because I'm sitting here on Death Row, but because a man is dead. He's gone. I know how I felt when I heard about the people that died in that DC-10 air crash that day; I know how I feel about the people that died in the Jonestown mass suicide. People just getting killed all the time. It bothers me when I hear about anyone getting killed in a car accident or a wreck or shot in some stupid argument. Somebody blows the head off of somebody else. Or these cops with their throw-down guns, because they were chasing somebody and they thought he had a gun. Now that person is dead and they try to weasel out of it by hiding behind their badge and claiming that it was just an accident. You know, accidents will happen. Only he's dead. "It could have been one of us—if he had a gun."

I was here when they killed Gilmore. They just had us on the one side then. I remember how quiet it was when we heard. You could hear a little bit of profanity in the background and the disgust. "I knew they was going to get him," or something like that. When they killed Gilmore, it hit me more than Spenkelink.

Gilmore—there was a man jumping up and down, screaming, hollering and cussing the judges to their faces and saying that he wanted to die, to go ahead and do it. He'd much rather have death than to serve in prison.

He didn't want to live in their prison. He didn't want to be under their rule from then on. He wanted them to give him death.

I have to think the man really didn't want to die, but he wanted them to make a move to show their hand. And they killed him.

He probably didn't want to live in prison and that right there he was telling the general public that most men fear living a life in prison with no hope for parole more than they do death, because death is something they have never experienced before, and many feel, as I do, that it's just the end, the conclusion.

But Gilmore let the public know. He was saying to the public that we on Death Row would much prefer death to life without parole in prison.

They didn't like Gary Gilmore. They think he just took the easy way out, the coward's way out. In a sense, I can see it.

They felt the same when David Lee Powers was here on the Row. He's one I never could quite figure out. He was the one on Death Row that they had to force-feed. I think he's still in Rusk State Hospital or over at The Walls.

The man is highly intelligent. He's deep in his thoughts. He wrote a great deal of poetry. I used to read a lot of it and we talked a lot. He's very much against the establishment.

The thing I couldn't understand was his being so much against the establishment but still giving his life up, be willing to starve hisself to death.

The Man, they still get their wish in the end, you know: his death.

You should fight them all the way instead of giving up. Other Death Row inmates wrote him letters: "This is not the way to go. Not the way to do it. It's the coward's way out. It's yours to decide."

When —— was saying he wanted to die but he wanted his execution televised, a lot of them didn't quite see where he was coming from. They thought he was crazy and pretty well disliked him for saying it because it would look bad on them. The way —— explained it was, "Man, I'm guilty. I did it. They want to kill me for it. It's what I got coming. Let them come on and kill me, but I want 'em to televise it."

It's one thing for a person to sit there and condemn a man to death—but then to have it shown on television?

If it's such a terrible thing, you shouldn't have it.

Right. They wouldn't want it on TV. You wouldn't want your son or kids watching it, so why have it then? It's the old double standard.

I'm not sure I'm going to get a reversal. You can never be sure. They do it the way they want to do it.

But I feel that if it comes my way, if they say, "It's time for you to go," I'm not just going to let them walk me in there. I don't think no man is that strong. He crazy if he just walking down and set in the electric chair. He crazy. Regardless of how pretty it looks painted yellow or green or whatever. I'm not going to set in it. I'm not going to lay on no bed and just stick my arm out there and tell them, "Here you are, go and kill me."

I fear that after I've gone through all the procedures and they still don't reverse my case, I'm going to make them shoot me. I'm not going to let them stick no needle in my arm.

You don't have your choice of where you want to die, you know, but you do have a choice in committing suicide. And that's what that is—suicide. If you lay there.

I'm not saying a person shouldn't be punished if he killed someone or sent to some sort of mental institution. But killing them, it's not going to solve nothing.

I don't know how much that man get for sticking that needle in a person's arm, how much he get for pulling that switch on that chair. But it's not worth it.

You take a man, you throw him in one of these little cells, and you keep him here for years and years, and he has no idea whether he's going to be executed in the end or not. Just the waiting, I feel that is cruel and unusual punishment.

Of course, I feel that capital punishment itself is cruel and unusual. But the Supreme Court ruled that it wasn't. I would like for them to rule, not on the punishment itself, but the mental agony that one has to go through while he's waiting to be executed.

You sit around and it's day in, day out. You got no idea what's going to happen to you. You can't make plans for the future. That probably doesn't sound hard to some people. I'm sure a lot of people, until you're in this position, can't understand what it is, you know, to say, "Next year I'm going to do this. On my son's twelfth birthday I'm going to do this for him." Until you're in this type position you don't realize what not being able to look forward to something means.

There's no help for it, but it works on you day by day.

Like sometimes I catch myself sitting around thinking about, "When I get out I'm going to—" Then *boom*! "Hey, you might not get out. You can't say that."

I go into bouts of depression periodically when I get to thinking about it. Mostly, I try to keep my mind off of it, which I can't do. But you try the best that you can. There's not a whole lot you can say about it, because it's more or less of an inner thing. It's hard to put that mental agony into words.

I wish I could say that I was prepared for death, but if I did it would be a lie, because in my personal opinion, there is absolutely no way that one can prepare for it. Because death is the ultimate. To the best of our knowledge, there's nothing after it. In Zen Buddhism they say that you'll be reborn in forty days, but there's nobody around to give you that guarantee. If one could prepare for it, if one knew that there was a life after death, if there was such a thing as reincarnation, it wouldn't be so hard to accept things. Accept death in itself.

I realize that, as the saying goes, from the day you are born, you're dying from that day on. But most people don't think of it like that. Most people, they sit around and they say, "Sure, I'm going to die, but not today, not tomorrow. Maybe sixty or ninety years from now, if I'm lucky. Then I'll die."

But when you're in my position, you say, "Well, wow, maybe, just maybe I'll see the trees bloom next year. Maybe when the robins come back, I'll be prepared to see them." That's really how you think.

I used to have a cell and you could look out the window and you could see the trees as they bud in the springtime. And then you'd see the leaves and stuff fall off them in the wintertime. You sit there. "Wow. I really hope I see this again."

You think in extremely smaller terms. You don't think in terms of longevity. It's more or less just one day to the next.

And when you get off into a position like this, well, it's my personal opinion that you're never more aware of life until you're close to death. That's my personal opinion. And believe me, I am very aware of life. And I hope to go on living it as long as possible. But if it don't work out like that, well, that's the way it goes. I'm a firm believer in that, when my number comes up, I'll go. Whether it's here or out there.

But that's always after the fact. Somebody dies and you say, "His number came up."

Right. Well, I got in that habit when I was in Nam. You know, like if you get involved in a firefight and there's all kinds of shrapnel and rounds flying by you and you say, "If my number comes up, I'm gone." But at the same time you realize, by all rights I shouldn't have lived through that. And you actually begin to believe that when your number comes up, you go, and not before. You can look at some things and say, "Hey, no way was I supposed to live through that."

When the guy on the side of you doesn't.

Yeah. Right. I guess that's why I got in that habit. And that is one thing you never know: when your number is up. You never know, you never know.

But here, anytime that they take you back and sentence you to an execution date—it's normally thirty days away—and within that time you really wonder: "Wow. Is my number up? Will I be here on the thirty-first day? Will I see the sun rise that morning?"

I've had execution dates set on me twice. I'm still here.

The death penalty don't affect me that much. I'm not worried about being executed. The only time it really bothers me is, I get depressed sometimes because of the mail situation. I get depressed when I see my parents suffering because of this crime that I was involved in and the death penalty that I'm sentenced to.

I'm punishing my people because the court's punishing me. And that's not right. They haven't violated any laws, but they have to be put through all of this because I violated the law.

Is there any way to avoid that?

Not that I know of. I can't really say. This waiting and waiting and waiting. The courts have plenty of patience because they go home at night. They see their kids.

Somebody doing a five-year sentence or ten years or even a life sentence in Texas, they know that the man is going to come home. He has a chance of making parole. But they have no idea with the death penalty. We might be executed. If they start executing, it could just snowball and everybody could go faster and faster.

But we don't know. Maybe they won't, and maybe they will. You never can tell. The executions could start next month or they could start next year or they could never start at all. We have no idea of knowing. We're just waiting.

And day after day, seeing the pain it puts your people through to have to see you wait . . .

I can wait. I think I can wait here for ten years. And be all right. But the pain it's putting my people through makes you want to do something about it, and there's nothing I can do.

Just sit here and wait.

These people here, they don't care. They don't care. I feel they just as soon kill you and get it over with.

I read a lot. DAs are saying it's taking too long. What does that sound like? He wants a man to just die, you know. If he violated his rights or crossed him, railroaded him, it don't make to him no difference. I feel that they feel that a crime has been committed and somebody got to pay for it.

They want publicity for their career, that's what I think it's all about. I might be wrong. I don't know if you have ever set off in a trial, all through a trial and listened to some of the comments that a district attorney makes. He don't know anything about this person personally. But then he gets up there and makes comments like he been knowing him all his life.

I feel that if Texas ever start executing, they're going berserk with it until somebody puts a stop.

I've talked to two or three of them that will readily say, "I'll never get out." But the majority of them, even the ones that got this death penalty and can get two or three more, they're talking about, "I'll be home by Christmas." They said the same thing last year and the year before that. The only people they're fooling is themselves. You ask them why.

"I don't know, I don't know."

They're just fooling themselves.

Just before my case got heard in the Court of Criminal Appeals, the Supreme Court ruled and upheld the constitutionality of the death penalty.

Was that Jurek?

Yeah, Jurek. That was a real shock to everybody here. When they had knocked it out in '72, they said it was cruel and unusual because it didn't give the jury enough leeway. In our opinion, the current system was set up the same way. We thought that the jury didn't have enough leeway the way it was set. If you're found guilty, then the jury goes out and they decide whether you are or will be a continuing threat to society, and whether you intentionally caused the death of this person. If they answer those questions yes, they have no choice but to give you the death penalty. We felt the Texas death statute would be knocked down because of that. But it wasn't, you know. And that sent just about everybody here into a shock. "Wow. What is the Supreme Court doing? This can't be happening."

And for all the guys here, I believe that did away with all the illusions right there.

First time a lot of them really thought they might die?

Right. We were all under the impression that the Texas death statute would be totally knocked down. Matter of fact, that's what all of our lawyers were thinking, too. But it didn't work like that. "Surprise!"

Then my case was heard and it was affirmed in November. It really didn't shock me. I felt that I should have got a reversal, but what I said was, "Oh, the hell with it. Fuck it. Big deal."

That's the way I take most things. If there's something that I can't change, I try my best not to worry about it. What's that: *que será, será*. That's the way I try to take things. I feel like, why waste time worrying about something that's there that you can't change. What you do is, you move on to something else, something that possibly you can change, you know. It has helped me retain my sanity so far.

There are murderers in prison. There are rapists in prison. There are arsonists in prison. There are murderers doing life sentences, many of whom were tried for capital murder. For one reason or another—whether it be plea bargaining or just blind luck leniency—they escaped with a life sentence rather than the death penalty.

I don't think that the death penalty in Texas is a valid form of punishment. I don't think that it deters crime. It's a gambling proposition. There's a fifty-fifty chance involved. If you secure a conviction for capital murder, you have two choices of punishment: life imprisonment or the death penalty.

Something that galls me greatly is the situation that we have in Texas known as plea bargaining. It was involved in my case. The prosecution, rather than go to the expense of carrying out a trial—which is usually protracted over at least a thirty-day period of time involving a good deal of expense to the state and to the taxpayer—they will offer life imprisonment. To plea bargain in Texas, you must waive your right to appeal. When you sign the waiver, you have life imprisonment. You go to TDC with no right to appeal, you have signed away your rights. I think that's an atrocity.

I don't think it's a way to do things, and apparently the legislature in Alaska has also felt that that's not the way to do things because they have just overturned their plea-bargaining statutes. I think that is just the first of several states. Plea bargaining is a cop-out. That's the phraseology: a cop-out. In order to save the state the time and expense, they will offer a man something that they think he will accept in order to secure the conviction.

Some men consider themselves lucky to get a plea, and in some cases, I can see where that might be valid. In my own case, there's no way that I would do it. If I were offered life imprisonment tomorrow for pleading guilty, I would turn it down.

Do you worry that you'll be executed?

No.

You don't think it will happen?

There are two ways for me to consider worry. Number one: Am I afraid to be executed? No, I'm not. Number two: Do I think that the people in the United States will have a change of heart or just become cognizant of the fact that the death penalty is not a valid form of punishment? From everything that I've heard, the consensus nationwide is that the death penalty is valid. But I do think that times are changing, and I think that opinions are changing. And I think that the death penalty will, again, be overturned constitutionally.

The general belief is no one is going to die. But last week a clown in Georgia was trying to make them kill him.

Alabama.

Alabama. He has some tempers flaring. "Let him come down here and we'll kill him."

If I wanted to die, rather than drag all these people in, I'd just do it myself. If I had that kind of nerve. I don't believe I could do it. That may be the reason there's so many down here that ain't done it. They might could do it to somebody else, but couldn't do it to theirself.

'Cause everybody thinks about it, everybody thinks of making them come. I've talked to lots of people and everybody thinks about making them do it.

But something happens. Your mother writes you and she misses you and you remember something, a goody from home. Your little girl just lost her front tooth. Something like that. You forget about doing it.

Then they swear they didn't think about it. I've thought about it a lot, and I ain't gonna do it. I'm thinking about it again, but I'm not going to do it.

A whole lot of guys figure they gonna strike the death penalty off. I don't believe they will. I know they gonna let it go on. They gonna start killing because the southern Baptists believe in killing.

In the Bible, in the New Testament, Jesus say, "There will come a time that mens will kill and think they're doing my work." And this is the time now. They all killing. And they think this is God's will.

Look here, let me explain something to you. In the Old Testament, where it said if a man take another man's life he should die, then right under there they say if they catch a lady an adulterer, she should die. But Jesus told all them bunch of sinners, I believe it was in John 8, these men brought this lady to Jesus, tempting him, saying this lady should die. She should be stoned to death. But Jesus say, "The first one of you have never sinned cast the first stone."

Man have used God's word in bad ways. They don't really understand. They just want to live the part that they can see a way to do their dirty work with.

Some people think that they will win an appeal and be acquitted. Some people think they will be commuted. Some people contend to the very end that they were innocent. Some people contend that they won't be executed in the final say, for whatever reason. Some people are just waiting for the death penalty to be overturned. And some people are resigned to the fact that they are going to die.

I don't really think anybody wants to die down here. I can't help but think that Gilmore had a death wish. He more or less forced the state of Utah to execute him. As far as I've been able to ascertain, there are no such people here, and most assuredly I'm not one of them.

I'm not afraid to die. I've been too close to it too many times. If I were to go out tomorrow and be run over by a bus, I'm not afraid of that. I'm not afraid to have a needle put in my arm and be executed. But it perturbs me greatly to think that somebody is going to deprive me of my right to say, "Well, I want to go out and get run over by a bus."

I'm not the type to lay down and let them do it. I'm going to fight it to the very end. That doesn't mean that I'm going to be kicking and screaming. I'll fight it legally through the courts. And if my time comes and I'm called, I'll still be complaining about it. But I'm not afraid of it.

Are most men?

Some of them are deathly afraid of it. I don't think, probably, the majority of people ever really resign themselves to the fact that they are mortal. I've completely realized that I'm going to die. It's just a matter of time. But I would like to have more to say in how I go.

Do people talk about it?

Very little. There's no one that is so hardened that, as far as I can see, they would make light of it. It's always a specter that hangs over you. You're cognizant of the fact that it's there, but even though it is there, it's like the moon: it comes and there's nothing you can do to stop it. You live with it.

To me, the death penalty is no more oppressive than a life imprisonment. Either way, it's something that's extremely distasteful, and something that I don't look forward to.

You don't think it's more oppressive than life imprisonment?

It's an end. To someone that's always been an outdoor type, incarceration is extremely distasteful. While I wouldn't be suicidal, I've considered myself to be a survivor. If my sentence is commuted or if I secure another trial and get a life sentence, I'll take it and I'll do it. Because I am a survivor. I do what I have to do, whether it be distasteful or not.

How many people on the Row believe that the state is going to do it to them?

There ain't none of them.

Right now, there's I think five that's most likely to be executed. And they're not afraid theyself.

If they'd a been in here to execute anybody, I'd a been the first joker to go, and that would have been two years ago.

Because I stood up in that court over in McKinney, Texas, and I told 'em, "You drop that appeal now. I'm firing that appeal attorney. Your kangaroo courts, you can stick it and ram it," I said. "Mister, the state has done heard my case, now execute me."

They wouldn't do it.

My attorney stayed on the case for six months without pay to clear his own name. That's the joker that got me that stay of execution in Marshall without my permission. By rights, I should have walked on that charge, by law I should have. But they couldn't do that. Now, I can write to him right now and he won't even answer a letter. I got the grievance committee investigating him right now.

Me, myself, I really believe that it can happen. In fact, I know that they are serious. I truly believe that if I don't get a reversal or somebody reaches in to give me a hand somewhere, that I will be executed. There's no doubt in mind that I will.

I came to this conclusion a couple of years ago when I had learned to accept it. I'm not going to let it drive me off the deep end.

But I'll tell you what. You can go up and down this Row, just say the twenty people on one-row, and I doubt if you could get five people tell you, "Yeah, I believe they will execute me."

Well, I *do* believe. I have no illusions about that whatsoever.

I try to tell people that all the time, you know. I say, "Man, these people are *serious*. They will *kill* you." Oh, no, no. I say, "Well, why do you think you're here?" I say, "That's what you here for, whether you realize or not. You not doing no time. You setting here waiting to be executed, and you best get that through your head right now."

It's in every man's mind. We know that we are going to get out of here one way or another. Either we're going to walk away free, we're going to walk away into population, serve a life term or some sort of term, or we're going to leave here feet first in a box. We know that we're not going to be here. We don't know how long or if there's any hope or any idea of when we might be leaving here. But we know we won't live here for the rest of our lives. We just don't know when.

I've had a death day set on me three different times. And each time, facing death wasn't no problem. It was the up, the stay of execution, the kickback on it. That's what really hurts you.

My last time, I got within three days of execution.

I was ready to go on. It didn't bother me a bit. And turned around, come up with a stay of execution. That's what hurt. Like to put me in a state of shock.

As far as that goes, a man just lives and survives on Death Row.

Postscript

Our Point of View

We do not believe that the death penalty does anyone in our society any good. We do not believe that it prevents deaths, that it makes society better or nicer, that it satisfies any moral need, that it does anything, in fact, but perpetuate a faith in the effectiveness of violence as a solution to grim human problems.

Many inmates on Death Row argue against the deterrent effect of capital punishment. They point to the filled cells of J-21 and J-23 as evidence. "If it's such a deterrent," one said, "how come we're all here waiting to be executed?" That argument is, of course, defective. Death Row, like all prison units, represents the individuals for whom deterrence, whatever its strength, failed. No bank robber was deterred completely by the laws against bank robbery; no drunk driver was deterred completely by the laws against drunk driving. But that doesn't mean no one else was, and neither does it mean that those offenders themselves weren't deterred in some other instances. More important, Texas hadn't, at the time of these interviews, executed anyone for fifteen years. Texas had a death sentence, but it didn't yet have a death penalty.

But there has never been any decent evidence that the death penalty was any better a deterrent than a long prison term. The only factor that seems consistently significant in the literature is the likelihood of apprehension and punishment.

We do not believe capital punishment is any more or less a deterrent than a long prison term, but we have no more way of proving that than do those who argue that there would be a deterrent effect if the penalty were carried out with some regularity, and if there were some way it could be applied fairly.

There is, we think, only one justification that a reasonable and rational person can maintain for the death penalty, and it is a justification that is not itself rational. It can be maintained only because it is a matter of faith, hence not subject to critical examination. It goes like this: Because the state kills without anger, it has the right to put to death those individuals it believes are evil.

Some who argue the state's right to kill refer to the Bible, which is, of course, nonsense. How can one say that the authority to kill comes straight from Exodus, but that we can ignore the abominations detailed in Leviticus because they are no longer modern? God specifically prohibits capital punishment for Cain, the Bible's first murderer. The Bible is brought in to support a position already taken, not to develop one.

How do we know we're good? Because we can punish the bad. How do we know who are the really bad, the limit of the scale? They are the ones we can kill without ourselves inculcating any guilt. The real reason for the enormously complex and drawn-out process attendant upon a state execution is not to permit the condemned some surety that all his or her "rights" were protected; it is, rather, to enable that killing to occur without tainting any of the perpetrators.

Saying, "You killed, so in fairness you will be killed," is clearly inconsistent with the rest of our criminal justice punishment schedule. A man who writes a handful of bad checks is not himself made the subject of bad checks—he goes to prison for a length of time having nothing to do with the money involved, or he doesn't go to prison at all because this is his first offense or because he has a fine lawyer. In Texas, there are third-offender check writers who got probation at trial, and there is one third-offender check writer who got a life sentence at trial.

A banker who decides to steal some money doesn't kill a liquor store clerk, he simply writes some extra lines with his Parker pen. The death penalty, for all the current polishing, will continue to be the property of the poor, the badly represented, and the naive.

But even if the death penalty were fair, if the rich were killed as freely as the poor, we would still think it wrong. We think the reason, after all the arguments, is based on the answer to a moral question: Is it morally legitimate for us to do in a state of calm reason what someone for whose actions we have scorn and contempt did in a state of passion or a condition of amorality or stupidity? We can offer many excellent reasons for the necessity of prison; we cannot think of any that legitimize killing people in such calm.

There is no question that many men on the Row are guilty of terrible crimes. But we doubt it is necessary for the state to manage this kind of special society in order to treat that guilt. Surely there are many men in population who have committed crimes far more heinous than many men on the Row. The only thing that differentiates them is a legal technicality, or whether or not they agreed to plead guilty in exchange for a life sentence. In many cases, the only difference between a man who must die and a man who may be out of prison in twelve or fifteen years is that the former insisted on exercising his constitutional right to a public trial.

We think the real reason for the passionate incorporation of the death penalty is that it functions as symbolic cloture. There is little enough apparent cloture in the criminal justice mechanism. People are arrested and, according to police and public folklore, are let go time after time after time. Convicted criminals, according to the same bizarre misperception, are released from prison after minimal time, again commit crimes of terrible violence, and again serve short sentences. This is rarely true, and the abuses most often result from incompetent or illegal police or prosecution work. But no matter; the perception exists that the bad guys are getting away with it.

An execution is proof positive that the bad guy is not getting away with it. He won't be paroled; he won't have a soft job in prison; he won't escape; he won't feed at the taxpayers' expense. Justice is served; the case is closed.

The symbolic function of a state execution extends far beyond the immediate killing of a specific human being. The function has nothing to do with deterrence and probably little to do with desert. It is, rather, about the sense of completeness and confidence and certitude given the society as a whole. See, there are absolutes, folks.

The process is complex and detached and distanced. No one is responsible for this death. The juries merely decide on the facts, the judges merely utter the sentence prescribed by law, the prosecutors and lawyers are just doing their jobs. The warden is sympathetic and, on the last night, does everything he can to make the condemned comfortable. There is no one to be angry at.

The participants are turned into agents, not people: the Condemned, the State, the Executioner. A priest stands by and certifies that it is a moral event. Witnesses make it a certified happening. A doctor swears death occurred humanely and on schedule and completely. All those people do topsy-turvy jobs. The doctor is trained to save lives, the priest is dedicated to love, the warden is there to restrain people who have hurt other people.

And before it, before that dramatic moment, are the terrible years about which the men in this book speak so painfully and eloquently. The death penalty is not merely the clinical and rational killing of someone the state has convinced itself is freely killable; it is also the long and special torture of that person in a kind of prison like no other.

"Nothing extenuate," cries the guilty and self-doomed Othello. This book is not about these men's crimes or their deserts, finally; it is about ours. Nothing extenuates our dedicated maintenance of this house of rational death. This book is not about those men and what they have done; it is about us and what we are doing. It is a book about vile crime.

Coda

"Blood on the concrete, on the walls, all the murders . . ."

A little before two a.m. the morning of March 17, 2022, while he was proofreading the galleys for this book, Bruce got a text message from Kerry Max Cook:

> I have something to tell you. Can I call you or is it too late/ Of course it is so I will just tell you: the Ellis Unit where you filmed, it's been turned over into a youth facility for kids. I just found that out a few days ago. The former death row walls are painted with pretty flowers and children symbols. What a great new thing to add as an epitaph to the book!

Bruce responded, "Call now," which Kerry did.

Kerry said that he'd gone for a job interview.

"They mentioned the Ellis Unit. I said, 'I've got a lot of memories there.' He said, 'They've turned it into a place for children, for kids.' I said, 'What?' He said, 'Yeah, the death row cellblock is now been painted bright yellow with flowers and children pictures and so forth. It's where they hold the youthful offenders now.' When he said that, when he told me that story, Bruce, I just saw blood on the concrete, on the walls, all the murders that I saw there. It was such a violent place just stained by the patina of such suffering. Don't you remember how asphyxiating that place was when you and Diane were there?"

"To make that into a kiddie place is so bizarre."

"It is to me, too. Do you remember Raymond Riles? He was a nut job. We called him King Moto. He wanted to be called King Moto. He called himself King Moto. He was in the news a year ago, still on death row, oh my god, that man was so mentally ill. Ray Charles could have beaten that case."

"I read that a court decided he never should have been there in the first place because he was nuts from the beginning."

"And so was Brandon. Remember Thelette Brandon. He was three sheets to the wind. That man, how a jury looked at him and determined that there was not something wrong with him! Some of these people, it was so obvious. Nothing but prejudice and hatred and racism caused their convictions."

"I remember Brandon was never not in motion. He was always moving."

"Sitting on the toilet and bouncing up and down. Always at the bars, talking. About the Russians and the Chinese, always going on. He never stopped."

"And Dominique Green. He got to Death Row years after you and Diane were there. I was invited to Rome, Italy, by a European antideath penalty group. I'm walking with this cardinal in this church, in this little narrow hallway, and it's torches on the side. It's like a dungeon. And he stops, he stops at this wall, and he says, 'Kerry, did you know Dominique Green?' I said, 'Yeah." He said, 'He's buried here. He's interred in the wall.' I knew that kid. He came to prison as a kid. He was like seventeen. I watched that kid grow up on Death Row. Bruce, he should not have been executed. That kid was savable. He was under the Law of Parties thing, you know? He didn't kill anybody. One of those tragedies. [Green arrived on Death Row August 17, 1993, three months after his nineteenth birthday. He was executed September 26, 2006, shortly after he turned thirty.]

"This new program, it's got a name. They've got a soccer court. I can't believe it. A basketball court. That old death row yard that you filmed in, that's still there. They still recreate in there. Oh, my god. I'd love to see that. I'd give anything to see that as a free man. Anything.

That place has these incredible deep, deep memories. I couldn't walk in that hall without being so incredibly overwhelmed. To think that there's just kids running up and down playing with basketballs in those hallways, those paintings, goldfish on the walls. Air conditioning. They're putting in air conditioning! Yeah!"

Texas can send kids as young as fourteen to prison serving adult time. But federal law mandates that they be kept separate from older inmates until they turn 18. They'd had a special unit for them on the Clemens Unit, but there was a sex scandal, a number of staff firings, the forced retirement of the Clemens warden, and the juvenile unit being moved to J-Block on Ellis. The rest of Ellis still houses the same kind of repeat, violent offenders as when we were there. The only difference is that one block at the far end of the corridor now holds kids too young to drink or vote. Lauren McGaughy described the new unit in the *Dallas Morning News* (June 1, 2018):

> Two deck chairs sit underneath a palm tree, empty and inviting. In the distance, yachts sail on calm waters. The outline of a coastal city stands out in relief against the blue sky. The murals here depict a fantasy belied by prison life. Look right, the simple paintings evoke an unencumbered island existence. Look left, bars separate the red-brick room from the yard outside. In the distance, the walls are topped with barbed wire. This wing of the O.B. Ellis Unit in Huntsville, 86 miles north of Houston, used to house death row inmates. Soon, it will be the new home of the COURAGE Youthful Offender Program, where the state incarcerates teen inmates who are tried as adults and convicted of serious felonies. . . .
>
> A mural greets new arrivals to the new YOP wing at the Ellis Unit. Seven stairs painted with seven words remind teen offenders what COURAGE means here—'Challenge, Opportunity, Understanding, Respect, Acceptance, Growth, Education.'
>
> Pass through the door and it's all fresh paint and new fixtures. The wing is bright, with large floor-to-ceiling windows and extra exhaust fans to keep the space a bit cooler during Texas' triple-digit summers. There's a long metal table for chow time, rooms for one-on-one-counseling, and, outside, a new basketball court. . . .
>
> The teens in YOP will eat, live and get counseling within the walls of their separate wing to ensure 'complete separation from adult offenders.' The guards, who will be specially trained to deal with teens, will be dedicated solely to the youth wing. There is a medical triage unit in house, so the young men won't have to leave if they sustain a minor injury, and the wing also has two 'additional separation' cells so teens who act out or need extra protection can be housed individually here.
>
> Ensuring adult and youth offenders are never alone together could help avoid another incident like that at Clemens last year.

> In fact, the only time YOP inmates will come face-to-face with adult prisoners will be when they make the short trip to the prison classroom.

The man who interviewed him, Kerry said, "wants to get me in there to talk to those kids. I said, 'Yeah, I'll do it.' In that same day room? Are you kidding me? Do you know how many people died in that day room, Bruce, after you left? Murders, man. The gangs, they really got bad. Aryan Brotherhood and others. Gangs got really bad after you left. They just took over. It was a killing field. You were pre *Ruiz v. Estelle*. You would not recognize J-21 or J-23. In the '80s and '90s after you left, we had a lot of different murders. They locked down J-21 and J-23. They took a welding crew in there. They welded these deep diamond fences across all the cell doors, they made fencing between the cellblock and the row so the guards could walk on the other side of it with a Plexiglas shield. They put screens over the windows. It was a tomb. It's a concrete tomb. A steel and metal tomb. They would have to take all that out to put the kids in there, I'm sure."

"When I was there," Bruce said, "it was like any other cellblock except nobody got out."

"Those days have been gone. It was a dungeon. Everyone hated it. That's what they threatened you on. In the work program, if you get a disciplinary, if you talk back to the officer, they'd say, 'You want to go to J-Wing?' Everyone knew it as the dungeon. It was horrible. It's where they put the gang members. The Aryan Brotherhood, the Mexican Mafia."

"I was there before thee *Ruiz* decision came down. The gangs hadn't gotten a foothold in the prisons."

"When *Ruiz* happened, that's when the gangs got the foothold. They filled in the vacuum. When federal judge William Wayne Justice ruled that the Texas prison system did constitute cruel and unusual punishment in violation of the Eighth Amendment, that's when the gangs filled the vacuum and stepped in. It became Guantanamo, just brutal. I saw so many murders while I was there. It was a bloody war zone. And it was lock-up twenty-three hours a day.

"That diamond screen that they welded across all the cell doors, all twenty-one cells on the three rows. Bruce, it was so dense between the screen that was on the cell door to the screen that you had to look through that separated the cells from the row so the guards could walk outside so the inmates couldn't throw urine and feces on them, to the screen that was on the windows. It was dark twenty-four hours a day in your cell pretty much because light could not penetrate that metal. Can you imagine the years I did in that kind of situation? It was brutal psychologically."

"I'm surprised you're not blind."

"My eyes are pretty bad."

The triple-wire screens were before the 1991 move to Pulunsky Unit, but they foreshadowed it. No more could the condemned men play chess or checkers by reaching through their cell doors; no more could they help one another with their cases; no more could they hold out mirrors between the bars to see other people.

Kerry has been having a particularly hard time since COVID-19 hit. Because of his murder conviction, he can't be hired for most of the jobs he's qualified for, and COVID shut off the intermittent income he'd been getting from lectures and conferences.

He talked a while about his case. He is still fighting to get a declaration of innocence. His lawyers have been waiting for six years for the county to turn over some key exoneration documents. An appellate court ordered them to deliver the documents in 2019. They keep not arriving.

"I've got a team that want to fight and not settle. I'm tired. I'm really tired."

"It's been a long time. I'm not surprised that you're tired."

"Forty-four years, Bruce. You met me when I was twenty-one years old. I'm still unexonerated. I'm still fighting. I'm about to turn sixty-five."

After that third murder trial, Kerry Max Cook was off of Death Row. He's never been free of it. Nor are we.

www.ingramcontent.com/pod-product-compliance
Lightning Source LLC
LaVergne TN
LVHW010352080826
844660LV00004B/255

* 9 7 8 1 4 3 8 4 8 9 2 9 2 *